CURRENT

MIND
OVER
MIND

MIND OVER MIND

THE SURPRISING
POWER OF
EXPECTATIONS

CHRIS BERDIK

CURRENT

CURRENT
Published by the Penguin Group
Penguin Group (USA) Inc., 375 Hudson Street, New York, New York 10014, U.S.A. • Penguin Group (Canada), 90 Eglinton Avenue East, Suite 700, Toronto, Ontario, Canada M4P 2Y3 (a division of Pearson Penguin Canada Inc.) • Penguin Books Ltd, 80 Strand, London WC2R 0RL, England • Penguin Ireland, 25 St. Stephen's Green, Dublin 2, Ireland (a division of Penguin Books Ltd) • Penguin Books Australia Ltd, 250 Camberwell Road, Camberwell, Victoria 3124, Australia (a division of Pearson Australia Group Pty Ltd) • Penguin Books India Pvt Ltd, 11 Community Centre, Panchsheel Park, New Delhi–110 017, India • Penguin Group (NZ), 67 Apollo Drive, Rosedale, Auckland 0632, New Zealand (a division of Pearson New Zealand Ltd) • Penguin Books (South Africa) (Pty) Ltd, 24 Sturdee Avenue, Rosebank, Johannesburg 2196, South Africa

Penguin Books Ltd, Registered Offices: 80 Strand, London WC2R 0RL, England

First published in 2012 by Current, a member of Penguin Group (USA) Inc.

10 9 8 7 6 5 4 3 2 1

Grateful acknowledgment is made for permission to reprint an excerpt from "he died April 9, 1553" from *The Night Torn Mad with Footsteps* by Charles Bukowski. Copyright © 2001 by Linda Lee Bukowski. Reprinted by permission of HarperCollins Publishers.

LIBRARY OF CONGRESS CATALOGING-IN-PUBLICATION DATA
Berdik, Chris, author.
  Mind over mind : the surprising power of expectations / Chris Berdik.
    pages   cm
  Includes bibliographical references and index.
  ISBN 978-1-59184-509-6 (hardback)
  1. Expectation (Psychology)   2. Thought and thinking.   3. Cognitive psychology.   I. Title.
  BF323.E8B47 2012
  153.4—dc23
  2012019144

Printed in the United States of America
Designed by Carla Bolte • Set in Palatino LT Std

To

ISABEL AND OLIVER

for whom expectations
were invented

life is not all that
we think it
is, it's only what we
imagine it to
be and for us
what we imagine
becomes
mostly so.

—Charles Bukowski, "he died April 9, 1553"

CONTENTS

(YOU WILL) GET WELL SOON

MIND
OVER
MIND

PRELUDE] **A MARVELOUS THING**

In the summer of 1784, the most learned men in Paris warned King Louis XVI of a gathering threat to his government and the moral fiber of his subjects. It was an ominous, mysterious force, impossible to see, touch, taste, or smell, even though its effects were everywhere and terrifying to behold. The name of this menace? *Imagination.*

They had seen imagination's power firsthand while investigating a healer named Franz Anton Mesmer, whose unique treatments had become a sensation in Paris. Mesmer cured people of nearly every malady by moving his hands around them to re-balance their "animal magnetism," which he said was an all-connecting, cosmic energy. A German by birth, Mesmer began his healing practice in Vienna and then moved on to Paris in 1778. Soon, well-to-do Parisians flocked to his clinic to be "mesmerized." Some of his most ardent followers were in the royal court, including Marie Antoinette. The demand for Mesmer's services became so great that he trained a cadre of new magnetic healers who either assisted him or started their own healing practices.

A visitor to Mesmer's Parisian clinic would enter a large hall darkened with thick purple curtains and filled with tall mirrors meant to reflect and intensify the invisible energy. The eerie tones of a glass harmonica filtered in from an adjoining room.

In the middle of the hall stood the *baquet*, a large circular oaken tub about a foot high, filled with water, powdered glass, and iron shavings. Dozens of patients seated themselves around it. Those closest to the *baquet* would hold one of several jointed iron bars that pierced its lid. Others would connect to them by grasping a long rope passed from patient to patient, or by holding hands.

After everyone was arranged in a silent circuit, Mesmer would enter the room wearing a long flowing cloak of lilac silk embroidered with celestial symbols. He would approach his patients and stare into their eyes. Occasionally, he would tap them with an iron wand or gently lay his hands on them. He would make sweeping gestures to channel the magnetism wherever it was needed.

As Mesmer worked his way through the crowd, patients would cough, spit, or cry out. Suddenly, one of the patients would begin to convulse. This was the "crisis" that presaged a cure, and it was contagious. As one witness described it, the hall eventually became a jumble of flailing limbs, "wildness in the eyes, shrieks, tears, hiccupings, and immoderate laughter." Some coughed up blood. Others vomited. Many fainted. Mesmer's attendants would quietly escort those with the most violent symptoms into a well-padded side room. Yet once the crises faded, the patients were at ease and seemingly refreshed. Usually, they reported feeling much better.

The extreme popularity of these dramatic cures sparked controversy and public denunciations by leading French physicians. When the uproar spread to the royal court, the king, who would soon lose his head to the Age of Reason, demanded an investigation in the name of science.

He appointed a royal commission that included such notables as Antoine Lavoisier, "the father of modern chemistry," the astronomer Jean-Sylvain Bailly, who calculated the orbit of Halley's Comet, and a doctor whose name would become synonymous with terror, Joseph-Ignace Guillotin. To lead the commission, the king chose the elder American statesman Benjamin Franklin, who lived in the village of Passy, just outside Paris.

Their investigation of mesmerism led to the world's first placebo trials, using sham procedures to test a medical treatment. Not only that. The commission's report was the first account of the placebo phenomenon itself. The outcome was a condemnation of Mesmer and animal magnetism, as well as the power of the mind to shape reality. The king's investigators drew a bright line between the real world and the fevered realm of imagination that threatened it like a pestilence. More than two centuries later, that line has barely begun to fade.

HOW FAITH BECAME SCIENCE

"Animal magnetism," Mesmer once told a curious physician, "is not what you call a secret. It is a science, which has principles, consequences, and a doctrine."

Indeed, Mesmer believed that his cures were as scientific as they come. He based his medical theory on some of the biggest discoveries of the age—the magnetism surrounding the earth and the gravity that kept it orbiting the sun. These immense forces touched everything and ruled the cosmos, Mesmer reasoned. Why couldn't they guide the workings of our organs and other vital tissues?

After years of training in theology, Mesmer had switched to medicine at the University of Vienna where he wrote a dissertation titled *The Influence of the Planets in the Cure of Diseases*. Our bodies have magnetic poles just like the earth, Mesmer wrote, and being largely made of water, we are as tidal as the oceans. Our physical health is sensitive to the rotation of stars and wobbles in planetary orbits, he argued, because these celestial phenomena are governed by the same "universal gravitation by which our bodies are harmonized, [like] a musical instrument furnished with several strings."

While Mesmer cited Galileo Galilei, Johannes Kepler, and Sir Isaac Newton in the foundation of his medical theory, it was the work of two Catholic priests that ultimately shaped his healing techniques.

The first of these was Maximilian Hell, a Jesuit astronomer at the University of Vienna, who cured people's stomach cramps by touching their bellies with magnets. Mesmer befriended the priest, and soon tried the magnets on his own patients with encouraging results. Eager to distinguish himself from his Jesuit mentor, Mesmer published a "Letter on Magnetic Treatment" in which he one-upped the priest by describing himself as a magnetic King Midas.

He claimed the ability to summon magnetic energy in "paper, bread, wool, silk, leather, stone, glass, water, various metals, wood, men, dogs." In short, he wrote, "everything that I touch."

Mesmer had shifted the locus of magnetic healing from cosmic gyrations to himself. The echoes of divine healing were obvious, but Mesmer insisted his theory was as scientific as Newton's *Principia*. Thoughts, beliefs, and expectations had nothing to do with magnetic healing, let alone divine intervention. Magnetism blanketed the earth, and these healings were simply more evidence of its ubiquitous reach. The proof was in the results. The magnetic energy was invisible, and Mesmer kept the exact mechanism of his control a secret, so a faith of sorts was still needed, but God was nowhere in sight.

God's absence was underscored by Mesmer's encounter with another priest, Johann Gassner, who claimed many illnesses were caused by demonic possession. As such, they were curable by exorcism, which Gassner performed before large crowds. Wielding a Bible and crucifix, Gassner would command the departure of whatever unclean spirits caused the headache, toothache, dizziness, or other ailments troubling his patient. Then, after a splash of holy water, the patient would collapse into convulsions. As Gassner spoke the final amen, the patient would recover and declare himself much improved.

By the time Mesmer began healing a handful of people with magnets, Gassner was casting out pathogenic demons throughout Austria and southern Germany to great acclaim. Nevertheless, German secular authorities were wary of charismatic religious leaders confronting Satan in their midst. In Germany's not-too-distant history, thousands of people had been burned as suspected witches. When Prince Max Joseph of Bavaria launched an inquiry into Gassner, he asked for Mesmer's help. The magnetic healer happily obliged.

In public demonstrations, Mesmer triggered, and then quieted, convulsions in patients using commanding gestures, just like Gassner had in his exorcisms. It wasn't that Gassner was a fraud, Mesmer charitably concluded. Rather, the priest was healing with magnetism and mislabeling it God.

By vanquishing Gassner, Mesmer burnished his scientific bona fides and put the finishing touches on his healing technique: the curative crisis instigated by tapping into the cosmic essence.

Within a few years of setting up shop in Paris, Mesmer's healing business was booming. He had expanded from one *baquet* to four, prescribed specially "magnetized" water, and even magnetized a tree near his house for use by the poor who could not afford a session with the master. Mesmer had more clients than he could handle. What he didn't have, and what he craved more than anything, was the respect of the scientists and physicians he considered his peers.

Desperate for acceptance, Mesmer began presenting them with certificates of cure signed by his patients. First he approached the French Academy of Sciences, then the Royal Society of Medicine, and finally the Faculty of Medicine of Paris—the last of which grudgingly agreed to observe him but were not impressed. In fact, when a respected doctor named Charles D'Eslon publicly supported magnetic healing, his colleagues scratched D'Eslon's name from their membership rolls.

Most physicians of the time were fond of blistering, bleeding, purgatives, and enemas. They considered Mesmer's noninvasive techniques to be nothing more than hocus-pocus. Far from accepting Mesmer as one of their own, the French medical establishment was aching to prove he was a huckster. When the king finally called for an investigation, they had their chance.

LIES IN PURSUIT OF TRUTH

In 1784, the seventy-eight-year-old Franklin was enjoying his eighth year as a permanent guest at the leafy estate of Jacques-Donatien Le Ray de Chaumont, a wealthy merchant and former munitions supplier to the American rebels. Franklin was a celebrity in France. He never lacked for company, including government ministers, courtiers, scientists, and inventors.

That summer, however, Franklin had visitors of another sort—a parade of sickly men, women, and children, including a bow-legged girl with the jerky symptoms of Saint Vitus' dance, an asthmatic widow, a man hobbled by a tumor in his leg, another beset by headaches and chilly feet, a boy with tuberculosis, a severely constipated old woman, and another woman who was partially blind and in chronic pain after colliding with a cow. With the arrival of the patients, limping, wheezing, and groaning, at Franklin's borrowed château, the bucolic stage was set for the world's first placebo experiments.

Mesmer stonewalled the king's investigation. D'Eslon, however, had become a student of Mesmer and had since established a magnetic healing practice to rival his mentor. D'Eslon used the same techniques as Mesmer. Their patients swooned and recovered with equal fervor. Thus, the commission considered D'Eslon's magnetic healing to be a suitable substitute for their inquiry.

For his part, D'Eslon was eager to defend mesmerism's cures and possibly regain his own credibility. He invited the commission to observe his healing sessions, but the investigators weren't so interested in the *effects* of magnetic healing. They wanted to know whether magnetism, which Mesmer and D'Eslon referred to as a cosmic "fluid," was responsible for the cures. If not, then Mesmer was a fraud and magnetic healing treatments were dishonest. Case closed. The commission could ignore the question of whether any patients were in fact being healed, and if so, *what* might be healing them.

To prove that magnetic cures were "the fruits of anticipated persuasion," as the king's investigators suspected, they needed a unique kind of experiment—placebo experiments. The patients were chosen by D'Eslon, then blindfolded by the investigators and subjected to all manner of tricks. The commissioners quizzed patients about where on their bodies a nearby mesmerist was directing the healing energy. They triggered convulsions in one patient by impersonating D'Eslon, and in another by giving her water they falsely claimed was magnetized. Later, in Franklin's gardens, the commissioners blindfolded a frail twelve-year-old boy and told him that he would be brought to several trees, including an apricot tree that D'Eslon had magnetized. In truth, they led him only to normal, unmagnetized trees, but the boy fainted anyway.

"The experience is therefore entirely conclusive," the commissioners wrote in their report to the king. Magnetic healing was caused by expectations, not by the ebb and flow of a universal energy. The term "placebo" had yet to enter medical parlance, but the word they used instead, "imagination," carried the odor of phoniness that has followed placebo effects ever since.

At one point during the experiments at Passy, D'Eslon took Franklin aside and conceded that imagination might play a role in the treatments. Nevertheless, he argued, "imagination thus directed to the relief of suffering humanity would be a most valuable means in the hands of the medical profession."

D'Eslon had made a similar point a few years earlier in a letter to his fellow doctors defending Mesmer. He supported the notion of a ubiquitous healing energy, but added, "Besides, if Monsieur Mesmer had no other secret than to be able to cause the imagination to act effectively to produce health, would he not have a marvelous thing?"

His contemporaries' answer was a resounding no that still echoes today.

Mesmer rejected the investigators' findings, not least because he claimed to be the only true master of magnetism, despite all the healers he'd trained. Still, the shame of the published findings drove him back to Germany and Austria, where he spent the rest of his days in relative obscurity.

Mesmer would go down in history as one of medicine's greatest quacks, and the commission that exposed him would define the placebo's role for centuries—a fantasy used to highlight what's real by contrast, a lie used in pursuit of truth.

UNLEASHING IMAGINATION

At Passy, the king's investigators knew they had glimpsed a phenomenon that went beyond debunking Mesmer, and even beyond the healing arts. Their report lingered on imagination as an "active and terrible power," with otherworldly and spooky overtones. "The effects strike all the world," they wrote of it, while "the cause is enveloped in the shades of obscurity."

Ironically, these learned men balanced their aversion to imagination with a hearty appetite for speculation. Imagination was not just the enemy of reason, they concluded, but a fomenter of rebellion. "The multitude are governed by the imagination," they wrote to the king. "It has been usual to forbid numerous assemblies in seditious towns as a means of stopping a contagion so easily communicated."*

In their report, imagination was part charlatan and part bogeyman. To summon it was to dabble in the dark arts. More than two centuries later, we are not so easily spooked, but the self-fulfilling prophecies of the mind—from a sugar pill that eases pain to a run on the bank—are still seen as evidence of our gullibility and the ease with which we detach ourselves from reality. In this light, we

---

* If the specter of a wild-eyed, imagination-addled citizenry wasn't enough to scare the king of a restive nation, the commissioners had a second, secret report guaranteed to unsettle him as the husband of a restive wife. This secret report suggested that mesmerists were bringing women to orgasm, which the commissioners considered a grave threat to France's moral fiber. Much like the threat of imagination-kindled rebellion, they warned, "there is nothing to prevent the convulsions in this case from becoming habitual, from producing an epidemic transmitted to future generations."

are as likely to be cured by a placebo as we are to hear voices in the wind or see the face of Jesus in our oatmeal.

The power of expectations surpasses our capacity for self-deception, however. In fact, our real world is in many ways an expected world. What we see, hear, taste, feel, and experience is produced from the top down as much as it is from the bottom up. Our minds organize chaos. We fill in blanks with well-learned forms, patterns, and assumptions. Our predictions for the near and distant future bend reality.

Granted, if you push the idea of an expected reality far enough, then you end up raving on street corners about summoning riches with visions, and inviting catastrophe with worry. But the power of expectations need not undermine reality. Our expectations are the ever-present filter of it all, but not the all itself.

This book seeks to untangle the complex interplay between what we assume will be and what is. You'll learn why flipping the eye chart can improve people's vision, why sugar pills heal ulcers in French patients but not in Brazilians, why people feel full after eating imaginary cheese, why wearing knockoff sunglasses can turn people into cheaters, why blurry vision can help cricket batters, and why interviewers consider applicants more qualified when reviewing their résumés on heavier clipboards.

I use many terms in the pages ahead, including imagination, expectations, placebos, and anticipation. They are not one and the same, but they all reflect the mind's habit of jumping to conclusions, and the surprising power these conclusions wield. If we can unlock the power of expectations, then we can maximize their potential and avoid their pitfalls.

The chapters that follow offer a mix of history, scientific research, and stories—about gambling addicts, wine geeks, counterfeiters, ex-convicts, and Olympic champions—all revolving around a version of D'Eslon's "marvelous thing," our mind's ability to make something out of nothing. The book explores how expectations rule our preferences and can make us desperately crave what we don't even like. I'll describe how our fast-forward brains anticipate every move we make, and how this special fore-sight can be sharpened, or completely undone by expectations. I'll investigate the assumptions that can win or lose championships, change who we think we are, and set us up for a lifetime of success or failure. Finally, I'll return to the medical placebo and observe its slow emergence from Mesmer's shadow and the stigma of deception.

Our brains can't help but look forward. We spend very little of our mental lives completely in the here and now. Indeed, the power of expectations is so pervasive that we may notice only when somebody pulls back the curtain to reveal a few of the cogs and levers responsible for the big show.

Exploring the vast influence of expectations brings up humbling, even frightening possibilities. We might discover just how little contact we truly have with bedrock reality, and how much of our time, effort, and emotion we devote to watching and worrying over shadows. On the other hand, the power of expectations makes our reality coherent, meaningful, and open to the possibility of change, if we put our minds to it.

HEAD GAMES

1] RUNNING ON EMPTY

Why are we thrilled by the crack of the starter's pistol or the referee's opening whistle? The contest of strength, speed, or endurance has begun. The game is under way. That split second is the pinnacle of sports expectations, which go way beyond who will win and who will lose. Indeed, they push up against our limits. And then they keep going.

On a breezy day in May 1954, a twenty-five-year-old medical student named Roger Bannister stepped onto the soggy track at Oxford University. He knew the time to beat, and so did thousands of spectators who had come to watch him run. The long-standing world record for a mile was 4 minutes and 1.4 seconds. But beating the world record wasn't enough. Ever since Bannister failed to medal in the 1952 Helsinki Olympics, he'd dedicated himself to running a mile in under 4 minutes.

Bannister knew that some doctors believed his goal was impossible, and possibly life-threatening. In a book about that race at Oxford, Bannister wrote, "I felt at that moment that it was my chance to do one thing supremely well. I drove on, impelled by a combination of fear and pride."

When Bannister finished in 3 minutes and 59.4 seconds, a jubilant crowd rushed the track. The record Bannister beat was nine years old. His new record stood for less than two months. Remember who beat it?*

The fact is that while few of us will ever run a 4-minute mile, it's no longer newsworthy. Today it would likely earn no better

---

* John Landy of Australia ran a 3:58 mile on June 21, 1954.

than ninth place at international track competitions such as the Wanamaker Mile. Bannister's achievement remains remarkable, because 4 is a nice round number, and because it symbolizes our ability to push beyond limiting expectations and bust the myths of impossibility—like Sir Edmund Hilary scaling Mount Everest in 1953 and Chuck Yeager breaking the sound barrier in 1947. Bannister's legs powered him through that mile, along with a heart and lungs strengthened by years of preparation. Still, he needed something else to beat 4 minutes. He needed to believe it was possible.

Defining human limits is a mean business, something "the man" has always done to keep us down. Consider how much better the "best" is now than it was a century ago. In 2012, the current high school record for the 200-meter dash beats the 1912 Olympic gold medal time by a full second and a half, and the top high school marathoner would finish more than 13 minutes ahead of the 1912 gold medalist. The assumption that the future promises ever more astounding athletic feats fascinates audiences and motivates competitors. Suggesting that the days of "faster, higher, stronger" are numbered is about as popular as farting in church.

Of course, there *are* limits, not only for the mile, but for human athleticism more generally. The pace of new world records is slowing in competitions of pure speed, power, and endurance. At some point, these limitations will hold us back *despite* our steadfast refusal to accept them. What then? Change the rules? Change our bodies? Change the Olympic motto? Or do we need to change our minds?

Reflecting on the final sprint of his legendary mile, Bannister wrote, "My body had long since exhausted all its energy, but it went on running just the same. The physical overdraft came only from greater willpower."

How far can willpower take a runner's legs? How much of our muscle power is mind power? As athletes push up against our physical limits, the question looms large.

ARE WORLD RECORDS GOING EXTINCT?

In 2004, *Nature* published a short piece extrapolating the trends in world record times for men and women running the 100-meter dash from 1910 to 2252. Because women's times were improving faster than men's, the authors concluded that women would one day be running faster than men, possibly before the end of the century.

Among the article's many critics was Geoffroy Berthelot, a statistics-minded researcher at Paris's Institute for Biomedical Research and Sports Epidemiology.

"If you just extrapolate the data, then you eventually say that the 100-meter record will be under one second," Berthelot says. "But you can't go beyond the physiological limit. And while we don't know exactly where that is, we know you can't go beyond zero. You can't arrive before the start."

Actually, Berthelot seems to know fairly precisely where the limits are, at least in some cases. In several swimming events and the sprint competitions in track, he thinks we've already reached them. A 2008 paper he coauthored looked at the progression of world records in Olympic events since the first Games in 1896. It concluded that performance in 13 percent of the events had already plateaued, and half of them would most likely max out within two decades. The paper's title, "The Citius End," suggests that the Olympic spirit might soon need to be redefined.

In a 2010 follow-up analysis, Berthelot and his coauthors went beyond world records and collected the top ten performances each year for seventy events, including thirty-six track and field events between 1891 and 2008 and thirty-four swimming events between 1963 and 2008. Plotted on a graph, the top performances improve in fits and starts. The steeper slopes hint at something unusual—a war's end, a game-changing new technique, better equipment. Or doping.

For Berthelot, the fact that some world beaters likely cheated only strengthens his argument that the end is near for pure athleti-cism. In early 2012, a federal grand jury found no basis for charges of illegal performance boosting against Lance Armstrong, seven-time winner of the grueling twenty-one-day, 2,000 mile Tour de France. The news was vindication for Armstrong, who maintains he won all those races clean.

Nevertheless, so many top cyclists have been found guilty of doping, including nearly all of the cyclists who finished second and third behind Armstrong in his Tour victories, that the sport seems in danger of moving to a drug-enhanced level of perfor-mance expectations. There's a potential tipping point after which the athletes who take drugs to push beyond their natural limits are no longer the exception. They become the new normal.

"Things were just getting faster and faster," said cyclist Frankie Andreu in a May 2011 segment on *60 Minutes* about doping alle-gations against the U.S. Postal Service's cycling team. Andreu is one of several former members of the team, which Armstrong captained, to admit the use of performance-enhancing drugs. "There's 200 guys flying over these mountains, and you can't even stay in the group. And it's just impossible to keep up." It was ei-ther dope or go home, Andreu said. So he doped.

There are plenty of people who have no real problem with that. They dismiss anti-doping efforts in professional sports as much ado about nothing, a crusade beset by double standards. At its core, the argument over sports doping is about our expectations for athletics. What do sports at the highest levels mean to us?

If the answer is striving for victory, overcoming failure, and, ul-timately, pushing the boundaries of human athleticism, then we should try to keep the contests as clean as possible. Roger Bannis-ter was lionized because he embodied a new sense of possibility for what human beings could do—what *we* could do. That was what captivated the world, not the absolute number of seconds that he ran.

Still, it would be naive to suggest that's all, or even most, of what we want from top-level sports. We don't pay good money to sit in the stands and be inspired. We want our team to win. We expect to be entertained. If this is what we want, then why not legalize performance boosters, so long as they're reasonably safe. After all, dunking a basketball from the foul line is pretty cool, but dunking from the three-point line would be totally unreal.

The Achilles' heel of the entertainment rationale, though, is that everything gets boring when it becomes routine. Soon enough, it will be obvious that the Wow! threshold is being advanced by drugs rather than effort or dedication or sheer daring. How entertaining would it be to watch contests that boil down to who has the best drugs?

Having said that, what about the Wow? Some sports, particularly the raw tests of speed and endurance, seem at risk of losing their allure, for both competitors and audience. What would it be like to watch, or train for, the Olympics if we knew we'd already seen the best there ever will be?

One can expect cutting-edge equipment to continue nudging some records along, although sports-governing bodies are increasingly wary of allowing technology to set the pace.

In 2008, many top swimmers, such as Michael Phelps, began wearing a new type of full-body swimsuit made of a high-tech, water-repellent fabric. In the eighteen months before the international swimming federation's May 2009 decision to ban the full-body suits, more than a hundred swimming world records fell, including the seven Phelps set at the Beijing Olympics while winning an astonishing eight gold medals.* Berthelot notes that while the federation banned the new swimsuits, it authorized the introduction of angled starting blocks that give swimmers an extra burst of speed as they enter the pool.

New and better equipment has always been a part of superior athletic performance. At a certain point, however, drawing some

---

* As of this writing, more than two years after the ban went into effect on January 1, 2010, there have been only eight new swimming world records.

admittedly arbitrary line makes sense. It would feel just as lame to root for the athletes with the best technology as it would to cheer those with the best muscle juice.

Another way to keep some of these competitions exciting might be to slice victory by the thousandth of a second. After all, since American sprinter Jim Hines first beat ten seconds at the 1968 Olympics, there have been fifteen world records in the men's 100-meter dash thanks to measuring to the hundredth of a second, rather than the four measured in tenths of a second.

"But you're just resampling the curve. It doesn't change the dynamic," counters Berthelot. By dynamic, he means the great slow-down of human athletic progress. "You're still reaching the plateau, but you're more precise in describing that plateau."

True, but Olympic sprinters don't run (and we don't watch them run) in order to ratchet up the slope of human athletic progress. The quest is to do it faster. Period. If more precision allows a finer determination of this, then scale may not matter. They didn't time races to the hundredth of a second in 1921 when the American sprinter Charley Paddock ran 100 meters in 10.4 seconds, two tenths of a second faster than the old record. Was Carl Lewis's world record in 1988 less celebrated because it edged the old time by only a hundredth of a second?

Swimming and track events are still marquees on the Olympic schedule. Still, appealing to an audience is one thing, and motivating the athletes is another. Most of the events on Berthelot's watch list are contested in relative obscurity. Olympic audiences might find the prospect of a new record, even one notched by a thousandth of a second, worth a sliver of their television viewing time every four years. Will it be enough to motivate runners, though, who must train for years to compete for an ever-diminishing chance at greatness?

Berthelot isn't too worried. "If there are no more world records," he says, "then maybe we'll have to focus on the competition itself."

OUTSMARTING FATIGUE

If athletes truly are approaching our natural limits and if surpassing these limits thanks to drugs and technology feels hollow, then higher, faster, stronger may increasingly depend on the mind's ability to wring the last drops of speed, strength, and endurance from the muscles, heart, and lungs.

This won't be easy, according to traditional exercise physiology, where the standard account of fatigue is purely physical. At a certain point, our lungs and hearts just can't keep up with the muscles' demand for oxygen and nutrients. Lactic acid builds up as a last-ditch energy source. Then our muscles start to quit. Our bodies do all they can, and then can do no more.

Archibald Vivian (A. V.) Hill, a Nobel-winning British physiologist, came up with the basics of this explanation in the 1920s, and it remains the core of textbook accounts. In the late 1990s, however, a South African sports physician and exercise physiologist named Timothy Noakes started to question whether the heart, lungs, and muscles truly governed fatigue.

If a body just kept exercising, on and on, until it was utterly spent, he wondered, why weren't more athletes succumbing to heat stroke, heart attacks, and fatal dehydration? Why weren't more competitors collapsing and even dying from exertion? Noakes found his first clue in a paragraph of Hill's original writings that had been largely overlooked for decades.

"When the oxygen supply becomes inadequate, it is probable that the heart rapidly begins to diminish its output, so avoiding exhaustion," Hill wrote. To prevent serious damage to the heart, he suggested that "some mechanism (a governor) slows things down, as soon as a serious degree of [oxygen] unsaturation occurs."

Hill speculated that this mechanism might be part of the heart muscle itself or in the brain. Noakes suspected the latter, and he went further. While Hill thought the protective slow-down kicked in when things reached a crisis point, flipping the emergency off switch when catastrophe was at hand, Noakes proposed that the brain sees fatigue coming and that an anticipatory "central governor" (named for Hill's "governor" concept) rules endurance via these expectations.

Noakes and his colleague at the University of Capetown, Ross Tucker, built on the theory of "teleoanticipation" proposed in 1996 by German exercise physiologist Hans-Volkhart Ulmer. According to Ulmer, it's all about the finish line. The exercising brain starts there and works backward to regulate exertion.

Let's say you're an experienced, albeit recreational runner of 10K races. Before every race, your brain's central governor uses previous running experience to predict when your lungs will start to burn, how your legs will feel, and how long you'll need to exert yourself. If it's really hot out, or if you're already a little dehydrated, then the central governor takes that into account and sets a safe pace.

As you run, your brain adjusts its initial expectations using feedback from your senses and bodily systems to ensure that you have what it takes to finish with a little bit, but not too much, to spare. Then, to keep your pace in line with these expectations, the brain quietly adjusts the number of "go" signals it sends to your muscles. Accordingly, when you're surprised by how far you are from the finish, that sluggishness that washes over you is protective. It's the brain cutting the throttle in anticipation of trouble.

For example, Noakes and Tucker had expert cyclists ride a stationary bike at whatever speed translated into a constant rate of perceived exertion (RPE). For reference, the RPE for exercise tests can go from 6 "very light" to 20 "maximum," and the cyclists pushed themselves to an RPE of 16, between "hard" and "very hard." They were told to stay at that level until the researchers stopped them. Meanwhile, the researchers varied the temperature of the lab—setting it at either a comfortable 15° Celsius (about 60° Fahrenheit) or a sweltering 35° Celsius (about 95° Fahrenheit).

They monitored the cyclists' core temperature and heart rate during the exercise, which continued until the cyclists' power output fell to 70 percent of starting levels. In the hot room, performance dropped off much faster. That's not surprising, except that the cyclists' power decreased well before they actually got hot. There were no significant differences in heart rate either. In other words, the heat didn't catch up to the hot room cyclists. Their anticipatory brains made sure that didn't happen by putting on the brakes ahead of time.

Or consider the ability of highly trained endurance athletes to speed up for the last bit of the race, the so-called end spurt. This suggests that up until that point they'd been running (or swimming, biking, whatever) at a slightly less than optimal pace, holding something in reserve, just in case. As the finish line nears, uncertainty decreases, and the central governor can go all in.

Is it possible to trick this central governor into keeping fatigue at bay? Yes. For example, research shows that energy drinks aren't what you think they are. Or, rather, they are exactly what you think they are. Let me explain. The body takes a long time to transform ingested carbohydrates into useful fuel. Metabolic studies show that taking a swig of Gatorade or a slurp of energy goo won't add much to your energy stores for at least an hour. Meanwhile, exercising bodies make use of fuel already on board, known as glycogen, which is stored in the liver, muscles, and other tissues.

Fatigue follows glycogen depletion. In a purely physical analogy, the car runs out of gas. Then it stops. The central governor theory, however, suggests that your legs go wobbly because the brain is making a calculated prediction and slowing things down to keep everything safe. Imagine if your car wouldn't let you drive past a highway exit after the fuel light illuminated. There's still some gas in the tank, but the brain holds it in reserve, because the body can't function without it, let alone finish the race.

In 2009, British physiologists asked cyclists to ride a long distance on a stationary bike as fast as possible. At regular intervals during these time trials, which lasted about an hour, the cyclists rinsed their mouths with a sweet liquid and then spat it out. The rinse was either rich in carbohydrates or just distilled water. Heavy doses of artificial sweetener ensured that both energy-rich and energy-absent liquids tasted the same. Even though the cyclists didn't swallow anything, they rode significantly faster and generated more power when they swished with carbohydrates, compared to the placebo solution. Moreover, this extra pace didn't speed up heart rates or increase the cyclists' perceived exertion.

What could explain this? Somehow, independent of sweetness, the mouth was sensing the carbs and telling the brain that more energy was on its way. Thanks to the expectation of replenishment, the brain freed up more of the body's stored energy.

Notably, a few years earlier, one of the researchers led a study in which cyclists doing similar speed trials were intravenously given either a carbohydrate solution or a placebo—saline that subjects were told was carbohydrate solution. Not only were these carbs not spit out, they were actually given a metabolic headstart, shooting directly into the bloodstream. Yet, unlike the swish-and-spit scenario, the injection of a new energy source did not boost the cyclists' speed compared with the placebo. Without the expectations communicated by the mouth's carbohydrate sensors, the brain wasn't getting the message.

PUSHING LIMITS: DUPING AND DOPING

Shortly before retiring, the legendary Australian swim coach Harry Gallagher admitted to doctoring stopwatches in training so that his swimmers believed they'd gone slower than they actually had.

"I tricked them into putting out greater and greater than they had before," Gallagher told an interviewer. In the end, he tricked his swimmers into winning nine Olympic gold medals and setting more than fifty world records. "I wasn't fibbing to them," said the wily coach. "I'd manipulated time on my side."

This ruse may backfire for pessimistic swimmers. In 1990,

psychologist Martin Seligman gave varsity swimmers a personality test that pegged them as optimists or pessimists. At practice,
coaches gave these swimmers falsely negative times. When given
another chance, only the optimists improved. The disappointed
pessimists swam even slower, which the researchers saw as a
symptom of learned helplessness. "The expectation of future failure," they wrote, "works by undermining the incentive to try."

The fact that even highly trained athletes can be tricked into
better (or worse) performance bolsters the theory that expectations ultimately set our physical limits. Research into the placebo
effect in sports has been spotty, not least because the ethics review
boards at universities, research institutes, and government agencies that must okay all studies find it easier to justify deception on
behalf of medical breakthroughs rather than faster splits. Nevertheless, there's good evidence for an athletic placebo effect.

In the first of these studies, done in the 1970s, placebo steroids
increased the strength of trained weight lifters. Over the next two
decades, the only other sports placebo investigations were follow-
ups on the weight-lifting research, including a 2000 study of na-
tionally competitive power lifters who believed they were testing
a new fast-acting muscle builder. The researchers collected data
on the subjects' maximum baseline lifts and gave them placebo
tablets to take while training. A week later, the subjects increased
their maximum lifts between 3 and 5 percent, which was a significant improvement given that these were well-trained athletes at
the top of their sport.

After another week, before a second round of testing, half of the
athletes were told the truth. What happened next made perfect
sense on one level, but no sense at all on another. Lifters were
weakened by the truth. Their maximum lifts returned to baseline
levels.

The researchers suggested that their study might help anti-
doping initiatives by calling the bluff of supposed performance
enhancers. *See, it's all in your head. Lay off the juice.* Still, the
knowledge that one's mind had summoned extra physical strength

(and that, by contrast, the chemical performance enhancer was bogus) was not enough to bolster performance. The lifters who knew the truth couldn't lift as much as they had while under the placebo's spell. If they wanted to get stronger, they needed belief. Strength gained from a chemical was apparently easier to believe than strength from the mind alone, no matter the facts.

Even without the aid of placebos, however, there is evidence that you can think yourself stronger. In a 2004 study out of the Cleveland Clinic, people who repeatedly imagined exercising a particular muscle increased that muscle's strength. Before you join a mental gym, though, consider that most of the effects have so far been limited to a single finger or elbow muscle. Plus, to get measurable strength improvements, the subjects in these studies had to imagine doing a single piece of monotonous resistance training, from a first-person perspective, over and over and over. "It's the most difficult kind of visualization," says Vlodek Siemionow, a biomedical engineer at the Cleveland Clinic. "You must be strong willed to do it."

In the meantime, about a dozen other investigations have shown a sports placebo effect in the past decade, occasionally in the myth-busting role inherited from the investigation of Mesmer. In 2010, University of Wisconsin researchers tested the Power Balance bracelet, a silicone wristband embedded with two dime-sized holograms that, according to the bracelet's makers, "resonate with and respond to the natural energy field of the body" to improve flexibility, balance, and strength. Power Balance had sold millions of bracelets (at about thirty dollars apiece) since it set up shop in 2006. Its Web site boasted a "power balance team" of high-profile athletes and endorsements, including Drew Brees, Shaquille O'Neal, and Red Sox second baseman Dustin Pedroia, who called the bracelets "the next level in athletic performance."

But the Wisconsin researchers found that athletes performed just as well with a placebo bracelet as they did wearing a Power Balance bracelet on the flexibility, balance, and strength tests that the company used to demonstrate the bracelet's effectiveness. Other researchers soon replicated these results.

In November 2011, a federal court hit the bracelet's makers with a $57-million judgment in a class-action lawsuit that charged the company with "inappropriate marketing claims." The makers of Power Balance then admitted that there was "no credible scientific basis for the claims" they used to hawk their bracelets, declared bankruptcy, and offered refunds.

In other research, dummy performance boosters (and false feedback) have helped runners and cyclists push their limits, often significantly, though not in every case. For instance, British sports psychologists gave cyclists two different placebo doses of caffeine for separate 10-kilometer time trials. The placebo caffeine improved speed somewhat with the "low dose" and more so with the "high dose." When told they were getting a placebo, however, the cyclist's performance dropped below baseline.

Sometimes sports placebos aren't about what's added but what's taken away. Researchers gave weight lifters a placebo dose of caffeine along with the suggestion that it would boost their strength. After a baseline lift, some of these folks also benefited from surreptitiously reduced weight, enhancing their belief in the power of the drug. For the final lift, the normal load was restored. The athletes whose expectations had been bolstered by the false feedback lifted more weight with less muscle fatigue than both the control group and those who were simply told they were being given caffeine.

The authors of this study alluded to a central governor acting to prevent a "catastrophic" physical breakdown. "In this context," they wrote, a placebo may signal the central governor to "inhibit its brake." In other words, athletic placebos don't create strength, speed, or endurance out of thin air. They help athletes access what is already theirs.

Likewise, placebos may help athletes simply by easing the precompetition anxiety that can speed up metabolism, waste energy, and take a toll on attention. "If you tell people that they have an advantage, then you remove anxiety and people just perform better," says British sports psychologist and triathlon coach Chris Beedie. "For most of us, there's always going to be this little area of psychological headroom we can tap into."

Using varied expectations, Beedie and colleagues were able to raise and lower the performance of cyclists by giving them an inert gelatin capsule before they rode a series of sprints. They told one group that it was a drug that had been shown to boost performance in short-distance cycling such as these sprints. They told another group that the drug helped in longer-distance races, but tended to hurt sprint performance. The cyclists with high positive expectations for the phony drug improved, compared to baseline, while the group with negative expectations for the drug did worse.

In 2010, German researchers studied the effects of omens and good luck charms on several types of performance, including golf putting. Subjects were more accurate when an experimenter told them that their golf ball had been a lucky one for previous subjects.

Thus, wearing a "balance bracelet," ingesting a dummy performance booster, or utilizing other trickery to shore up self-efficacy could be just like rubbing a rabbit's foot or wearing lucky underwear—a little something to soothe the jitters that threaten optimal performance. Many athletes, and not just the openly devout, put their performance in God's hands. The research suggests that faith could help these athletes simply by reducing their anxiety, whether or not their prayers are answered.*

In sum, there are two main ways that placebo expectations can smooth over an athlete's self-imposed speed bumps—the anxiety relief that comes with belief in a performance booster, or specific, automatic triggers such as those in the carbohydrate swish-and-spit study.

---

*Unless you have the kind of quid pro quo faith exhibited by Buffalo Bills star receiver Stevie Johnson. After dropping a game-winning touchdown pass against the Pittsburgh Steelers late in the 2010 season, Johnson tweeted his frustration with the Lord: I PRAISE YOU 24/7!!!!!! AND THIS HOW YOU DO ME!!!!!

The latter mechanism raises the possibility of phantom doping. For instance, morphine is banned in athletic competitions because enhanced pain tolerance could be a competitive edge. What if an athlete could get similar effects from placebo morphine?

In 2007, Italian researchers held a friendly pain-tolerance competition between randomly assembled "teams" of athletic subjects. The athletes would endure arm tourniquet pain during two weekly "training" sessions, followed by a "competition" on week three. The team that collectively endured the most pain would be deemed the winner.

Some of the teams were openly given shots of morphine during their training sessions, while others were given no treatment. On competition day, the researchers told everybody (except the folks in a no-treatment group) that they were getting a shot of morphine. In reality, it was just saline. The team conditioned with morphine endured the most pain, even though a full week had passed since their last real dose. Subjects who were not conditioned with earlier shots of morphine, but were simply told they were getting the painkiller, had smaller, but still significant, pain relief from the placebo injection.

For now, athletes are only banned from taking morphine just before a competition. The drug is not prohibited outright. Presumably an athlete could legally train with morphine or a similar painkiller and then take a placebo dose on the day of competition. Even if it was deemed illegal to do this, morphine clears urine within a few days, and placebo effects in the study occurred a full week after the last real dose.

"Do opioid-mediated placebo effects during competitions have to be considered a doping procedure?" the researchers asked in the study's write-up. If the major sports governing bodies ever do consider phantom doping to be cheating, it would be the first-ever ban on athletic expectations.

In the meantime, athletes are free to trick their brains into easing up on the emergency brake however they would like, whether that's popping a placebo, wearing a good luck charm, or spending a few moments reflecting on athletes like Roger Bannister, who did the impossible.

The current fastest mile was run in 3 minutes, 43.13 seconds by Hicham El Guerrouj of Morocco in 1999. *That* record has stood for more years than the one Bannister beat. Indeed, the last record for the mile to survive so long was set in 1895. Still, thanks to Bannister's legacy, no one will declare a 3:40 mile impossible, or even three and a half minutes. Who dares say it will never happen?

2] IN THE ZONE

It was another chance for English soccer glory. The squad facing Portugal in the quarterfinals of the 2006 soccer World Cup overflowed with talent, just like every English team in the tournament's history. Yet ever since England won the World Cup in 1966, the nation's high hopes for its team were repeatedly dashed. After so many heartbreaking exits from the international stage, the sky-high expectations for the team were always darkened by the question: how will they blow it this time?

A zero-zero tie at the final whistle, the match against Portugal came down to a best-of-five penalty kick shootout to decide the winner. England had never survived a World Cup shootout. It was indeed another chance for England, but nobody on the team looked all that happy to have it.

In soccer shootouts, teams take turns sending a player up for a set shot on goal from just twelve yards out. The goalies must wait for the kick before they can move off the goal line. Goals are expected. At the international level of play, 85 percent of on-target penalty shots score. The real question is who will mess up? Soccer skill matters, but it's secondary in these contests. Luck matters, too. Mostly, though, it's about the pressure of expectations—who will handle it, and who will crack.

With the shootout against Portugal tied at one, Steven Gerrard, a star English midfielder, stepped up to the penalty spot. The Portuguese goalkeeper had already saved a shot from another English hero, Frank Lampard. But Portugal squandered that opportunity when its second shooter misfired and hit the left goalpost.

This was Gerrard's chance to make things right. He was

England's player of the year and a scoring machine. He'd netted twenty-three goals the previous season in the English Premier League and two goals so far in the World Cup. He was just the man England needed, but that knowledge did not sit well with him. As the play-by-play announcer put it to the millions glued to their TVs:

Steven Gerrard is ashen-faced!

Gerrard shot low and to the right. The keeper guessed correctly and knocked the ball wide. England was devastated, but all was not lost. Even after Portugal's next shooter scored, putting them up two goals to one, England could draw level if their fourth shooter managed to convert. This time, the opportunity to save England fell to defender Jamie Carragher. When Carragher stepped to the penalty spot, the English fans in the stadium clutched their faces and closed their eyes.

Nerves are drawn so tight, to breaking point. [The ref blew his whistle.] *Carragher!*

Carragher's shot was low and straight down the middle. It was the easiest of the Portuguese keeper's three saves, a World Cup record. Moments later, the Portuguese striker, Cristiano Ronaldo, calmly walked up and blasted home the winning penalty kick. The official score of Portugal's victory over England was three to one on penalties.

There was lots of conjecture about why England lost, yet again. Their captain, David Beckham, had left the game just after half-time on a bum ankle. Not long after that, the ref ejected English playmaker Wayne Rooney for stomping on a Portuguese defender who fell after a rough attempt to steal the ball. The ejection forced England to play down a man for much of the second half. Still, the team held on. Supported by a stadium filled with roaring English fans, they played with passion and gave themselves a chance at victory. Clearly, they had the skill to win. Their valiant second half showed they had the fight, too. Why did they lose? Maybe because, at some level, that's what they expected to do.

The spectacle of sports stars choking under pressure is morbidly fascinating. In isolation, these episodes seem like aberrations and a testimony to what happens when things go horribly and unexpectedly wrong. Superficially, they are the sports equivalent of a multicar pileup on the highway. Choking is much more than that, however. In fact, a closer look at these improbable failures reveals the essence of sport.

First, the potential for athletes to wilt under pressure amplifies the excitement of big games and humanizes athletic superstars. In the shadow of every glorious upset there cringes a choker, often a whole team of them. Choking exposes the double-edged sword of high expectations.

Second, by looking into how top athletes falter, we better understand how they succeed. Studies suggest that one of the first things choking athletes lose is their ability to anticipate, a skill gained from years of practice. Athletic anticipation is automatic. In fact, it's embodied in the athlete's next move, and it's increasingly seen as the key to world-class performance. Yet this special foresight is fragile. It can be completely undone by the expectations of anxiety. Choking is mastery in reverse. Caught up in a choke, expectations eat their young.

THE CURSE OF ENGLISH PENALTY KICKERS

The self-destruction of the 2006 World Cup was all too familiar to the crestfallen English. Two years earlier, Portugal beat them in another quarterfinal shootout at the European Championships. Penalties were also their undoing in the 1998 World Cup, the 1996 European Championships, and the 1990 World Cup. Even when not playing for the national side, top English players had a reputation for buggering up penalties in big games.

This woeful history is of special interest to Geir Jordet, a sports psychologist at the Norwegian School of Sports Sciences. His laptop is loaded with clips of top English players shanking penalty shots or blasting them into the keeper's arms, and then collapsing into steaming piles of superstar failure.

Jordet wants to know what turns top athletes into chokers, and elite English footballers are excellent case studies. They are watched, discussed, and written about obsessively by a soccer-mad nation that simultaneously expects greatness and disappointment. They are top-form professional athletes, among the world's best, playing in matches they've dreamed about their whole lives. Time and again, they crumble.

"The irony is that I'm not that interested in penalties. But I'm immensely interested in athletes dealing with pressure, and penalty kicks happen to be the most extreme case of that," says Jordet, himself a former semiprofessional soccer player and coach. "When the shooter hits the ball, I lose interest. Everything of importance has already happened."

Jordet's fascination dates to 2004. He had recently moved to the Netherlands, whose national team faced Sweden in a quarterfinal of the European Championships. The game was decided by penalty kicks. The Dutch missed once, but the Swedes missed twice and were eliminated. Jordet interviewed the players from both teams and asked them to relive the shootout. Armed with their recollections and archival data on other major shootouts, he started building a model of penalty kick psychology—a web of player, team, and historical expectations that can ensnare any shooter, but seems especially sticky for British soccer stars.

Over the years, Jordet has watched hundreds of penalty shots in major international tournaments. He scrutinizes the players' preshot routines—Where do they look? How do they walk? How much time do they take? He looks for the psychological cracks that predict a miss. Jordet knows that penalty takers only seem alone as they await the referee's whistle. In reality, they are crowded at the penalty mark by a host of expectations.

Players and coaches don't much like shootouts, which they

deem a high-pressure lottery that's impervious to practice. The French soccer star Christian Karembeu once compared shootouts to Russian roulette. "Someone will get the bullet. You know that," he said. "And it will reduce them to nothing."

Contrary to this sort of fatalism, Jordet has found that the outcomes of penalty kicks actually follow logical patterns.* In general, the more important the game, the fewer goals are scored in the shootout. More goals are scored on shots one and two than on later attempts. Forwards score more often than midfielders, who, in turn, score more than defenders. The most important variable, however, is anxiety. Unsuccessful shooters wear it all over their faces.

Jordet and his colleagues have learned to spot the telltale behaviors of players who miss critical penalties in big matches. In general, they take quicker shots and tend to turn their back on the goal rather than backpedal while awaiting the whistle. Both are avoidance behaviors. The goalkeeper is a threat, Jordet reasons, which is why more anxious players look away. In fact, just being there is a threat—to a player's self-image, to his reputation, and to his legacy—which is why anxious players hurry their shots. They want to get it over with. They want to escape.

Avoidance behaviors relieve the pressure a bit, but they also rob shooters of their focus. That makes sense. More perplexing is the link Jordet has found between expectations and shootout success. Specifically, he's shown that penalty kicks are kryptonite for soccer superstars.

In the first of these studies, he ranked the status of every player taking a penalty in a high-profile shootout over three decades of international tournaments. Players with "current status" had already won an award such as FIFA player of the year. "Future-

---

* Goalies typically guess and jump to one side as soon as the ball is struck. Thus, even a weak shot scores if the keeper is flailing in the opposite direction. To scrub some of the luck from the equation and to better differentiate quality shots, Jordet always does two levels of analysis—one based on overall goals and misses, and the other looking only at shots where the goalkeeper guessed correctly.

status" players received similar recognition, but *after* their shoot-out appearance. Finally, there were "no-status" players who never won a major individual award.

The current-status players—the stars—did the *worst* of all three groups, scoring just 65 percent of the time. By contrast, players granted future status netted 89 percent of their penalty kicks. Meanwhile, the no-status players, aka plebeians in cleats, scored 74 percent of the time.

A high level of soccer skill helped penalty takers convert. One could assume that future-status players have the same (or nearly the same) talent as current-status players without the individual accolades. And players who were later recognized for their abilities scored the most often. Current recognition of that talent, however, and the expectations that go along with it, seemed to tangle up the feet of star players on the penalty spot. In addition to their low scoring rate, current-status players were much more likely to miss the goal completely.

When Jordet counted only those shots where the keeper jumped to the correct side of the goal, current-status players fared even worse. They scored just 40 percent of the time. The future-status players again did best, converting on 86 percent of these chances.

During a break at a recent sports psychology conference, Jordet shows me a video of a current-status English player, John Terry, taking the potential winning penalty kick for Chelsea in the final game of the 2008 Champions League. Terry is nicknamed "Mr. Chelsea," and he earns about $200,000 a week.

"Chelsea has never won the Champions League.* They're one of Europe's richest teams, and Terry's their superstar," Jordet says. It's pouring rain as Mr. Chelsea walks to the penalty spot and awaits the whistle. "See him fiddling with his captain's band," says Jordet. "He's preoccupied with it." When Terry shoots, he

---

*That changed in May 2012 when Chelsea won its first Champions League title in a comeback victory against Bayern Munich.

doesn't just miss. He slips and falls on the sodden field while clanking one off the right post. He stays down, burying a tearful face between his knees.

British penalty takers are hurt by more than star-studded expectations. After all, many national teams have high-status players and do just fine in penalty shootouts. The British players have something else to deal with—the intense collective expectations for their team held by fans and players alike.

Jordet analyzed the shootouts in major international tournaments over three decades involving eight European soccer powers, which he defined as a country that had won at least one of these tournaments. He gauged the status of each team in three ways—previous tournament titles (including years since the most recent title), the number of times a club team from the nation had won the Champions League,* and the percentage of shooters who were current status according to the aforementioned definition.

What did he find? The higher a team's overall status, the fewer penalties it converted and the more its shooters displayed the telltale avoidance behaviors. The best illustration was England. With the highest average number of Champions League winners and the second-highest average of celebrity players on its roster, they were rock bottom on penalty kick conversion. In six shootouts, English players scored just two thirds of their penalty shots, and *only half* of those when the keeper guessed correctly. They were the most rushed by far, followed by Spain and the Netherlands, which were also near the bottom of the scoring pack. English players also did the most to avoid looking at the keeper.

"This suggests that English players, in these contexts, may experience extraordinarily high expectations and pressure," Jordet wrote. Okay, but certainly England's not the only soccer-mad country that expects its national team to triumph? Why do they choke so much more than, say, German or Brazilian players?

---

*Elite club teams have international rosters, but these clubs are still dominated by players born in the country the club represents. On average, about eight of the starting eleven players in the fifty-two club teams under study were native-born.

In *England Expects: A History of the England Football Team* (2006) British journalist James Corbett argues that England's players have been "overwhelmed" by an "inexorable sense of expectation." What's more, these presumptions of soccer greatness are dogged by a history of falling short. To play for England, Corbett writes, is to shoulder "the insatiable hopes, dreams and delusions of its people," and generations of disappointment.

The English players in 2006 knew their history. "Of course, you can't help but think about Southgate, Batty, Pearce, Beckham and Waddle, and all those penalty nightmare misses of old," noted defender Ashley Cole, who would have taken the next penalty shot if Carragher hadn't missed. "It lurks in your mind somewhere, adding more pressure and a little bit of fear."

In 2011, Jordet again analyzed three decades of penalty shootouts from major tournaments. He compared the performance of penalty takers based on their team shootout history, taking into account the number of previous wins and losses, and whether the shooter had been on the squad in the most recent contest.

Penalty takers on teams with a history of shootout losses scored less often than shooters on teams with no shootout history or a history of winning. The differences were greater when the shooter was on the team during its previous shootout. In that case, 87 percent of the shooters scored if their teams had a winning shootout history, but just 63 percent scored if their teams had a history of blowing it. Meanwhile, players on teams with no shootout history scored on 76 percent of their shots. Finally, the shooters whose teams had a dismal history of two or more shootout losses converted just 46 percent of their chances.

A first reaction might be: no kidding, losing teams field less-talented shooters and tend to lose penalty shootouts while good teams win. The data argues against that, however. Despite their inability to win games decided by penalty kicks, teams with a history of shootout losses won more tournament games overall than teams with no shootout history or teams with a history of shootout wins. The teams that struggled the most with penalty kicks also fielded more high-status players, according to Jordet's definition.

Jordet's studies reveal correlation, not causation. Still, his results provide fuel for speculation about the psychological profile of the penalty shot choker. It's the interplay of personal, team, and national expectations that's poisonous to the penalty taker. Imagine that you're an English soccer star, stepping to the penalty spot for your national team. Lurking in the background is the expectation that any top-level player should score on a shot this close, especially one like you who's been singled out and honored for soccer greatness. Now imagine you're on a team that really *should* win more often than it does. When you step up to the penalty mark, all of those expectations are waiting there for you, making very fertile ground for any kernel of self-doubt.

Weaker players on less-storied teams can step up to the penalty mark in major tournaments and hope for the best. They may feel proud, maybe even lucky, that they made it this far. Soccer superstars on favored teams with a checkered history have no such luxury. Not only do they expect a lot from themselves, but they also carry a nation's hopes for redemption. They will either break the curse of history or add another infamous, blundering chapter. There is no middle ground.

I THINK I CAN, UNTIL I CAN'T

In the mid-1980s, renowned psychologist Roy Baumeister published a study that ignited decades of scholarly debate about when athletes choke under pressure. Baumeister suggested a potential home field *disadvantage,* or a "home choke" effect among athletes playing in the most important games. Using data from every baseball World Series, League Championship Series, and National Basketball Association semifinals and finals, he found that teams fared poorly when they played at home with a chance to clinch a multigame series, winning just 41 percent of these games.

A decade later, however, other researchers replicated the analysis with fresher data and the evidence of a home choke had disappeared. Then a 2010 meta-analysis spanning ten sports found a significant home field advantage in every case, *especially* for high-pressure games such as playoffs and championships.

Baumeister questioned the methodology of home choke critics and pointed out recent rule changes* that helped the home team. He also emphasized that he had never questioned home field advantage in general. Instead, he argued that supportive audiences had the *potential* to endanger performance. To make his point, Baumeister moved from the messiness of archival sports research to a lab study in which subjects counted backward by 13 out loud starting from 1,470, or played a video game for cash prizes, all while being watched. The audience was either a good friend who would share the prize for an outstanding performance, a neutral observer, or an adversary who would claim the cash if the subject messed up.

How did subjects supported by a friendly audience perform? When the tasks were easy, they did about as well as subjects in the other two groups. When the tasks were challenging, they did worse than everybody else, *but they thought they did better*. Why? All of the tasks featured a trade-off between speed and accuracy, and both counted in the subject's score. In front of a friendly audience, people were more cautious, improving accuracy somewhat but losing even more on speed. In the write-up, Baumeister and his coauthors wrote that supportive audiences may "elicit a self-protective orientation that takes precedence over achievement goals and may detract from performance quality." In other words, people don't want to screw up and risk the esteem of their "fans." They try harder, but in the wrong ways. At the same time, supportive audiences can "help people feel better and help them think they are doing better," even when they're not.

---

* For instance, since 1986, World Series games follow the rules of the home team's league regarding the use of designated hitters instead of pitchers (notoriously weak hitters) in the batting lineup.

So what happens when an athlete chokes under pressure? According to Baumeister, choking is worse than expected performance "under circumstances that increase the importance of good or improved performance." A number of sports psychologists have since argued that this definition is too mild. Choking, they say, isn't missing your putt by a few extra centimeters or dropping a couple percentage points in free throw accuracy, as it's framed in some research. Athletes know when they're choking without measuring or adding up the score, because everything comes unglued. Confidence in success and ability is suddenly, and inexorably, replaced by visions of failure and futility. The sheer improbability of that failure gives it a stink that's very hard to scrub clean.

Certainly, the quintessential choke is more than an athlete not quite meeting her usual standards. Nevertheless, at the highest levels of sport, ever-narrowing slivers of time separate victory and defeat. Count to two out loud. That's the difference between Jamaican sprinter Usain Bolt winning three gold medals at the 2008 Olympics and going home with no medals at all.

With that in mind, if expectations have even tiny effects on the performance of top athletes, they may be decisive, no matter what they're called. It's worth taking a deeper look into the athletic skills that high pressure and anxiety can undermine, and what new strategies may keep choking at bay.

EXPECTATIONS KILL ANTICIPATION

The show is always the same. One by one, the baseball all-stars step to the plate only to be struck out . . . by a girl . . . throwing underhand. In 1996, the "girl" was Olympic softball pitcher Lisa Fernandez. Fresh off a gold medal, and standing all of five foot six, Fernandez struck out Major League sluggers Bobby Bonilla and David Justice. In 2005, the pitcher was Jennie Finch, who'd recently won her own softball gold medal. Albert Pujols, Mike Piazza, and Barry Bonds couldn't touch a single pitch from Finch.

There are several reasons why big-league hitters have no problem with 95 mph fastballs but can't handle a 70 mph softball. The biggest one is anticipation. Experiments show that elite athletes don't have quicker reflexes than the rest of us. In most tests, the average reaction time by pro or Joe alike is about 200 milliseconds.* That's how long it takes to carry out a response that your brain has already ordered up. It's also about half the time that a pitch is in flight, whether it's a softball thrown from 43 feet or a fastball hurled from 60.5 feet. That leaves a hopelessly tiny speck of time for the actual swing decision. The only way a batter stands a chance is to see the future—to predict when and where the ball will cross home plate—using pre-pitch clues from the pitcher's windup. Major League players have spent years learning to read the movements of baseball pitchers' arms and hands. This ability runs on automatic. Conscious thought is too slow. Facing a windmilling softball pitcher, baseball players are robbed of this foresight, and they go down swinging, or not—Barry Bonds didn't even wave at the three pitches Finch threw to strike him out.

Sports scientists have long known that anticipation is critical for elite athletes. There simply isn't enough time to track a professional player's fastball, tennis serve, or hockey slapshot in flight, process that visual information, decide the appropriate action, and send the motor commands to the muscles. Only recently have researchers started to find out *how* this anticipation works, when it doesn't, and how it can be enhanced. The answers are important, not just to curious scientists, but to every athlete and coach looking for an edge.

Study after study shows how highly skilled athletes outpredict novices when watching stop-action films of a basketball leaving the fingertips of a free throw shooter, or a tennis player's racquet just making contact with the ball on a serve. While expert athletes seem able to glimpse the future, this skill relies on neural wiring that we all share.

* Go to www.humanbenchmark.com to test yourself.

According to the "common coding" theory proposed in the late 1990s, our brains control our movements in the future tense, by anticipating their effects. Athletic expertise sharpens these predictions, but they support almost every move we make.

When you play catch, for instance, your brain anticipates the destination of the baseball zipping your way, specifically where the catch should take place. This "forward model" of the catch coordinates every other movement required for the effort—do you need to twist your arm for a backhand grab, reach down to your shoelaces or jump to reach the ball, or just start running because this one's over your head?

A prime candidate for generating these predictions are "mirror neurons," discovered accidentally by Italian neuroscientists in the early 1990s. The researchers were using electrodes implanted in the brains of rhesus monkeys to record neurons that fired whenever the monkey reached for a peanut. One day a human experimenter happened to reach for a peanut as the monkeys watched. Bang! The same neurons started crackling.

Follow-up tests indicated that these mirror neurons don't just mimic, they collectively represent "action ideas" that the brain accumulates and keeps at the ready. For instance, the same neurons fire when a monkey rips paper, or watches somebody else rip paper, or when the monkey hears paper ripping. Once learned, the neural pattern for "ripping paper" waits in the monkey brain and can be cued by perceiving its effects.

Much of the evidence for human mirror neurons has been less direct. In 2010, British researchers compared the predictions of expert and novice badminton players watching stop-action videos of badminton shots while in a brain scanner. The videos paused just before the racquet hit the shuttlecock. Experts were much better at anticipating where on the court a shot would land, and the predictive accuracy correlated with the amount of activity in brain areas where mirror neurons had been found in monkeys.

That same year, UCLA neuroscientists found the first direct evidence for human mirror neurons. They studied epilepsy patients whose brains were already implanted with electrodes (to help pinpoint the origins of their severe seizures). They asked these folks to watch or perform grasping motions, along with smiles and frowns, while recording more than a thousand neurons. Just as in monkeys, a substantial number of neurons in these patients fired for both observing and doing, with specific patterns of neural activity linked to specific actions.

When we learn how to hit a backhand in tennis, shoot a jump shot, or downhill ski, there's usually a heavy dose of step-by-step instruction. Teachers and coaches break down skills and strategies into small pieces that newbies practice repeatedly, learning gradually and consciously, always on the lookout for errors to be corrected. So our action ideas when we're learning a sport are relatively clunky and shortsighted. As we master these skills, our brains off-load them to the faster, automatic system that guides our movements with increasingly refined forward models. The more we practice, the more accurate and farsighted these predictions become.

This superior anticipation isn't a given, however. It's intimately linked to how well an athlete is playing. While motor anticipation runs on automatic, the slower, conscious brain knows when a performance counts and when it doesn't. It mulls the expectations of the fans, and it knows the score. Indeed, it's so used to analyzing everything and calling the shots that it habitually reacts to anxiety and fear of failure by butting in and disrupting the automatic anticipatory system—either with worries and distraction or with too much attention to the details of well-learned techniques. In doing so, the conscious brain mucks up the very performance it aims to save.

In 2007, psychologist Rob Gray wanted to investigate the connections between athletic expertise, performance, and anticipation. Gray set up a home plate in his lab and told novice and expert baseball players to stand there for virtual batting practice using a computer-generated pitcher on a large projected baseball diamond. Every pitch was right down the middle, although the computer randomly varied height and speed. Thanks to a motion sensor attached to the end of the bat, every swing was tracked in three dimensions.

At first, the batters received immediate performance feedback. After a swing and a miss, a disembodied umpire yelled "Strike!" A boisterous crowd cheered hits and groaned at weak grounders. An announcer called both fouls and home runs. Then, after a few dozen practice swings, all post-swing feedback was delayed until the batter used a cursor to predict where on (or off) the field they expected the ball to land. After making a prediction, the batters watched the hit unfold.

Gray and his team plotted a grid over the field and compared every prediction with the ball's actual landing spot. The expert baseball players were better than the novices at both hitting and predicting. The experts also seemed to do their best when they kept their focus on the outcomes of their swings, rather than the swings themselves. They made more accurate predictions of where the ball would land when they were hitting well, and less accurate predictions in the midst of hitting slumps.

"We think that when the expert players went through a period of misses, they tried to change something about their swing. They started overcontrolling it," says Gray. "They turned their attention inward as opposed to performing well."

In short, they choked. When novice players focused on their swings, their ability to predict also went south, but this inward focus did wonders for their hitting. In other words, beginners and chokers focus on technique. Experts focus on what's next.

WHEN FORESIGHT ISN'T 20/20

We've seen that high expectations in sports are fertile ground for anxiety, which messes up performance by disabling a key element of athletic expertise—anticipation. What can be done to keep pressure from short-circuiting the athletic mind?

At a 2010 sports medicine and coaching conference organized

by Cricket Australia, a handful of cricket coaches found a surprising new training tool to ward off choking: blurry vision. For the uninitiated, cricket is a bewildering sport. It shares a lot with baseball, in that there are batters, fielders, runs, and outs. In cricket, however, the ball is "bowled," rather than pitched, at a batter who stands in front of a wicket made of three wooden "stumps" topped by two wooden "bails." There are no fewer than ten ways to get a cricket batter out, but a common one is a swing and a miss on a bowl that hits and dislodges part of the wicket. In top-level cricket, bowls can be as blistering as any fastball.

At the conference, the coaches learned of a study in which researchers used contact lenses to blur the vision of expert cricket batters. The lenses created four levels of distortion ranging from no change to legally blind. Surprisingly, a little blur didn't hurt hitting performance. In fact, batters hitting medium-paced bowls of approximately 60 mph weren't fazed by anything less than the highest level of blur—a degree of fuzziness that blends bowler with background. Even when facing faster-paced bowls, in the range of 80 mph, the batters had no trouble until the second-worst level of blur. Somehow, batters knew where the bowl was heading, even without a clear view of it in flight.

A follow-up study showed that these predictions were the most accurate when untouched by conscious thought. The best predictions were wrapped up in a player's practiced reactions. Once again, batters' vision was blurred. Their task was to predict where the bowl was heading—first verbally, then by pivoting their lead foot in the expected direction, and finally by swinging. It turned out that these expert cricket batters couldn't verbally predict bowl direction to save their lives. They did only a little better with the foot pivot. They were consistently accurate *only when swinging.*

What really grabbed the cricket coaches' attention was that a little blur actually improved the batters' nonswinging predictions of bowl direction. A similar effect had been found in a 2009 study of blur on tennis players anticipating a serve.

How could blurry vision help a cricket batter track a ball that reaches him in less than half a second? The researchers cited a two-tiered theory of human vision proposed in the mid-1990s: one level is the more recently evolved visual system for detail and color, which produces a fine-grained interpretation of everything we see. In addition, there's an older visual system keyed to movement and contrast, in which clarity is sacrificed for speed and anticipation.

In motion predictions, detail is secondary. For example, expert badminton and tennis players can outpredict novices on the outcome of a serve using only "point-light videos" of twenty bright dots showing a player's joints, forehead, and racquet (think: animated Lite-Brite). The cricket research went further. It suggested that when the real task is movement prediction and reaction, detail can get in the way.

Maybe the athletes weren't as accurate with verbal predictions because describing something is a conscious task for which the brain habitually turns to the fine-grained visual system. Blur is a detail filter, forcing the batter's brain to switch back to the action-oriented visual system, thereby improving the critical skill of anticipation. That idea hooked the coaches on blur and prompted several of them to contact the researchers for a pair of their special goggles to help their slumping players.

"They use it as a training tool to change the focus of batters who are a little bit out of form," says David Mann, an Australian optometrist and one of the researchers who did the cricket studies. "Often, when guys aren't batting well, they're thinking too much about what they're doing and not going with their instincts."

ESCAPE ANXIETY OR EMBRACE IT

Other than wearing somebody else's glasses, how can athletes ward off choking? How do we keep the anxiety born of high expectations from short-circuiting the anticipatory reflexes that are essential for a winning performance? There's no single answer and no miracle cure.

Peak athletic focus is forward-thinking and goal-oriented. Choking turns this focus inside out in multiple ways. It is a hydra of self-defeat. Sometimes anxiety prompts distraction—by the crowd, perhaps, or an athlete's own worries. Other times, the pressure turns focus inward, and athletes overcontrol their movements. They become hyperfocused and scrutinize the mechanics of their performance instead of simply performing. Both types of choking stem from misplaced attention, but they call for very different counterstrategies.

According to Jordet, penalty kickers rush their kicks because their primary focus is to escape the pressure. Scoring a goal becomes secondary, resulting in more hurried shots, more devastating losses, and more tears.

However, for athletes prone to hyperfocus, slowing down can make things worse. In one recent study, for instance, psychologist Sian Beilock asked both experienced and novice golfers to use either a standard putter or a goofy, strangely weighted S-shaped putter. Everybody putted one hundred times at five distances after being told to putt as quickly as possible while still trying for accuracy. In another round of putts—the order was counterbalanced—subjects putted after being told to take as much time as they needed for utmost accuracy.

The results revealed an irony of time pressure. Taking it slow helped the novice golfers and the experienced golfers when given the strange, S-shaped putter, but the extra time hurt the experienced golfers using a standard putter.

Sometimes more time just means more opportunities for the conscious mind to barge in and make mischief. "Haste doesn't always make waste," Beilock writes in her book, *Choke: What the Secrets of the Brain Reveal About Getting It Right When You Have To* (2010). She and other researchers have also warded off choking with a little distraction—having golfers count backward as they putt, or asking basketball players to sing a song as they shoot free throws. Keep your conscious mind occupied, in other words, and it won't get in your body's way.

One anti-choking strategy that manages to combine taking one's time and letting well-learned skills run on autopilot is routine. Kickers in the National Football League thrive on routine. So do the best NBA free throw shooters. One study of free throws in a stretch of recent NBA playoff games found that shooters hit 84 percent of their shots after following their routine (number of bounces, deep breaths, glances at the basket, wiping forehead, and so forth) but only 71 percent of their shots when they deviated. That may not seem like a huge difference, but consider how many basketball games are decided by clutch free throws in the waning seconds.

Perhaps a more fundamental way to keep anxiety from derailing athletic anticipation might be to bypass traditional step-by-step skill learning in favor of effects-focused instruction. If the expert brain focuses on outcomes, then why not skip right to that and avoid the incremental, rule-based learning that comes back to bite athletes under pressure?

This "implicit learning" approach is championed by kinesiologist Gabriele Wulf. Since the mid-1990s, she has shown that beginners learn sports skills more quickly—including soccer throw-ins, tennis backhands, golf pitch shots, and slalom skiing—when their instructions focus on external effects rather than technique. For instance, focus on the trajectory and landing spot of a backhand rather than footwork, backswing, or the contact point of racquet and ball.

Or maybe we could simply change our expectations about our ability to perform under pressure. In a 2012 study, subjects threw a ball at a target from seven meters away. Then everybody completed a personality questionnaire. The researchers randomly told some subjects that their answers suggested they would likely thrive under pressure, while giving nonspecific feedback to control subjects. Finally, everybody tried again to hit the targets, but under pressure this time. They were videotaped, offered cash prizes for hitting the target, and given a goal of improving their accuracy by 15 percent. Nearly 90 percent of people who were told that they'd likely do well under pressure met that accuracy goal, compared to only about 27 percent of the control group.

Other researchers taught runners to reinterpret symptoms of anxiety, such as sweaty palms and stomach butterflies, as feelings of excitement. Runners ran faster when they were led to believe that their pre-race jitters meant they were getting amped up for the competition.

Another idea for choke resistance, championed by the Dutch kinesiologist Raôul Oudejans, is to ratchet up anxiety during practice. Traditionally, practice is a time for focused preparation that is optimally free from pressure and distraction. Even in competitive scrimmages, nothing really counts. Oudejans suggests that making practice a little uncomfortable can prepare athletes for the pressure and anxiety of game time.

In one study, he worked on free throws with two semiprofessional basketball teams. First, the players took two baseline tests of accuracy, one without pressure and another for higher stakes— a sizable cash prize for accuracy, an attentive audience of coaches and players, and videotaping with the understanding that experts would later evaluate each shooter's technique. In the high-stakes test, shooters were also told to imagine that every free throw was a potential game winner.

Then, at the tail end of nine regular practice sessions spread over several weeks, each player shot a few extra free throws, either normally—bounce, bounce, shoot, bounce, bounce, shoot— or under high-pressure conditions like the ones mentioned above. In a final session, the players' free-throw performance was tested again, both with and without the high-stakes manipulations.

Before the training, the extra pressure reduced overall shooting accuracy by about 5 percent. In the post-test, the team that had trained normally had a similar drop-off in performance under stress. By contrast, the team that had trained with anxiety had no such trouble. In fact, they were *more* accurate when shooting under pressure. This brings us back to Jordet. At many meetings with soccer coaches he was told that penalty shootouts were so uniquely stressful that practicing them was beside the point. Shooters at the penalty spot may want to escape, Jordet says in an interview, "but the coaches are the biggest escape artists of all. They don't practice these things. They don't think about it or plan for it, because they'd rather not see it happen."

As Jordet's research accumulates, however, coaches are gradually being converted. He has worked with the Dutch national team and with a number of professional club teams in Norway, the Netherlands, and Belgium on overcoming the pressure of a shootout. Independently, word is spreading about not rushing penalty kicks. In terms of average time per shooter, the 2010 World Cup featured the most "relaxed" penalty shootout in the tournament's history—deciding a round-of-sixteen match between Japan and Paraguay. Japan lost that one, but a year later, their women's team took their sweet time and calmly upset the Americans in a penalty shootout to win the women's World Cup.

THE "HOT HAND" DEBATE

Jordet's research suggests that a penalty shooter's past successes and failures, even the performance history of his team stretching back for decades, can ultimately change the speed and trajectory of his or her shot. In other words, a history of failure makes failure more likely when the stakes are high. This idea runs smack into a decades-old controversy over the "hot hand" and "cold hand," which is the notion that an athlete's early successes or failures can affect subsequent performance.

The argument started in 1985, when psychologists Thomas Gilovich, Robert Vallone, and Amos Tversky investigated the common belief that basketball shooters can get "hot" after making a few shots in a row, thereby increasing their chances of hitting the next one. While it has received much less attention, the trio of scholars also scrutinized the belief that missing a few in a row could mean a player had gone "cold" (i.e., was choking) and was more likely to miss his next shot. Does success beget success? Does failure breed more failure?

The basketball players, coaches, and fans surveyed by the researchers certainly believed this. But Gilovich and his colleagues found otherwise. They analyzed a season of the Philadelphia 76ers, a team that took the rare step of recording the outcomes of its players' shots and the order in which they took them. It turned out that shooters were *more likely to score after a miss, and more likely to miss after scoring,* the opposite of what the hot hand/cold hand beliefs predict.

Collectively, after making a shot, there was a 51 percent chance players would make the next one. After missing a shot, however, their chances of making the next basket *rose* to 54 percent. If they'd made their previous two shots, then their chances of scoring on the third dropped to 50 percent. But if they'd missed two in a row, then they had a 53 percent chance of making number three.

The researchers concluded that the common belief in the hot hand stemmed from a misunderstanding of randomness. If you flip a coin some huge number of times, chance will give you heads half the time and tails the other half. However, if you just look at, say, ten of those flips, the distribution may not look "random" at all. For instance, the odds of getting at least five heads or tails in a row with ten flips is about one in five.

Gilovich, Vallone, and Tversky also looked at shooting data from three professional basketball teams and found that streaks of various lengths—both hits and misses—did not happen more often than the players' overall shooting percentage would predict. Of course, basketball players, unlike coin flippers, must contend with defensive pressure, and some shots are harder than others. The researchers minimized those differences by analyzing free throws, where there's no defense and the shot is always the same. They studied free throw data from the Boston Celtics and found that players averaged 75 percent on their second shot whether or not they made the first one.

In the years since, other researchers have searched for evidence of the hot hand in several sports, using statistics in the manner of good scientists. A review of these studies published two decades after the original concluded that statistical support for the hot hand is "considerably limited," although a few hints of it were seen in sports such as bowling and horseshoe pitching where competitors repeatedly attempt the same shot without defensive pressure. One study also found a weak hot-hand-ish effect in tennis and another found one in volleyball.

What may goad athletes and sports fans is that straight-up statistical tests of the hot and cold hand turn players into probability robots. For example, a basketball player who makes 40 percent of his shots is treated like a ten-sided die with four sides that say "hit" and six that say "miss." Roll that ten-sided die the same number of times as the player shoots in a season, and you'll likely get results that statistically match the actual games, including the frequency and length of shooting streaks.

Gilovich and company were careful to note that the "hot hand" they were testing was the prevalent "success breeds success" model. But as others have argued, it might be useful to dispense with unbroken streaks as the test of hot and cold hands. Even those who believe that success begets success know that all streaks eventually end. They just don't know when. Judged in terms of probability, that means that a little success begets more success, but then *even more* success inevitably begets failure. What kind of magic is that?

In addition, what if we also put aside aggregate statistical analysis and simply looked at performance ups and downs in isolation? For instance, take our 40 percent basketball shooter. Imagine that he makes just 6 out of 20 shots one night and then hits 10 out of 20 shots the next. On a third night, this player manages only 2 out of 20. Then, on a fourth night, he nails 14 out of 20. Did he get hot on that fourth night? Did he go cold the night before?

Despite the ups and downs of these four games, our shooter obeys the laws of probability by making 40 percent of his overall attempts. If the hot hand must defy probability, then we have no evidence of it here, and we can extend this sort of variability over an entire season with the same results.

Is it nevertheless possible that on the night that our human shooter hit 14 out of 20, he benefited from confidence and lowered anxiety due to some early baskets? Is it possible that this extra confidence was in the mix of factors that made this particular night so successful, and that its absence helped seal his fate on the 2-for-20 night?

What else might cause these performance ups and downs? Variable defensive pressure from opponents could partially account for it. Maybe our shooter was able to work in a little more practice before his above-average games, or he made better shot selections on these nights. All of these are possible; indeed they are likely.

What is not possible, if a hot hand effect does not exist, is that swings of confidence due to past performance influenced this variation. If the cold hand doesn't exist, then choking under pressure is just probability catching up with an athlete at the worst possible time. If the hot and cold hand are complete fictions, then self-confidence can have nothing to do with performance unless one argues that an athlete's self-confidence is affected by *everything but* recent performance.

As the philosopher Steven Hales noted in an essay about the hot hand, the skeptics don't simply argue "that success makes people too optimistic about future success, or that the internal sense of being hot is sometimes wrong. Rather, the skeptics maintain that [the belief in a hot hand] is always wrong. This is a bitter pill to swallow."

The denial of the *cold* hand seems even harder to swallow. It may be logically inconsistent, but a performance ceiling due to training, technique, and overall athleticism seems more solid than a performance floor after an athlete fouls up big with everything on the line.

The scientific case that success can, *at least sometimes*, breed more success (and vice versa) is known as momentum psychology. Jordet, for one, positions his penalty kick studies as evidence for momentum in sports. Even when past successes and failures are not pinned to the foot of the current penalty shooter, he concludes, "positive or negative vicarious experiences may have strengthened or weakened the players' self-efficacy in the penalty shootout, thus producing higher or lower performance, respectively."

Jordet opens one of his studies with a quote from soccer star Michael Owen of Manchester United. "There is nothing so nerve-racking as a penalty shootout," Owen says. When you stand at the mark awaiting the whistle, "your body simply doesn't belong to you." The question at these critical moments is whether it also belongs to your expectations or just to the laws of probability. It may be both.

CONSUMING EXPECTATIONS

3] THE BIG WANT

In her worst years, Jeri B. could lose more than a thousand dollars a night, just for fun. Her gambling started at the dog track and then moved on to Foxwoods Casino in Connecticut.

"I was there the day Foxwoods opened," she says. "I spent every cent I had and drove home on gas fumes."

When Jeri went bankrupt in 1994, she owed more than $100,000. Jeri didn't think of herself as an addict. She wasn't hopelessly impulsive or manic or big into drinking, drugs, or risky living. She had a college degree and a steady, high-paying technology job. She was no stranger to hard work and responsibility. After declaring bankruptcy, Jeri laid off the gambling, and she was debt-free in ten years. Still, the craving never left her.

By 2004, flush with new credit cards, Jeri had found a new casino much closer than Foxwoods—just keystrokes away, in the flourishing world of online gambling. In no time, she dug herself another six-figure debt.

When it comes to activating the brain's reward system, the expectations of wanting are more powerful than the here and now of liking. We often think of desire and the objects of our desire as inseparable. We think it is the indulgence itself—the luscious ice cream, the rush of nicotine, or the flood of coins from a slot machine—that motivates us. To a greater extent, however, it is the expectation of these rewards, the luxurious anticipation of them, that fires up our brains and compels us to dig in, take a drag, or place another bet.

Does this seem like a distinction without a difference? Maybe, until we confront a story like Jeri's. She didn't enjoy winning. She enjoyed gambling. Anticipation is what kept her at it, day after day. Put simply, addiction is a grotesque and overgrown form of motivation. It is motivation without end, accomplishing nothing but self-destruction. Yet, the compulsive thoughts that hijacked Jeri's mind and ruined her life sprang from the same mental machinery that gets us out of bed every morning and keeps us working and striving to reach our life goals.

While liking fades, wanting never quits. In a healthy brain, that's a good thing. Our brains aren't greedy. They are future-obsessed. Survival of the fittest depends on the ability to spot what's new and different and the motivation to prepare for it. From an evolutionary standpoint, enjoying the moment doesn't get us very far.

Nevertheless, too much wanting can blind us to dangers, diminish our performance, and make us work doggedly for what we don't even like. We try to ignore, resist, or smother wanting with straight-up denial and self-control, but maybe there's a better way. If we unwind the expectations at the root of wanting, then we can see how these expectations can get the better of us, and how we might get the better of them.

CHANGING THE WANTING EQUATION

The world is fat. In 2010, the Organisation for Economic Cooperation and Development reported that in nearly half its member nations, at least 50 percent of the population was overweight. In 1980, obesity rates in the industrialized world were usually well below 10 percent, the report noted. Since that time, they had doubled or tripled in many countries, and the OECD analysis of childhood obesity rates projected an even pudgier future for most member nations.

Obesity has been a top public health enemy for years. As our waistlines expand, so do our rates of diabetes, heart disease, and stroke. The fattening has persisted even as supermarket shelves and fast food menus are stocked with more low-calorie options.

The surgeon general has issued warning after warning, and gym memberships have skyrocketed. Despite all this, we keep getting fatter. Why can't we stop eating?

A few years ago, a group of psychologists came up with a novel way to slim us down. They convinced people that the unhealthy foods they crave had made them vomit at some point in their childhood. False memories diminished cravings for strawberry ice cream, peach yogurt, and egg salad, and affected actual food decisions. Only one food proved impervious: potato chips.

It seems wacky, but the suggestion that we fight obesity with false vomit memories indicates how difficult wanting can be to tame. Plain old information about why something is bad for you rarely works. Smoking causes lung cancer.* Not in me. That burrito supreme is a caloric tsunami. So what, I'm hungry.

The persistence of unhealthy habits in populations that, by now, clearly know better has sparked the development of new self-control strategies that don't require temptation to be reasoned into submission, including giving others the power to restrain us when we can't restrain ourselves. For instance, most casinos keep lists of people who have volunteered to be barred from entry. In 2010, MasterCard introduced "In Control" credit cards that held customers to a budget and pestered them with e-mails and text messages if they overspent. Likewise, Web sites such as ultrinsic .com and stickK.com let people wager real money on meeting their self-control goals or voluntarily endure public shaming if they fail.

Willpower, whether our own or borrowed, is clearly important for both avoiding unhealthy temptation and keeping us focused on longer-term goals, as we'll cover in more detail in Chapter 8. Nevertheless, we may be missing a big part of the self-control puzzle by reducing it to a struggle between a nay-saying, civilized brain and a primitive, hedonistic "lizard brain."

*The relative ineffectiveness of the plain-speaking surgeon general's warnings led to the graphic redesigns—such as pictures of tracheotomies, babies in smoke-filled rooms— introduced in 2012.

Our reward system is not just a party animal from whom we must hide the cookies, booze, and credit cards. Wanting isn't all id. Our reptilian brains play a big role in what we crave, but so do the parts of our brain we consider far more enlightened. In the split second before we make a decision, our reward expectations are a constant work in progress, shaped by memory, emotions, and the appeal of competing desires. Our brains' reward systems get a buzz from anticipating immediate, tangible goodies like ice cream as well as more abstract prizes such as discovery,* mastery of a complex task, or good health and a long life.

The ability to resist temptation may have as much to do with changing the balance of our expectations as it does with our powers of self-denial. A group of researchers at Caltech showed this by scanning the brains of self-reported dieters. In the first round of scans, subjects were shown a range of food images, from broccoli to candy bars. They then rated each food on separate scales of healthiness and taste. The researchers presumed that the dieters had two distinct "goal values" for food—an immediate desire for tastiness and a longer-term desire to be healthy.

In a second scanning session, a computer picked one food for each dieter that the subject had initially rated neutral for taste and healthiness. They asked the subjects to choose between this neutral food and every other food for a potential post-scan snack. To ensure that they were getting truthful answers, the researchers gave the decisions real consequences. They told their subjects that one of their snack choices, picked at random, would be served to them after the scanning session. In other words, if you picked boiled spinach and passed on a Snickers bar in order to seem virtuous, then get ready to eat yer spinach, Popeye!

About half of the dieters, henceforth the "non-self-controllers,"

---

* Even monkeys crave discovery, it turns out. When presented with two pictures that predict a reward that randomly varies in amount, the monkeys favor the picture that gives some hint about how big the reward will be. This advance knowledge doesn't change the size of their reward. So, knowing doesn't give the monkeys any tangible advantages. Nevertheless, the monkeys want to know what's coming, and they change their behavior in order to find out.

consistently chose the foods they rated higher in taste during the first scanning session. Meanwhile, the "self-controllers" more frequently chose foods they earlier rated higher in healthiness.

What did the brain scans say? The difference between the two groups was revealed in the ventromedial prefrontal cortex (vmPFC), a central cog in the brain's reward system. Overall, the more that a particular food sparked activity in a subject's vmPFC during the second scanning session, the more likely he or she was to choose it for a snack. However, stark differences emerged when researchers compared the strength of this prefrontal reward signal with the subject's initial taste and health ratings of the chosen food.

Specifically, vmPFC activity in the brains of non-self-controllers at the moment of decision reflected only the food's initial taste ratings. Taste was the only reward that mattered to them. In the minds of self-controllers, however, a food's healthiness ratings also factored in.* This increased their expectations of reward for something healthy like broccoli when matched up against the neutral snack, while decreasing the relative allure of a delicious yet unhealthy snack like chocolate.

The frontal and subcortical areas of our brain's reward system are constantly chattering back and forth, engaged in multiple feedback loops, gauging the expected value of different rewards. Self-controllers weren't simply better at denying themselves something they wanted. Their long-term goals of staying fit changed the balance of their reward expectations. They didn't overcome the power of wanting. They harnessed it to the pursuit of better health.

FILLING UP ON EXPECTATIONS

It's useful to remember that wanting has a purpose. It gives us the motivation to pursue a goal, whether that's a long-term goal like

---

*The extent to which a food's healthiness made it more desirable was correlated with activity in the nearby dorsolateral prefrontal cortex (dlPFC). This led the researchers to surmise that the dlPFC may be the part of the brain that sees the value in long-term goals, such as staying fit, and adds those considerations to the wanting equation signaled in the vmPFC.

running a marathon or a shorter-term goal like eating a juicy cheeseburger. Once that goal's been achieved, wanting moves along.

We can speed this process up or slow it down by changing our expectations. For instance, we can satisfy our hunger by consuming a mix of real calories and placebo calories, as British psychologists showed in a 2011 study. They offered a strawberry-banana smoothie to students who had fasted for three hours before coming to the lab. Prior to serving the smoothies, they showed each subject a plate filled with the ingredients, ostensibly to ensure that the subjects weren't allergic to anything, but really to mess with their minds. While all the smoothies contained the same amount of strawberries and bananas, some subjects saw modest portions of fruit while others saw plates that were overflowing.

Before enjoying their smoothies, students rated their hunger on a sliding scale ranging from "not at all" to "extremely." They used a similar scale to rate the fullness they expected from their liquid lunch. Not surprisingly, people shown the heaping piles of fruit expected a lot more from their smoothies—about 40 percent more fullness on average. What's more surprising is that these expectations were fulfilled.

The students agreed not to eat or drink anything caloric for three hours after their smoothies and to check in with the researchers every hour to tell them how hungry they felt. People who expected more from their smoothies were less hungry and more full at every time point. Even after three hours, they were more full than they'd been when they had arrived at the lab. By contrast, in just two hours smoothie drinkers who saw less fruit up front felt hungrier and less full than they had before lunch.

Other research shows how placebo calories can have real effects on our metabolism and digestion. Participants in one study were given a 380-calorie chocolate milkshake, but they were told it was either a 620-calorie "indulgent shake" or a 140-calorie "sensishake." The researchers took blood samples from the participants before and after they drank their milkshakes to measure ghrelin, a peptide released by the stomach that makes its way to the brain with this message: "Feed me!" The brain responds by generating the familiar sensation of hunger. As you eat, the stomach slows its release of ghrelin and hunger abates. The blood concentration of ghrelin in people who thought they were indulging dropped steeply, but it barely budged in people who believed their milkshakes were low-cal.

We are often warned about the perils of mindless eating. For instance, studies have found that dieters often overeat a food they believe is lower in fat and calories, or order a more scrumptious dessert after choosing a salad over fries, thereby undoing the advantages of their initial healthy choice. The thought is that people let down their guard. They stop monitoring their intake and eat without thinking. The milkshake study, however, suggests that thinking a lot about what we eat can be a double-edged sword. Being in a diet frame of mind, simply believing that we're eating foods with fewer calories and less fat, may keep us hungrier than we otherwise would be. Labeling food as "diet" and ourselves as dieters may keep cravings alive.

Because our minds are future-obsessed, the pleasure of liking is fleeting. Wanting persists, however, as its expectations move on to a new target. Psychologists have various names for this cycle: "the hedonic treadmill" or, simply, "adaptation." We get used to things. The fifteenth bite of a banana split is nowhere near as much fun as the first, and that's independent of your stomach filling up. It's a top-down process that begins even before the first bite.

Two years ago, psychologist Carey Morewedge asked a group of people to imagine doing two simple tasks repeatedly—put quarters into a coin-op laundry machine and eat M&M's. The ratio of quarters to M&M's varied. Some subjects imagined eating ten M&M's for every imaginary quarter they put into the laundry machine. For other, the ratio was just the opposite. One group in a second experiment was asked to eat many cubes of imaginary cheese. After all this, the researchers casually offered the subjects an actual bowl of M&M's from which they could eat as much as they wanted.

People who imagined eating the most M&M's ate the fewest real candies. Imaginary *eating* was key. Subjects who simply imagined placing M&M's in a bowl ate just as many real M&M's later as anybody else. The effects were also food-specific. In the follow-up experiment, people who imagined eating lots of M&M's gobbled up just as much cheese as anybody, while the group who'd just indulged in an imaginary cheese feast ate less.

STRETCHING OUT ENJOYMENT

The inevitability of adaptation means the best way to stretch out the pleasure of something we like may actually be to interrupt it repeatedly. In a 2009 study, researchers asked people if they'd rather watch a sitcom with or without commercials. Overwhelmingly, subjects predicted that they'd enjoy watching uninterrupted shows more. However, when another group of subjects actually watched these shows without being given a choice about commercials, those subjects whose viewing experience was interrupted by ads rated it as much more enjoyable.

The researchers also found that people derive similar benefits from getting interrupted while listening to their favorite music or enjoying a massage, and from *not* breaking up the experience of unpleasant stuff like hearing really loud guitar feedback. Of course, this is just the opposite of what we expect. We think interruptions of pleasant experiences will detract from our happiness. And we think splitting up the unpleasant experiences with a break or two will make them easier to endure. As a result, we often intensify and drag out what's boring, annoying, and painful, while hurrying along life's most pleasant moments.

Underestimating adaptation is part of what psychologists Timothy Wilson and Daniel Gilbert call "miswanting," which we do routinely. For instance, most of us believe that we'd be happier if we made twice as much money as we do now, and even happier if we made ten times as much. Yet almost every year a study makes headlines by showing that wealth brings happiness only up to a point. A 2010 study led by the Nobel-winning economist Daniel Kahneman analyzed a Gallup survey of one thousand Americans and found that emotional well-being increased with income, but didn't improve beyond annual earnings of $75,000. The same year, the economist Richard Easterlin replicated results he first published in the 1970s indicating that the happiness of a nation's people doesn't correlate with national wealth—a finding now known as the "Easterlin Paradox."

Easterlin's 2010 analysis expanded the range of nations studied to include both developed and less-developed countries on several continents. While Easterlin found that getting richer does make people happier in the short term, the relationship falls apart within a decade of the initial upswing in wealth.

There are a number of intermingled reasons why getting richer doesn't seem to bring the sustained happiness we expect it will. For one thing, we're prone to what Kahneman calls a "focusing illusion." Our expectations of greater wealth are too keyed on the money and the new things it could buy, and they neglect the fact that the rest of life, with all of its quirks, frustrations, and disappointments, keeps humming along.

Plus, we seem wired to measure our satisfaction in relative terms and are prone to disappointment. So are our closest evolutionary relatives. In the 1920s, the engagingly named Otto Tinklepaugh found these same tendencies in rhesus monkeys. A monkey would watch Tinklepaugh hide lettuce under one of two cups. The animal would be removed from the room, then brought back and released. He would go straight to the lettuce cup and happily enjoy his reward.

In a later experiment, monkeys watched Tinklepaugh place some bananas under one of the cups, which he would secretly swap with lettuce after the monkey was taken away. It goes without saying that monkeys much prefer bananas to lettuce. Here are

Tinklepaugh's observations of a monkey returning to the room and searching for his expected banana but finding lettuce instead:

"Subject rushes to the proper cup and picks it up. Extends hand toward lettuce. Stops. Looks around on floor. Looks in, under, around cup. Glances at other cup. Looks back at screen. Looks under and around self. Looks and shrieks at any observer present. Walks away, leaving lettuce untouched on floor."

Both the focusing illusion and our relativistic reward expectations may make our brains seem spoiled or ungrateful. After all, it took a lot of work to get that promotion, earn that raise, and buy that bigger house. Instead of savoring what we have, our brains seem more interested in finding something new to want. Desire may indeed be at the root of suffering, as the noble truth of Buddhism teaches. Some amount of wanting, however, the motivational spark of expectation, is critical to any focused effort, whether the ultimate goal is enlightenment, inner peace, or the corner office.

TOO MUCH OF A GOOD THING

The more you want something, the more likely you are to get it, but only up to a point. Even nonaddicted brains go haywire when wanting gets too intense. Motivated people succeed. Over-motivated people fail. They cheat. They despair.

In 2009, British neuroscientists watched the brains of people lying inside a scanner playing a Pac-Man-esque video game. The subjects won either a small or relatively large cash prize for racing through a maze and capturing a certain number of prey.

With big money on the line, players made more mistakes and missed obvious turns in the maze that could have cornered their prey for easy capture. The more players wanted the money, based on follow-up questionnaires, the more action there was in their reward centers and the more their performance suffered. The allure of potential cash was too bright. It was all the brain could see.

Indeed, a laser focus on a narrow goal can blind us to things

we'd normally care about greatly, including the difference between right and wrong. A 2004 study found that people given an
ambitious goal for the number of words they could create by un-
scrambling a bunch of letters did slightly better than people told
to "do their best," although the difference in word production
wasn't statistically significant. What was significant was how
much more the subjects who were given a goal cheated. Indeed,
subjects in a "reward goal" group who were offered cash for
achieving the word-creation goal cheated even more.

The "reward goal" folks were given cash up front. They were
told to keep whatever they earned according to the number of legitimate words they created and put whatever money was left
over in a sealed envelope along with their unsigned score sheet
where they noted the number of words they had unscrambled.
They were then to slide that envelope into a box on their way out
of the lab. Everything seemed totally anonymous, but the researchers had a secret way to identify cheaters who inflated their
scores, because the final string of letters, noted on both workbooks
and unsigned score sheets, was unique for each subject.

It's noteworthy that people in the reward-goal group didn't
need to falsify their scores. They were given money up front, so
they could have simply walked out of the room with all the cash.
Nevertheless, they almost never did that. The amount of money
they took always matched the number of words they *said* they created, even when their actual performance fell short of their claim.
Maybe cheating felt less like cheating that way.

Even certain intrinsic motivators can backfire on us if we invest
too much in them. Take the goal of happiness. It seems like the
most benign goal there could be, but in a series of studies published in 2011 by psychologist Iris Mauss, people who valued
happiness the most were often the least happy. Simply put, the
more we value something, the higher our expectations are for it.
The student who values getting good grades views a B much differently than the student who thinks grades are beside the point.
That's no big deal in the case of grades. Students can be high

achievers even when they aren't satisfied with their marks. When happiness is the goal, however, the risk of disappointment that comes with rising expectations sets up a catch-22.

In a survey, Mauss found that valuing happiness was the most detrimental to actual happiness during periods of low stress, precisely those times when we assume our happiness should be at its peak. In a second study, supposedly about TV programming, Mauss and her team manipulated how much people valued happiness by having some of them read a fake newspaper article extolling the benefits of being happy. After this, subjects watched one of two film clips—either the uplifting story of a figure skater overcoming the odds and winning a gold medal, or the tragic tale of a husband enduring the sudden death of his wife. Finally, the subjects completed both explicit and implicit measures of happiness.

There was no big difference in happiness after watching the sad movie. People expected to feel bummed out by it, and everyone did. By contrast, people assumed they should feel happy after watching the uplifting movie, and that's exactly when people who valued happiness the most were at a happiness disadvantage. In fact, according to an implicit measure of emotion, people with high happiness expectations were *less* happy after watching the skater win a gold medal than after watching a man mourn his dead wife.

HOW LOSING CAN FEEL LIKE WINNING

We've seen how the expectations of wanting are powerful but malleable motivators. Shuffling these expectations changes what rewards we pursue and the satisfaction we get from them. In studies, the effects flow in both directions—placebo calories fill us up, but rejiggered expectations can also undermine the pleasure of rewards we used to love (just ask Tinklepaugh's infuriated monkeys).

We may never have total control over the expectations of wanting, but what happens when we lose control entirely? This is the fate of addicted brains. They are consumed with wanting and trapped in a cycle of pure expectation that is never fulfilled even as it destroys lives in the pursuit. How does the addict's expectations for reward stay consistently high despite the pain of past experience? Why couldn't Jeri stop gambling even after she lost everything?

Congress legalized casinos on Native American lands in 1988. Since then, legal gambling has spread to every state except Utah and Hawaii. Americans now wager about $100 billion every year, and lose almost all of it. Meanwhile, between 2000 and 2010, annual online gambling revenue jumped tenfold to nearly $25 billion.

As gambling grows, so does addiction. While compulsive gambling gets much less research attention and funding than alcoholism and other substance abuses, it offers a glimpse of the havoc that pure want can wreak in the brain independent of chemical disruption and dependency.

While there are many neurotransmitters pulsing through the brain's reward system, dopamine plays a special role in pure want. It is the brain's anticipation juice. Dopamine signals what psychologist Kent Berridge calls "incentive salience," which is what transforms mere predictions of a reward into the motivation to obtain it. It helps the brain fine-tune wanting—deciding what to want and how much to want it. We don't need dopamine to like a glazed doughnut. We need dopamine to want it. It's no accident that dopamine carries signals for rewards and for the muscle movements needed to go out and get them.

The death of dopamine neurons is behind the shaking and lost muscle control of Parkinson's disease. Not incidentally, doctors treating the movement disorder have long noted a "Parkinsonian personality"—introverted, slow-tempered, and risk-averse. These patients usually don't smoke or drink very much, let alone flush their life savings down a slot machine.

That caution is often shown the door, however, when Parkinson's patients take drugs that directly stimulate their dopamine receptors, known as dopamine agonists. About 17 percent of them develop an impulse control disorder. They become binge eaters, porn addicts, and shopaholics. The rate of compulsive gambling among patients taking these drugs shoots to three times that of the overall population. When they quit the drugs, their addictions vanish.

In the healthy brain, the thought of money is pure expectation, which for most people can assume any number of forms—a new car, a college education, or a whole world of goods and services. For the compulsive gambler, however, the expectations of winning money become a cycle of want that exists only to feed on itself.

In the gambling addict's brain, the expectations that tickle the dopamine system narrow and converge around one thing—more gambling. Given the odds, this means the brain of a compulsive gambler must somehow turn losing into winning.

Indeed, compulsive gamblers are more optimistic about their chances of winning any given bet, compared with nonaddicts facing the same odds. Gambling addicts are also hypersensitive to a jackpot's allure. A 2012 brain-scan study found that whether the odds were good or bad, raising the stakes of a bet led to a much stronger surge of activity in the reward centers of problem gamblers, compared to control subjects. Plus, while most people become more cautious after a big loss, gambling addicts believe they can gamble their way out of any hole. They chase their losses with even bigger bets, a strategy that typically backfires.

"In my mind, the disease somehow became its own cure," says Jeri. "How will I get out of this problem I'm in? How can I get the money to pay off my debt? Oh, I know. I'll gamble."

Finally, gambling addicts are suckers for the "near-miss" illusion—a lotto number off by one digit or a slot machine jackpot spoiled by the final spinner. Instead of seeing these outcomes as losses and feeling the normal, discouraging sting, addicts interpret them as encouraging signs that they're mastering the game, or that luck is turning their way. They bet even more.

The gambler's perverse pleasure in the near-miss is based in a hardwired cognitive reflex. Our future-oriented brains habitually seek out patterns, because they help predict what's coming next. Finding a pattern is like solving a little puzzle. Aha! Now we know what to expect. Our reward system gets pumped.

Our brains are so pattern happy* that they find patterns even when we know they don't exist. When people in brain scanners are explicitly told they'll be watching a randomly generated series of squares and circles, their prefrontal and reward centers still re-act to runs of several squares or circles in a row, or a long sequence of alternating square, circle, square, circle, square.

The gambling addict's brain takes this reflex to an extreme. In the mind of a compulsive gambler, chance has personality and purpose. Luck can be both wooed and mastered.

In 2010, the neuroscientist Luke Clark studied near-miss expectations in frequent gamblers, including gambling addicts. The subjects played a modified slot machine video game while Clark scanned their brains. Whenever the two spinners—both with six images in the exact same order—stopped at a match, the subjects won a small jackpot. Importantly, players could see both reels in their entirety, allowing them to judge how close a losing spin was to a win. When the reels were off by just one image, this was a near-miss.

Wins lit up everybody's reward systems about the same. In the brains of the addicts however, the dopamine-rich midbrain also got excited by near-misses. These brains interpreted some losses as winning-lite—I'm getting closer!—creating a pleasure of pure expectation and another motivational charge to spur more gambling.

The happiest times Jeri recalls from her gambling years were the drives to Foxwoods, fresh from the ATM—a few hours on the road with a wad of cash in her bag and nothing to do but savor the possibilities.

---

*For instance, after a coin flips to heads several times in a row, we tend to think the next one is more likely to be tails, because it's "due." In reality, every coin flip is a 50/50 chance for heads or tails no matter what preceded it.

"It's the anticipation that you've got a method this time. You're going to do it right this time," she says. "It's all that planning and expectation, which of course is just insanity."

In contrast to alcohol or drugs, where the reward is fairly certain albeit fleeting, a big part of gambling's allure is "the action," the tingle of excitement generated by uncertainty.* At the same time, the real possibility of loss doesn't register with most gambling addicts. The focus is steadfastly on the potential jackpot. The odds exist to be beaten.

"Dopamine engaging motivation is not a simple mechanistic process," says Martin Zack, a neuropharmacologist who studies compulsive gambling. "It's a process of meaning."

Everybody's brain has a certain background level of dopamine. Reward expectations of every sort provide extra dopamine pulses, which are felt more keenly if background dopamine levels are low. Eventually, though, an addict's compulsive tickling of the reward system causes this background dopamine level to rise, and tolerance ensues.

In the addicted brain, the reward value of longer-term goals, such as saving money for a child's college education or a trip abroad, no longer registers in the expectations switchboard of the frontal cortex. Neither do the warning signals that most of us would feel when we considered everything we could lose when taking a big risk. The only expectations that matter for a gambling addict revolve around placing the next bet. Meanwhile, the rising level of background dopamine drowns out the gambler's usual jolt of pleasure from playing the nickel slots. It takes bigger and bigger bets to regain the tingle.

Jeri's gambling followed all these patterns. She chased her losses with bigger bets. Her wagers grew as her addiction deepened. She lived her life on the anticipatory edge, fixated on the

---

* A few years ago, researchers found that uncertainty intensifies emotional reactions. People who repeatedly said, "I'm not sure what's happening," while watching five minutes of a happy or sad scene from a movie they'd never seen, had more extreme emotional reactions than people who watched the same clips while repeating, "I understand what's happening."

next chance for a big win—not for the pleasure of the jackpot, but for the pleasure of taking what she won and laying it all on the line.

"Most normal people think about gambling to win money. But for me, it was all about getting money in order to gamble," says Jeri. "The lying, the conniving, all of it. The more money you get, the more you gamble. It's just ammunition to blow your brains out."

Compulsive gamblers, like many addicts, talk about the pleasure that builds well before they get their fix. For them, Zack notes, gambling is an "as if" pleasure, forever mired in anticipation. "Its potential is limitless. It's as big as your imagination," he says. Or, as Foxwoods Casino put it in ads celebrating its twentieth anniversary in early 2012: "Be Anyone. Do Everything."

JERI'S ANSWER TO THE BIG WANT

About a dozen gambling addicts gather in the back room of a Congregational church outside Boston. They grab some coffee and cookies, take seats around a square of folding tables, and introduce themselves. "I'm powerless over gambling," they all say.

It sounds pretty simple and straightforward, but addictions are complicated. They have different effects on different brains, and no treatment—pharmaceutical, cognitive behavioral, faith-based, or otherwise—has been, or likely will be, a magic bullet.

Like all twelve-step programs, Gamblers Anonymous is meant to be a lifelong commitment, but less than 10 percent of gamblers who join the program stick with it for even a year. Other treatments, such as cognitive behavioral therapy, have fewer dropouts, but comparative studies suggest they are no more effective than GA in squashing the urge to gamble. In fact, most are no more effective than a no-treatment wait list.

For any therapy to work, an addict needs to confront the power of want, to try and shatter the never-ending expectations that drive them headlong into self-destruction. GA is Jeri's answer.

She started attending meetings in March 2006, and she hasn't placed another bet since. At the church, the addicts take turns reading passages from small red, yellow, and gray booklets—the literature of Gamblers Anonymous.

When it's her turn, Jeri offers a selection on "the dreamworld of the compulsive gambler."

"When compulsive gamblers succeed, they gamble to dream still greater dreams. When failing, they gamble in reckless desperation," she reads. "Sadly, they will struggle back, dream more dreams, and of course suffer more misery. No one can convince them that their great schemes will not someday come true. They believe they will, for without this dreamworld, life for them would not be tolerable."

It's unlikely that any therapy, current or future, will help all compulsive gamblers. More inroads might be made by using personality type, addiction severity, and genotype to determine who is most likely to be helped by which therapy. But such personalization is a tall order.

Meantime, one obvious thing separating those who stick with GA and those who don't is the strength of their belief in the program. Maybe that faith—that this addiction is beatable and here's how we'll beat it—is strong enough to drag the minds of some gamblers away from the dreamworld spun by pure want.

The readings at the meeting are adapted from the Big Book of the original twelve-step program, Alcoholics Anonymous, written during the Great Depression by a failed stockbroker named Bill Wilson, whose drinking eventually landed him in the hospital. According to AA lore, at the peak of Wilson's misery, a white light filled his hospital room, and he heard the Lord's message that he need never drink again. He never did.

The religious overtones have been softened in the twelve-steps, which require surrender to an agnostic "higher power" and have spread to recovery programs for every imaginable addiction. Gamblers Anonymous was founded in 1957 in Los Angeles, not

Las Vegas. Still, faith permeates discussion at the GA meeting, specifically faith in the program itself.

"The meetings are amazing, and I don't know how they work. I don't get it," Jeri says. "They say, don't try to get the program. The program will get you."

Some of the compulsive gamblers gathered at the church are also battling addictions to alcohol or drugs. They say confronting the urge to gamble has been their toughest fight. Along with the stories of bankruptcies, broken marriages, and suicidal thoughts are frequent tales of relapse, often invited by the hubris of trying to analyze, customize, and outsmart the program and do recovery à la carte. They know better now, they say. Real empowerment, as Step One indicates, starts with surrender.

Near the close of the meeting, one of those who rejoined the fellowship after relapsing offers advice to an older woman attending her first meeting who has sat silently and stone-faced all evening.

"If you wake up tomorrow morning and tell yourself, 'I don't have to gamble,' it will be a better day," he tells her. "I can tell you that, because I've been there."

4 ┐ ACCOUNTING FOR TASTE

The new batch of bug juice is nearly ready. It's a salty palate cleanser mixed under the watchful eye of G. M. "Pooch" Pucilowski, the head judge for California's largest wine competition. He's going to need gallons of the stuff. In a neighboring building, six dozen judges are well into the first of many twenty-wine flights. Arranged in panels of four, they will evaluate nearly three thousand wines in two days.

On this early June morning, the wine competition is the only action on the sprawling grounds of the State Fair in Sacramento. The livestock corrals are empty. The concession stands are locked tight. The waterslides are dry. But in the cavernous "pour room" a small army of red-aproned volunteers rushes to and fro among the cases of wine spread out in long, neat rows.

All bottles and glasses are numbered. One group of volunteers plucks the wines from cases to assemble the flights. Another pours and arranges the wine on carts that are wheeled to the exit. A third group shepherds the carts across a brick walkway to the judges' building. Runners take over from there. In each building, there's a sort of mission control tracking the flow of wine and the progress of the judging via computer and two-way radio. Every panel has a steward to clear glasses and ferry messages, and a clerk to record scores. The goal of all this regimentation is not just efficiency. If the judges knew the winemaker, or learned the price, or (God forbid) saw the label of the wines they drank, then it would be impossible to keep their expectations and assumptions from biasing their ratings. Tasting blind ensures that the gold, silver, and bronze medals are awarded based only on what's in the glass.

The California State Fair wine competition has been around since 1855, and Pucilowski has been chief judge for more than a quarter century. Serving the winning wines is a centerpiece of the State Fair every July. It's a celebration of California's vaunted wine industry, which is the vanguard of America's $30 billion wine market. In the last few years, it's also been a flash point in a wine-splattered battle royale over value, expert opinion, and the weight of expectations.

A tall man in his early sixties, Pucilowski looks much younger thanks to his tousled salt-and-pepper hair, trim goatee, and resort-chic style. Today, on the first morning of the competition, he's wearing a creamy, short-sleeved button-down with an open collar, linen pants, and black leather clogs. He's gregarious, charismatic, and constantly moving—a mix of showman and field general, which seems appropriate for a guy in charge of drinking on an industrial scale. He lets me wander among the judges' tables and eavesdrop.

"The nose was very flowery and pretty," one judge says of a Cabernet. "Yeah, it was a nice, smooth Cab," another concurs. "It wasn't going to punch your face out." The next wine in the flight is less favored. "It had a really tangled finish," one judge offers. His neighbor goes further. "I couldn't even taste it. I tried twice," she says, making a face. "It smelled like dead fish."

How do we judge the value of wine? More specifically, what makes one wine better than another? The easy answer is that these value judgments are all in the palate of the beholder. But are the palates of beholders truly their own? Do I really love this Pinot Blanc from the Willamette Valley, or do I love the story my friend tells as he pours it—about the wine's maker and his visit to the family vineyard, and the fact that the critic Robert Parker just gave it 92 points? It's not just wine. Every subjective experience can be radically improved or ruined by our expectations. Is this movie hilarious or hokey? Is this vacation just what I needed or another supposedly fun thing I'll never do again? The question isn't *whether* expectations figure into our individual tastes; it's how big a role do they play, and how deep must we go once expectations are removed to reach bedrock truths about our likes and dislikes.

IN VINO VERITAS?

People have been drinking wine ever since some lucky farmer accidentally fermented his fruit many thousands of years ago. Yet to most people wine remains something of a mystery. We accept that some bottles will cost five or ten times as much as the $15 wine we pick up for dinner. We may think we know the difference, but blind taste tests show we often don't.

Why might consumers pay $150 for a Châteauneuf-du-Pape when they can pay $15 for a Côtes-du-Rhône, other than an ignorance of decimal points? Maybe they're wealthy and like impressing people with expensive things. Maybe it's their anniversary or another special occasion, and a pricey wine feels more special. The most obvious reason is that people who spring for the $150 wine expect to enjoy it more than a $15 wine—ten times more for utmost rationality, but plain old more will do. Are those expectations justified? Among oenophiles, the debate runneth over.

The potential to be fooled by "cheap" wine in expensive bottles has been an issue for millennia. In the first century A.D., the Roman naturalist and wine lover Pliny the Elder observed, *in vino veritas*, but he knew that in wine there could also be deception. Complaining about the spread of diluted and adulterated wines throughout the empire, he wrote, "Trade morality has come to such a pass, that only labels and cellar names are sold."

Some of the most expensive wines ever purchased were several bottles of eighteenth-century Château Lafite said to have belonged to Thomas Jefferson. They were auctioned for six figures in the 1980s, and within a few years were widely suspected to be frauds. Even mid-market labels have been besieged by dupes. In 2010, the supermarket chain Tesco sold bottles of counterfeit Louis Jadot Pouilly-Fuissé, which typically go for about $20 a bottle, to customers in England. In 2011, British authorities seized hundreds of bottles of fake Jacob's Creek wine from Australia, or "Austrlia," as the misspelled label read.

Wine experts are far from immune to such trickery. In 2001, Frédéric Brochet, a wine researcher at the University of Bordeaux, fooled French sommeliers by having them rate a middle-of-the-road Bordeaux he had disguised in two different bottles—one a pricey Grand Cru and the other a cheap bottle of table wine. The experts much preferred the wine when it was poured from the Grand Cru bottle, praising it as "excellent, balanced and flavorsome." The same stuff from the table wine bottle was "weak, flat, unbalanced and volatile"—*le yuck!*

Part of the problem is that expectations are built into our brain's tasting machinery. We have thousands of taste buds, but they are blunt instruments. They detect salty, bitter, sweet, sour, and the savory taste of umami. They serve a critical purpose: determining what's edible. They don't make fine flavor distinctions.

Fortunately, taste buds aren't the end of it. We also smell what we eat and drink, and odor turns out to be the essence of flavor. At every meal, we sniff thousands of vaporized chemical compounds. Some are mixed into the air, and some are released by the heat of our mouths and ferried to our noses via the back of our throats. To a great extent, what we smell is both the anticipation and the fulfillment of a wine's promise. Each sniff delivers a one-two punch of memory and associations, not the least of which is the anticipation of alcohol's pleasant buzz.

Smell is more discriminating than taste, but that doesn't mean that our noses can't be fooled. Flavors most of us know by one name are actually elaborate chemical concoctions, measured in parts-per-billion, that our brains make whole. According to one flavor textbook, there are 213 known odor compounds in cheddar cheese, 356 in apple, 466 in grape, and 503 in cocoa. Many basic chemical recipes are common to smells that make us salivate and those that make us gag. Our reaction often depends on odor concentration and context.

In one brain scan study, researchers cued the same smell with the words "cheddar cheese" or "body odor." When prompted by "cheddar cheese," people found the odor much more pleasant, and the pleasantness ratings correlated with activity in the brain's reward circuitry, particularly the orbitofrontal cortex. Even in the absence of odor, a sniff of plain air, when cued by the same words, had the same effects in the brain. Another sniff study, from 2011, showed that our brains anticipate smells with predictive neural coding for specific odors (in this case, watermelon and Play-Doh) that form well before our first whiff and persist even when the actual odor is not what we expected.

Of course, we need not parse the slippery attributes of a wine's flavor to enjoy it and judge it worthy of the price (or not). Let's bypass flavor specifics and look more broadly at taste preferences. Do we like what we like, or do we like only what we expect to like? When we say we prefer the Krug Grande Cuvée bubbly to Veuve Clicquot, how much of that sentiment was formed before we took our first sips?

LIKING WHAT WE EXPECT TO LIKE

A few years ago, researchers led by Dan Ariely asked a similar question: do we dislike what we expect to dislike? They secretly dosed beer with a few drops of vinegar and served it to a group of unsuspecting patrons at a campus bar in a taste test with regular beer. Surprisingly, drinkers preferred the vinegar beer to the unadulterated lager by a margin of three to two.

The researchers suspected that telling people about the vinegar would make them say they liked the beer less. But would knowing about the vinegar actually change the taste, or would drinkers just be expressing their aversion to the idea? In a follow-up taste test, Ariely's team told drinkers about the vinegar, but varied the timing of their confession—telling some before they took their first sip, but waiting until after the taste test to inform others. In both cases, they told people about the vinegar before asking them which beer they preferred.

People who learned about the vinegar *after* drinking their beer would taste it without any vinegar expectations. They might not like hearing about the secret ingredient after the fact, but the taste experience itself would already be in the books.

By contrast, people who learned about the vinegar up front would have those unpalatable expectations sloshing around in every sip.

If disliking vinegar beer was just a negative reaction to the thought of it, then it shouldn't matter when drinkers learned the news. They'd dislike it equally. However, if vinegar knowledge actually changed the taste, then knowing about it up front would have a bigger impact on preferences.

As it turned out, when the researchers told subjects about the vinegar *before* they drank, 70 percent of drinkers favored the pure brew. When the researchers waited until *after* the tasting to disclose the secret ingredient, more than half of drinkers still preferred vinegar beer. Expectations don't just change what we think we should enjoy. They change what we experience in a fundamental way.

Still, compared to the visceral expectation of drinking vinegar, the expectations of a price or a brand name seem pretty abstract. Can they impact our preferences in the same way? In one early study of brand power from the 1960s, regular beer drinkers consistently preferred "their brand" when labels were visible. When the labels were hidden, they couldn't tell their brand from two similar beers, and their preferences were all over the place.

While marketers spend billions crafting the emotional appeals of labels and brands, prices are just numbers. Nevertheless, they are powerful preference makers. Specifically, we often assume that more expensive goods are better. Behavioral economists call this the price-quality heuristic. It's based partly on the assumption that price gauges demand by rational consumers. We think, *these running shoes must be fantastic, or they couldn't sell them for $200.* This becomes a self-fulfilling prophecy when we join the crowd and pay the premium. Granted, the price-quality heuristic is also supported by experience in many cases. Quality expectations based on price can be fairly accurate when it comes to products with more objective measures of quality like durability or performance. However, when it comes to "experiential goods," such as wine, food, leisure, or entertainment, the price-quality rule of thumb is far less accurate.

Unlike many of our basic consumer biases, our belief that price signals value doesn't have much of an evolutionary pedigree, or so psychologist Laurie Santos found after she trained capuchin monkeys to use money. The monkeys' currency consists of small metal discs they can hand over to a researcher in exchange for various food treats. In her "monkeynomics" research, Santos looks into which less-than-rational human consumer behaviors are shared by capuchins with cash. The monkeys are separated from humans by thirty-five million years of evolution. Any behavior with roots that deep will be pretty hard to shake. Conversely, behaviors that have survived that many millennia likely offer some advantages, despite being occasionally troublesome.

After six years of research, Santos and her colleagues have found that capuchins share most of the human consumer quirks they've studied so far. Like us, the monkeys fear potential losses more than they value potential gains of the same size. They also value something more once they "own" it than they did immediately before owning it, just like we do. In fact, so far the only consumer bias capuchins don't seem to share is the price-quality heuristic.

In a yet-to-be-published study, Santos and her team taught the monkeys that a cube of blue Jell-O cost one token but green Jell-O cost three tokens, even though they tasted the same. Later, the monkeys were offered a choice between green or blue Jell-O, but for free. If the capuchins had inferred that more expensive Jell-O was somehow more valuable, then they'd favor green. Yet the monkeys chose both colors equally. The researchers witnessed similar effects (i.e., none) after teaching monkeys that one "brand" of tasty cereal was more expensive than another.

"They understand what price means," says Santos, "but they're not affected by price in the same way that humans are." In other words, the monkeys know it costs two tokens to get two chunks of cereal that cost one token each. They also buy more of their favorite food treat when it goes on sale. But it seems they don't think one treat is inherently better just because it costs more. There may be a good evolutionary reason for some irrational consumer behaviors, but when it comes to inferring quality from price tags, that's all us.

The good news is, this suggests that our overreliance on price tags may not be as deeply ingrained as some other consumer biases. The expectations of price could be easier to overcome, Santos says, "if we just have the right experiences and pay attention to our real preferences."

WHEN IGNORANCE IS BLISS

So we like what we expect to like and our taste experiences can be fundamentally changed by a tidbit of up-front knowledge, such as a brand name or a price tag. The next question is whether our "real" preferences have been led astray, or if preferences shaped by expectations are the only real preferences we've got. Thus far, the research suggests that dividing real preferences from bogus ones is much easier said than done. For one thing, the pleasure derived from expectations is real, as researchers at Caltech and Stanford demonstrated. For a 2008 study, they asked people to taste five Cabernets while in a brain scanner.

The subjects were told the per-bottle price of each wine before tasting ($5, $10, $35, $45, and $90) and rated how much they liked it. In reality, there were only three wines—the $5 wine also posed as the $45 wine, while the $90 wine also slummed as the $10 wine.

Overall, the more expensive a wine supposedly was, the more people liked it. Subjects enjoyed the $90 wine the most, but not when they tasted it in the guise of a $10 bottle. In that case, they liked it a lot less than they did the $5 wine in its $45 disguise.

Conceivably, people might feel pressure to say they like a more expensive wine no matter their actual preferences. In fact, price changes did not alter the activity of the brain's primary taste areas, such as the insula and thalamus, responsible for basic sensory processing. The main brain area that did become more active as the price increased was the medial orbitofrontal cortex (mOFC), part of the ventromedial prefrontal cortex (vmPFC). Recall that this brain area seems to be a switchboard of expectations, assessing the value of a potential reward from all angles—*that wine looks delicious and it's expensive, but it smells a little funny, and I don't usually like Merlot, although I do like alcohol.*

The results suggested that the mOFC integrates "the actual sensory properties of the substance being consumed with the expectations of how good it *should* be" (my italics). While this top-down intrusion makes for gullible palates, the researchers saw an upside. "In a world of noisy measurements," they wrote, "the use of prior knowledge about the quality of an experience provides additional valuable information."

What's that value? Efficiency. Evaluating every new experience in detail would be tough on our brains. It would hog energy and attention that could be better used elsewhere. It would also be debilitatingly slow. As a result, our brains reach for a shortcut—the pre-experience of expectations.

In the 1990s, the psychologist Timothy Wilson, whom we met in the previous chapter, demonstrated the influence of these expectations using a selection of *New Yorker* cartoons. He asked people to judge how funny the cartoons were, but first told one group that prior subjects thought the cartoons were hilarious. The remaining subjects weren't told a thing. Everything was videotaped, so that independent coders could later measure how long people looked at each cartoon and how much they smiled and laughed. Based on those measures, the coders assigned subjects an "index of facial mirth" for each cartoon.

The funniness of the cartoons had already been established by panels of students in pilot testing. The first three had been judged really funny and the last three were, well, *meh*. The no-expectations crowd scored them accordingly—their median funniness ratings dropped significantly for the final three cartoons, and their facial mirth plunged into negative territory. By contrast, those who expected to laugh at every cartoon did so. In fact, they found the final three cartoons even *funnier* than the first three, and their facial mirth scores went crazy. They weren't just peer-pressured into saying the cartoons were funny. They were laughing their heads off.

How could this be? It turned out that people who expected to find the cartoons funny spent less time looking at them. According to questionnaires, they didn't think as much about the cartoons either. Faced with familiar stimuli, our brains do a quick "confirmation check" with a snippet of actual experience, Wilson surmised. If nothing seems grossly amiss, then expectations take over, and we happily laugh along.

Still, Wilson also predicted a "contrast effect" in the event that expectations veered too far from actual experience. At some point, the "funny" cartoons would be dull enough, or the "expensive" wine would be sufficiently nasty, that our experience would override our expectations. Ironically, with a contrast effect, expectations still rule the day, only in reverse. We are more bored by a movie's ponderous plot if our heads brimmed with fantastic reviews when we bought our tickets. And a lackluster wine will taste even worse if we expected greatness and paid for the privilege. The contrast effect also works in the opposite direction, by enhancing pleasant surprises. The only way to discover true preferences, it would seem, would be to avoid expectations altogether. Enter blind tasting.

WHO OWNS YOUR PALATE?

Blind wine tasting has long been the foremost arena for establishing reputations and settling quarrels over expectations of price and quality. For instance, when Californian wines trumped

French wines at a 1976 blind tasting in Paris, the French judges were shocked. That upset is often credited with "making" the California wine industry.

The stakes are higher now. The wine business is bigger than ever. Europeans have always been wine drinkers, but Americans are catching up. In 2010, Americans uncorked nearly four billion bottles of wine, making the United States the top wine-drinking nation in the world—by volume, the per capita crown still belongs to France. Meanwhile, wine sales in China quadrupled between 2000 and 2010. At the same time, the tenor of the debate over price and quality has changed. The occasional potshot against famous labels or an evening of fun with your wine-geek friends has become a barrage of serious research by psychologists and behavioral economists armed with loads of data aimed straight at expectations.

In 2011, a food-and-wine critic cum sensory perception researcher named Robin Goldstein published a "Blind Tasting Manifesto" in *The Wine Trials*, his annual guide to wines costing $15 or less that beat more-expensive competitors in blind tastings.

The manifesto poses three intertwined arguments. First, expectations—particularly those based on price—rule our evaluation of wine. Second, the experts who guide our wine expectations cannot be trusted. Third, your true preferences are out there, awaiting discovery via blind tasting.

"By questioning wine prices, you will become less of a slave to expectations and more of a student of your own palate," Goldstein writes. "Invoking only the simple, everyday miracle of the scientific method, you will have turned a placebo into wine."

To back up the first argument, that our preferences are easily swayed by suggestion, Goldstein cites many of the studies detailed in this chapter. He also draws on the results of his own research, based on more than six thousand blind tastings conducted for *The Wine Trials* and analyzed in collaboration with Anna Dreber and Johan Almenberg, a husband-and-wife pair of Swedish economists. In 2008, they published *Do More Expensive Wines Taste Better?* Not according to the data. On average, everyday wine drinkers actually enjoyed expensive wines *less*. The story was different for tasters who knew something about wine, but more on that later.

Goldstein's second argument is that our wine preferences are being hijacked and homogenized by marketers and tastemakers who can't be trusted, including magazines such as *Wine Spectator* and Robert Parker's famous 100-point rating system. Parker once told an interviewer, "I can make or break a wine." It wasn't an exaggeration.

To undercut the authority of such experts, Goldstein recounts a stunt he pulled the same year as his price preference study. He won a *Wine Spectator* "Award of Excellence" for Osteria L'Intrepido (The Fearless Tavern). The restaurant didn't exist, except for an online menu and an extensive selection of wine, including a "Reserve Wine List" of exorbitantly priced wines that had been panned by the magazine's critics.

Goldstein paid the $250 entry fee and filled out the application with a fake street address in Milan, an e-mail address, and a phone number that went straight to voicemail. He claims that the only contact from the magazine came from its advertising department, telling him that he'd won the award and asking if he wanted to buy an ad in an upcoming issue announcing the winners.

Snippets of the *Wine Spectator* reviews graced an annotated "Reserve Wine List" that Goldstein posted on his blog. For 110 euros, diners could order an Amarone Classico that the magazine's critic had likened to "paint thinner and nail varnish." For 135 euros, they could enjoy a "swampy, gamy, harsh" Barbaresco Asij, or spend 200 euros on a Brunello that "smells barnyardy and tastes decayed."

Before we dive into Goldstein's third argument, that blind tasting is the key to discovering our true preferences, let's spend a little more time with the experts, specifically wine critics. How sensitive are our palates to the taste expectations set by their descriptions of wine? When a critic suggests that a wine offers a blend of, say, "sandalwood, tobacco, and leather notes" or "layers of fig, persimmon, mango, and creamed Jonagold apple fruit," how does that inform what we taste? A few years ago, the economist Roman Weil gave everyday wine drinkers a triplicate test— three glasses but only two wines, with one repeated. He also gave them descriptions of both wines written by the same critic to see if they could match words with wine.

About half of the subjects could tell the two wines apart, which is somewhat better than chance. But among these folks who presumably had the keenest palates, only half correctly matched the wines with the critic's descriptions. They would have done just as well by flipping a coin.

Weil's study appeared in the *Journal of Wine Economics* alongside an essay by the economist and wine enthusiast Richard Quandt in which he culled wine descriptors from top critics. Among the smells and flavors these experts discerned were: bacon fat, olive-tinged black currant, meaty fruit, seaweed, spice box, hot fig, and underbrush.

"Packed and tight, with sage, licorice root, black currant, plum and tobacco aromas and flavors supported by ferrous and hot stone notes," gushed a write-up quoted by Quandt. What could an everyday wine drinker make of this? Conjuring the aroma of licorice root and the flavor of hot stones is tough enough. Combining them weaves an impenetrable sensory thicket. Unlike the blunt signal of price, the flavor expectations of these florid descriptions are so unhinged from human capacity that they likely fly right by most readers' taste perceptions.

The expectations gleaned from a wine reviewer's overall approval or disapproval of a wine means more to most palates than does the purple prose. And nothing expresses approval like a gold medal or a grade of 90-plus points, both of which correlate with higher prices. Should this concern us? After all, it could simply mean that the best-tasting wines get the medals, the 90-plus scores, the accolades, and the premium price tags. To Goldstein, however, the whole enterprise smells downright barnyardy.

For example, every year *Wine Spectator* rakes in about $1 million in application fees for its Awards of Excellence, and the implications of Goldstein's hoax were clear—pay to play. In 2011, Goldstein collaborated with economists Craig Riddell and Orley Ashenfelter to compare the *Wine Spectator* award winners with independent Zagat reviews for more than 1,700 New York City restaurants. Controlling for quality of food, decor, and service ratings, as measured by Zagat, an award raised the price of a meal up to 48 percent, depending on the award level.

REAL PREFERENCES ARE EARNED

It's one thing to argue that a wine's price and critical acclaim are weak predictors of drinking pleasure, as Goldstein does in *The Wine Trials*. It's something very different to point out that, freed of expectations, average Joes and Janes prefer markedly different wines than the experts do, as Goldstein and his collaborators found in their price-signal study.

Recall that nobody in that study knew the prices of the wines they tasted. When the researchers superimposed their results onto a 100-point rating system, they suggested that the pricier wines averaged 4 points *lower* among everyday wine drinkers, but 7 points *higher* among the expert tasters. Had the experts' palates been educated, or corrupted? If they had learned about wine mainly from blind tasting, would they still prefer the expensive stuff?

In January 2012, Goldstein oversaw the launch of the Center for Sensory Perception and Behavior at the Culinary Institute of America. This research lab, based at the Culinary Institute's Napa Valley campus, was founded in collaboration with several prominent behavioral economists. Its mission is to investigate "the complex interactions between the physical properties of foods and drinks, the external cues in the environment, consumers' actual sensory experiences, and the behaviors that follow," according to a write-up by Goldstein, who is the center's first director. This goes well beyond wine, but wine is their first order of research business.

Earlier this year, the center cosponsored a conference of wine enthusiasts and behavioral economists to "explore the gap between subjective quality and price in the wine industry." The center's inaugural study will compare the effects of knowing a wine's region, bottle type, price, and other bits of context on sensory experience and preferences across different expertise groups—everyday wine consumers, winemakers, sommeliers, and wine critics.

The fact that *The Wine Trials* is a book recommending wines, which opens with a passionate call to own your palate, is a little bit awkward, but no big scandal. Consumers crave the guidance of others' opinions—hence the popularity of online customer reviews, despite recent allegations that merchants have been paying for five-star raves. Our empirical reach is limited, and there are only so many hours in the day. Left to fend for ourselves, the boon of choice can become a burden. Plus, Goldstein and his coauthors take pains to position their recommendations as "starting points, not endpoints," to be augmented with further blind tasting.

"Ours is a more modest project," Goldstein tells me. This is true. Few experts offering opinions go so far to undercut the value of expert opinions. On another level, though, it's less modest. The third argument of the manifesto is that wine judgments based on blind tasting are more honest and trustworthy than most, because they are untainted by expectations.

The manifesto's case for blind tasting gets thorny in a hurry. It isn't just an experts-be-damned call to like what you like. If the collective preferences of most wine drinkers drove the market, we'd be on "a dangerous path toward a bland convergence," Goldstein writes in his breakdown of a blind-tasting study by the Australian Wine Institute. That study found that consumers and experts have distinct preferences in Shiraz and Cabernet Sauvignon. So far so good, but Goldstein criticizes the study's authors' recommendation that winemakers cater more to mass-market tastes. Following such a strategy, he warns, "amounts to saying: if the prevailing taste is dumb, dumb down your wine," to which he adds, "If the consumer always already knows best, then how is he to learn?"

Learn what exactly? Goldstein's answer is that knowing our real wine preferences takes a little practice. Otherwise, we're just throwing darts. "There's a huge amount of bullshit in the wine world," he tells me. "That's because the methodology isn't rigorous, and because people aren't focused enough on honing and developing that ability to identify wines in blind tastings and notice things they like and don't like in wines."

In other words, if you don't even know what Pinot Noir should taste like, then how can you really identify the taste properties that make up a Pinot you enjoy, or reliably say you prefer one to another? It seemed that expectations were creeping back into the preference mix, albeit a variety born of experimentation and study (one hesitates to use the word "expertise") rather than marketing. After the bullshit expectations have been cleared away, there is potentially yeoman work do be done in building up a stock of these more wholesome expectations. Admittedly, the "work" is drinking wine. It nevertheless seems daunting.

Yet worth it, Goldstein insists, because if we can strip away the biases of outside expectations, then our true palates await discovery and fulfillment. Is this true? For some perspective, let us return to the California State Fair wine competition.

WHAT DO WE FIND WHEN WE TASTE BLIND?

As noted, the State Fair wine judges taste blind to ensure that they are free from the bias of expectations—just as Goldstein's manifesto demands. However, a long-term study of their judgments suggests that blind preferences change with the wind, and without expectations our palates may not know which end is up.

The trouble started in 2003, when the competition's organizers agreed to test the consistency of their judges. The idea came from one of their advisory board members, a winemaker named Bob Hodgson, who taught statistics for two decades at Humboldt State University.

Hodgson seems an unlikely troublemaker. He's mellow and somewhat taciturn, with wire-rimmed glasses, a ruddy complexion, and a white beard. He and his wife, Judy, started making wine on a whim as a young married couple in the early 1970s. At their Fieldbrook Winery, just north of Eureka, there's a picture of Judy stomping grapes while pregnant with the second of their three daughters.

Hodgson tries not to overthink wine, but he has an analytical bent, and for a long time something about wine judging didn't seem quite right. Every year, he would enter his wines in multiple competitions, and he was dismayed by their varied performances. Routinely, the same wine would earn a gold medal at one competition and come up empty elsewhere. Like most winemakers, Hodgson crowed about the awards his wines received. He posted them online and hung them on his tasting room wall. But unlike most winemakers, he didn't forget about the competitions that had dismissed those same wines as unworthy.

Wine medals don't indicate first, second, and third place as they do in the Olympics. They represent tiers of excellence, like the stars for restaurants and movies. A single competition can award multiple gold medals for Merlot, for instance, or none. Individual tastes play a role, but Hodgson felt that there ought to be at least a kernel of consensus on quality—not lockstep agreement, but some positive correlation of results.

If not, then the award on your tasting room wall might as well proclaim, "*Somebody* out there liked my wine." More troubling was the possibility that this same somebody might like your wine one day and dislike it the next.

Back in 2003, the State Fair's judges quickly sorted all the wines into medal contenders and also-rans on the competition's first day. If a wine got at least two out of four yes votes, then it progressed to the medal round. To test consistency, Hodgson and Pucilowski secretly gave some of the judges multiple glasses of the same wines in their flights. The judges' performance wasn't impressive. They often voted to retain and eliminate the same wines. Hodgson recalled a Zinfandel from his winery that was killed off twice by a panel but retained once. The next day, it earned a double gold medal.

The following year, the competition dropped the retain/eliminate round to give the judges more time with each wine. This did nothing to improve consistency. Hodgson translated the judges' scores, including the plusses and minuses often attached to bronze, silver, and gold, into a 20-point scale, with 2 points for every step between "no award" and "gold plus." If a judge scored the wine that was secretly repeated within a 4-point spread (e.g., between no award and bronze, or from silver plus to gold), then Hodgson counted that judge as consistent. Only 10 percent of judges met this mark. An equal number were wildly inconsistent, giving the same wine "no award" and a gold medal, for instance.

Hodgson and Pucilowski have tested the judges this way since 2004, and they get similar results every year. What's more, the small minority of consistent tasters in one year are often wildly inconsistent the next.

In 2008, after years of wrangling, Hodgson narrowly won the advisory board's okay to publish his findings. The study appeared in the *Journal of Wine Economics*, and in the wine world it was a bombshell. In early 2009, the State Fair's organizers felt compelled to post a video interview with Pucilowski on the wine competition's Web site, headlined, "Are Wine Competitions a Hoax?" No way, was the answer.

"It's subjective, you know. I like this. You like that," Pucilowski observes in the video. "We are attempting to say to consumers [that] in our judging, we found these wines worked really well. People really liked them. The judges really liked them. So you as a consumer may like them also." Elsewhere on the Web site, the language was much less conditional. Just above Pucilowski's "I like this. You like that" video was the exclamation, "Award winners truly are the best of the best!"

Hodgson takes pains to say that he, too, doesn't think wine competitions are a hoax. When I visited him at Fieldbrook the day before he was due in Sacramento for the 2011 State Fair competition, he noted the elaborate rules enforced to ensure blind tasting, adding, "their integrity is above reproach." The judges have a tough assignment. The current system may simply be asking too much of their palates, which is why Hodgson is trying to come up with a simpler system that will help blind tasting yield more consistent results.

I hitched a ride with Hodgson to the State Fair, and during the drive through the Klamath Mountains he explained his new wine scoring system. It's based on expectations.

"It's about how an ordinary person, or a wine buyer, would approach wine," he says. Using color and aroma, "they're going to form an impression of whether this is going to be a nice wine to drink."

This is the anticipation phase, rated from zero to 6. If you can't wait to take your first sip, give the wine a 6 for anticipation. If it looks murky or smells rotten, give it a zero. If your expectations fall below 3, then don't even bother to taste.

After you taste the wine, there are two more scores from zero to 6. One for the balance of acid, sweetness, tannins, and alcohol, and one for the finish, which Hodgson calls "satisfaction," based on whether the taster's expectations were met, not met, or exceeded.

"I want to keep it simple," says Hodgson. "I'm trying to make the judges' job easier."

ARE PREFERENCES TOO SLIPPERY TO TRUST?

The marketers and the magazines may have agendas when it comes to promoting one wine over another. It's very hard to imagine any ulterior motives driving the State Fair judges, however. They volunteer for this gig to help the rest of us zero in on some good wines. They spend a weekend sitting in a windowless room, swishing and spitting glass after glass for hours, so we don't have to. Still, the fact that these motivated and wine-educated blind tasters can't seem to evaluate the same wine consistently from one moment to the next is enough to make you wonder—as wayward and arbitrary as taste expectations may be, are most people's palates utterly lost without them?

Can we everyday wine consumers learn enough through blind tasting to reach some deeper truths about what we like and don't like?

Back at the State Fair, I ask Pucilowski if he thinks that discovering one's true preferences might be aided by a little learning. He scoffs at the idea.

"I tell people, just drink what you like," he says. "Screw the experts. You don't need a tasting like this to drink wines."

The gymnasium-sized room is full of judges nose-deep in glasses, spitting into small white plastic buckets and scribbling furiously amidst scurrying red-aproned volunteers. They've been at it for hours and will go again tomorrow.

Pucilowski says the only reason consumers might pay attention to wine competitions or critics would be to see if they agreed. If they did, then they could feel confident about following that critic's recommendations in the future. If not, then so long. This sounds very democratic and reasonable, but why should I expect my preferences to be any more consistent than these experts' seemed to be?

The 20-point rating system used by the judges at the State Fair and many other wine competitions is based on the work of Maynard Amerine, who taught viticulture and enology at the University of California, Davis, from 1935 until 1974, and deemed wine preferences far too wishy-washy to be trusted.

Amerine spent decades applying science to wine—determining the best growing conditions for grapes, making batches upon batches of experimental wines, analyzing them in the lab, and teaching rigorous analysis of wine's color, odor, flavor, and mouthfeel.

"It is vital for professional wine judges to have common, fixed standards for each type of wine," he wrote in his 1976 book on the sensory evaluation of wine.* "Generally, their personal preferences in wines do not come into play or are consciously ignored."

Amerine would have agreed with Pucilowski that nobody needs experts to drink and enjoy wine. According to Amerine, however, experts and consumers weren't really tasting the same stuff—consumers judged wine with superficial hedonism, while wine experts judged quality, something that consumers had no feel for. Quality should not change much from one expert to another, and certainly not in the same expert from one day to the next. It was this ability to detect quality that made experts valuable to wine consumers, Amerine argued, not preference matching.

At the end of the first day, about forty judges try out Hodgson's new system on a flight of twelve wines including two triplicates. Weeks later, Hodgson has crunched the numbers and analyzed the results. In a nutshell, the new system failed. Judges were no more consistent in their scores for repeated wines than before. In a presentation to the 2011 meeting of wine economists, Hodgson displayed a typical scorecard in which a judge gave different samples of the same wine straight 6s and straight 2s.

Hodgson isn't ready to quit, though. He'll refine the system and try again. He'll explain the ratings to the judges more thoroughly and be more careful about things like ensuring that all the triplicates are poured from the same bottle. "This is a work in progress," he says.

THE HOLY GRAIL OF REAL PREFERENCES

Once the expectations that inform our preferences are unraveled, what remains? Skeptics of blind tasting argue that trying to escape

---

*The book's coauthor was Edward Roessler, a longtime wine judge at the California State Fair and, like Hodgson, a statistician.

wine's context—the history and culture of the winery, the food, the company, the occasion, and others' opinions—is a fool's errand.

"Any number of conscious or unconscious influences from above can and do alter the degree of gratification one experiences from the primary sensations alone," read a 2010 letter to the editor in the *Journal of Wine Economics*. "Some wines are much better than others, but the satisfaction one gets from them is so much more nuanced in a social setting than in a blind tasting, the latter is but a pale shadow of the former."

Amerine believed that "pale shadow," the sensory evaluation, was the truer measure of wine. "It is the sensory quality of the wine in the glass that is important," he wrote. He advised wine judges to work under proper laboratory conditions—well lit, approximately 70 degrees, no distractions, no conversation with fellow judges, and definitely no labels. Amerine's book is illustrated with photographs of tasters in lab coats, eyeballing precisely filled glasses of wine in the privacy of unadorned booths. Shelves of beakers and graduated cylinders stand in the background.

This is hardly Goldstein's vision of blind tasting. The goal of his manifesto remains personal preference—still subjective and a bit shaky, but unbiased by reviews and price tags, and truly one's own. Nevertheless, skeptics warn of a pretension to scientific rigor and an exaggeration of the truth to be found in unvarnished sensory experience.

"Trying to eliminate all external factors beyond what's in the glass contributes to the sense of omniscience that we too often confer to wine critics," wrote *New York Times* wine writer and blogger Eric Asimov. "I'm not saying eliminate all blind tastings," he continued. "I am saying take them with a grain of salt. Do not award them an authority they don't possess. Let's stay humble about wine. Let's be comfortably ambivalent rather than so sure of ourselves."

Goldstein agrees that wine is best *enjoyed* with its context intact. But if you really want to be humbled, he says, taste blind. Challenge yourself. Discover the abilities and limitations of your palate. Armed with this knowledge, he argues, you can sift through the nonsense confidently, instead of just trusting the experts.

Indeed, while we may not want to rely on it, let alone pin medals on it, there is evidence that we have real preferences independent of expectations. First, there are the fairly consistent differences in the palates of experts and everyday wine drinkers found in several blind tastings. In a 2011 study, researchers compared average consumer ratings of Bordeaux wines compiled on www .cellartracker.com with three experts—Robert Parker, *Wine Spectator*, and Stephen Tanzer of International Wine Cellar. The three experts agreed with one another to a much greater extent than any of them agreed with the consumers.*

Perhaps even more persuasive evidence is a 2011 study that found the elusive "contrast effect" in wine tasters' reactions to prices. Another husband and wife research team of behavioral economists, Uri and Ayelet Gneezy, convinced a Southern California winery to vary the per-bottle price of their Cabernet. In exchange for a free tasting, winery visitors agreed to rate what they tasted on a 7-point scale. Depending on the tasting sheet used, visitors were told that the Cabernet cost $10, $20, or $40 a bottle.

But this was just the beginning. The winery had two different vintages of Cabernet, one of which consistently scored much lower than the other in blind tastings. The researchers tracked the purchases made by visitors who tasted each vintage of Cabernet at each price point. They found that the expectations of high prices can indeed backfire, suggesting that they collided with something solid, some core perception of quality.

Specifically, people bought a lot more of the "better" Cabernet when it was priced at $20 than when it was offered at a lowly $10. However, a price increase had the opposite effect for the "lesser"

---

*As the researchers admit, someone who goes online to rate the wine they drink may not be your typical consumer. Plus, there's no guarantee that any of the consumers tasted blind. Many of them likely knew a lot about the wine—the winery, the price, even a review— before tasting.

Cabernet. People bought far fewer bottles for $20 than they did for $10. The conclusion: higher prices may improve the allure of wine, but only if it's pretty good to start with.

"You have to make sure that you at least live up to the threshold of expectations," says Ayelet Gneezy. Otherwise, the high expectations of an expensive bottle can sour the wine within.

THE VALUE OF KNOWING WHAT YOU DON'T KNOW

Shortly after my visit to the State Fair I hosted a blind wine tasting of my own. Twelve of my friends and family members tried five Rhône wines, which retailed at three price points: $15, $30, and $60. All five bottles were selected and poured by my wife, who selflessly sat out the tasting to avoid skewing the results with her inside knowledge of what we were drinking. One taster was a true wine connoisseur, with two wine cellars and a palate that dazzles at dinner parties. The rest of us were wine bumpkins. Our flight included six glasses, with one wine repeated. Without discussion, tasters priced the wine in each glass and tried to guess the duplicate. Afterward, I asked everyone to mark his or her favorite with a smiley face on the score sheet.

Four of us, including our resident expert, placed three of the six samples in the correct price tiers, while chance would predict two correct. Two people, not including our expert, correctly named the duplicate, while five of us named the same incorrect pair. There was also a hint of consistency in our favorite wines. Collectively, three of the wines garnered all but two votes.*

As expected, most tasters put a smiley face next to a wine they'd priced highest. The winner, with six votes, was the 2007 Coudoulet de Beaucastel Côtes-du-Rhône ($30), and the runner-up, with four votes, was the cheapest wine served that evening, a 2009 Domaine de la Solitude Côtes-du-Rhône ($15). One of two $60

---

*Because some tasters had the good fortune of favoring the wine they thought was the duplicate, there were fifteen total smiley face votes.

bottles, the 2004 Pierre Gaillard Côte-Rôtie, received three smileys. Nobody liked the other $60 bottle.

I had encouraged tasting notes, and my guests obliged. Nobody detected meaty fruit, olive-tinged figs, or underbrush. They kept it simple: "rich and mellow"; "spicy, also yummy"; "something off"; "ick!" Describing his favorite wine of the evening, my brother gushed, "good." Our resident expert complimented the Côte-Rôtie with a "great nose!" Others called it smoky, peppery, or spicy. His wife hated it. "Smells yucky," she wrote, "tastes chalky."

This tasting wasn't scientific in the least. In conjunction with the real science, though, it gave me hope. While our blind wine judgments may have error margins as big as ocean liners, they are not entirely baseless. Somewhere out there, on a distant sensory horizon, there is something trustworthy that we might gradually approach, if never quite reach. It was a question of how much one cared, and it occurred to me that this was an undercurrent of Goldstein's manifesto. He wanted us to care more.

If we discount the portion of wine's pleasure derived solely from expectations, are we acting like Ben Franklin's commission dismissing the healing potential of mesmerism, just because its source was imagination? Possibly. Recall, however, that Mesmer claimed he could detect an invisible cosmic energy, much like the wine writers who claim to smell hot gooseberries and taste the limestone soils of distant vineyards. Blind wine tastings, like the placebo experiments of Franklin's commission, are worthwhile reality checks—even if they don't ultimately lead us to the mountaintop of pure, true preferences, and do no more than show us how much we don't know about what we really like.

We consider our likes and dislikes to be part of us. Naturally, we hold them dear. When we ponder how little of our world we truly understand, we at least want to believe that we know ourselves. The power of expectations does not obliterate this comforting notion, but it does tug at the covers. Expectations offer our palates bits of suggestion, some useful and some not. Their pleasurable effects, the research suggests, are real enough, and likely integral to the full enjoyment of a wine. Whatever we believe about our preferences, though, they are prone to change, subject to myriad influences, and benefit from frequent questioning as well as the occasional reshuffle.

"Even if you don't want to take the time, or don't care enough to learn anything about wine, which is completely fine, just the mere knowledge that you can be fooled into having a $100 experience from a $10 wine will make you think twice," Goldstein says. "Over time, it will lead you to have less of a bias against cheaper bottles, and maybe more skepticism toward expensive ones. I think that's a worthwhile trade-off, because you'll be drinking $10 wine much more often." Cheers.

5] *E PLURIBUS UNUM*

One evening in the fall of 1986, three constables barged into a London art gallery. They confiscated the art and arrested the artist, J. S. G. Boggs. His alleged crime? Officially, it was counterfeiting. More accurately, it was a conspiracy to create value.

Money was Boggs's muse. He drew it in exact detail, but with obvious flourishes, such as serial numbers reading E MC2 and LSD, or substituting his face for the usual head of state.

Boggs never tried to pass a drawing off as real currency, but he did spend his art. He offered Boggs Bills in lieu of cash to dumbfounded waiters, cab drivers, store clerks, and landlords, assigning each drawing a value equal to the bill it mimicked. When people turned him down, as they usually did, Boggs would pocket the drawing and pay his tab with legal tender. When people agreed to value the drawing as Boggs proposed, however, it opened the door to all sorts of magic.

If a waiter accepted a twenty-dollar Boggs Bill for a $14.40 lunch tab, for instance, Boggs would demand a receipt and change in real currency. He would sell the receipt and the change to an art collector for a few hundred bucks. The collector would then track down the waiter and offer hundreds more for the bill itself. A complete transaction, annotated and framed, could fetch a few thousand dollars at a gallery or auction.

Boggs's purpose was to shine an artistic light on how our minds conjure value—not just individually, based on unique tastes and desires, but collectively, based on the expectations that everyone shares our belief. Boggs Bills and the transactions they spawned created a whimsical reflection of that collective faith that we otherwise might not see.

Money is fungible—that is, your dollar bill is worth the same as my dollar bill—which makes it useful for trading less fungible things, such as an hour of labor for some groceries. Nevertheless, a dollar bill has no intrinsic value, especially once the government severed its tie with precious metals. Money sitting in your wallet is just paper. In your bank account, it's a number stored on a computer server that can be churned up into binary bits and sent to other computers to be reassembled.

In fact, since 2009, tech-savvy folks have been trading and spending a new currency called Bitcoin that has no physical form and exists only in encrypted online "wallets." Until 2010, Bitcoins were basically worthless, a programmer's bright idea and not much more. Then they started to catch on. Online exchanges opened up where Bitcoins could be bought and sold in other currencies, and a handful of online merchants started to accept Bitcoins as legal tender. As of this writing, these little nuggets of code are worth about $5 apiece.

Ultimately, the value of money is based on expectations of a future exchange, which requires trust that others will value the money just as we do based on their own expectations of future exchanges. Money is an act of faith in one another. It's just one example of value conjured from shared expectations. Similar beliefs and collective assumptions of value inform every choice we make as consumers.

It's tempting to think of value as a very personal question: what is this worth to me? The answer is up to you. To a degree, however, the answer is actually up to everybody else, because we are hardwired to want what we expect others will want.

If we ignore this social component of value, the results can be disastrous. But if we can recognize the influence of shared expectations, we may discover all sorts of ways to use their power for both personal and collective benefit.

WE HOPE IT SO

If you have a morbid sense of humor, then check out *Why the Real Estate Boom Will Not Bust* (2005) on Amazon.com. The book is by David Lereah, then a senior vice president and chief economist for the National Association of Realtors. On the cover, a house floats up from its lot, and a young family watches it rise above their heads. We can't see their faces, but we suppose their expressions have changed since 2005. Back then, they were likely amazed or awed, or possibly chagrined at being left behind. Today, they are petrified, or they ought to be, because they are about to be crushed.

Both the chief economist at Fannie Mae and a former member of the Federal Reserve board of governors gave the book a glowing review, as did many early readers. Most of the reviews, however, are post-bust.

"I found the pages much softer than Charmin," reads one. Another begs Amazon for a negative-star option. Some readers ironically give the book five stars as a cautionary tale for investors contemplating the next big thing. Even Amazon's book-recommending algorithm gets the joke, suggesting customers might also like *Dow 30,000, Dow 36,000, Dow 40,000,* or the dizzying *Dow 100,000.*

Why is it always so easy to believe the party will never end? After all, the story of every boom always ends with a bust. Always.

There were many reasons for the housing boom and calamitous bust—macroeconomic pressures, personal and political irresponsibility, regulatory hocus-pocus, and pure greed. What made it all possible, however, was the expectation that home prices would keep rising. It was a collective suspension of disbelief in economic gravity that made otherwise dubious, reckless, or loony choices feel rational. In such a world, home buyers didn't need to know the details of their mortgages, lenders didn't need to know if borrowers could handle the payments, brokers could sell wobbly loans to be chopped up and repackaged as solid investments that ratings agencies could stamp risk-free AAA, while federal officials blessed the whole enterprise as the American Dream. Ever-rising home prices would keep everybody out of trouble and make many very rich.

It's not that there weren't housing boom skeptics, among both experts and nonexperts alike. At its peak in 2005, amidst the gushing praise for Lereah's book, more than a few early readers called the boom's bluff.

"This book could be fatal to your finances," warned one of the early reviews on Amazon. Another suggested that a better title would be "Join the Greater Fools of America Club."

Most Americans were much more sanguine, buoyed by their faith in rising home values and the expectation that everyone would continue to believe. Thus, when the end came, it arrived with terrifying speed.

Triggered by the meltdown of mortgage-backed investments, the stock market lost nearly half of its value between September 1, 2008, and March 1, 2009. In six months, several trillion dollars of investment and housing wealth vanished. The fact that much of the lost wealth had been a mirage based on years of irrational expectations didn't matter. The fallout was devastatingly real. In 2008 and 2009, job losses topped six million in America and numbered in the tens of millions worldwide. Millions of people fell into poverty.

Amidst the wreckage, it's tempting to believe that people could never again be so ruinously naive. One suspects, however, that such hope is just our inveterate optimism at work once again. Our brains are wired to see the glass as half full.

Granted, a healthy economy depends on optimism, even the kind that defies the lessons of history. Optimism spurs entrepreneurship, encourages investment, and bolsters consumer spending that powers a thriving marketplace. Sadly, it also allows lessons of caution and prudence—so obvious in the rubble of a bust—to be forgotten in the next boom.

In 2007, Tali Sharot was among a group of neuroscientists at New York University that found the brain's optimism switch. They scanned people's brains while asking them to think about events they remembered or imagined in the future, based on cues such as "getting lost," "participating in sports," or "death of a loved one." The subjects rated each episode's intensity, how positive or negative it was, how far from the present it occurred, and how involved they were in the event.

The future was rosier than the past. Overall, people rated happy future events more positively than happy memories. Future happiness was also closer in time, and perceived with more detail and intensity than future misfortune.

Subjects' brains were the most engaged when they imagined happy future events, and two brain areas were particularly active—the emotion-driven amygdala and the rostral anterior cingulate cortex (rACC), the brain's switchboard of attention.

Being optimistic offers many benefits, but better fortune-telling isn't one of them. It's been repeatedly shown that mildly depressed people are more accurate than those of us with a normal (optimistic) disposition when it comes to judging their control over future events, their longevity, and the likelihood of various personal misfortunes. We all experience periods of struggle in our lives, and witness many more. How do we stay so sunny when we ought to know better?

According to Sharot, now at University College London, we are selective learners. Our brains process good and bad news differently, eagerly gobbling up new information if it suggests we should be more optimistic, but paying much less attention to more pessimistic facts. For a 2011 brain scan study, her subjects forecast their chances of experiencing all sorts of trouble—ranging from car theft to Alzheimer's disease. After each estimate, they learned the actual probability based on their demographic profile.

Subjects then had a chance to amend their forecasts in a follow-up scanning session. People were much more likely to adjust in the direction of the facts, if the facts indicated they should be more optimistic—for example, if they had estimated their chances of getting cancer at 50 percent while the average probability of somebody in their demographic being diagnosed with the disease was 25 percent. Their brains reflected this bias. Areas of the prefrontal cortex known for paying attention to errors and goofs, essential to learning, were much more active when people were corrected with facts that could be seen as good news.

What purpose might this selective learning serve? In the short term, our brains' optimistic bias frees us from endless conjecture about what might have been. It lets us face what's next with confidence. In the long term, that extra optimism may be what keeps us moving, doing, and propagating even though we know nothing lasts. As the biologist Ajit Varki recently argued, our instinctive optimism may have evolved in tandem with our brain's ability to contemplate the future, including the fact that no matter what we do, we all end up in the same mortal fix. Death's inevitability can be a real motivation sapper if you let it get to you, as it eventually gets to us all.

ARE YOU THINKING WHAT I'M THINKING?

Part of any asset's value is based on an expectation of how much others will value it. During a boom, the expectations-driven portion of value swells until it swallows up everything else. This is what happened to American home values between 2000 and 2006, when they jumped by 20, 30, and even 40 percent from one year to the next in some cities.

This self-fulfilling magic of an economic bubble is reminiscent of the famous scene from Don DeLillo's *White Noise* (1985) when Jack and his buddy Murray visit "The Most Photographed Barn in America."

"No one sees the barn," Murray tells Jack, as fellow visitors dutifully take out their cameras and tripods.

"Once you've seen the signs about the barn, it becomes impossible to see the barn," Murray says. "We're not here to capture an image, we're here to maintain one. Every photograph reinforces the aura. Can you feel it, Jack?"

Unfortunately, most of us can't feel it. We can't see a boom for what it is, because we don't recognize the influence that collective expectations have over our perceptions of value. Following the herd is for sheep, and we're not sheep, dammit!

In famous experiments on peer pressure in the 1950s, the social psychologist Solomon Asch gave people a task much simpler than judging the value of a house. His subjects compared the relative length of different line segments. For example, which of three line segments matches the length of an initial line segment displayed as a model? People were always tested in groups that were secretly composed of Asch's confederates, who, by design, answered first and sometimes gave the same blatantly incorrect answer. Finally it was the subject's turn to respond. Even when the rest of the group members were obviously wrong, subjects went along with their answer more than a third of the time.

This effect, which has been replicated repeatedly, is usually framed as a test of conformity and peer pressure. And yet it's not just about face-saving fibbing. More recent research shows that social pressure can actually change what people see, and what they value, too.

In 2011, researchers asked young men to rate photographs of women on a 7-point scale of attractiveness. The guys looked at face after face on a computer, and after each rating, they learned whether their peers had agreed. In reality, the peer feedback was generated by a computer programmed to rate some of the women 2 or 3 points more, or less, attractive than the subject did.

Then the guys rated each face again while inside a brain scanner. Not only did peer feedback sway their attractiveness ratings, it changed how their brains reacted to each face. The researchers compared brain reactions to faces that subjects had initially rated as equally attractive. Reward center activity spiked for faces that "peers" found more attractive, and it dipped for faces they'd rated as less attractive, while showing no change in reaction when peers agreed or when no feedback was given. In this case, beauty was in the eyes of the beholders.

In a separate experiment, researchers also scanned subjects' brains during their initial ratings of the women. After each rating, the screen would go blank and then display the peer ratings. Again, the reward center activity mirrored face ratings. In addition, no matter the rating, there was an extra reward center jolt when peers agreed and a dip when they disagreed. Peer pressure may be coercive, but being in the flow of consensus opinion feels great. Even if we could easily step out of the stream, who would want to? Sometimes, though, we would be better off if we did.

DUMB MONEY MAKES THE WORLD GO AROUND

The economist John Maynard Keynes once compared the stock market to a beauty contest in which the judges don't choose the faces they believe are the prettiest, nor even those whom others might judge the prettiest. "We have reached the third degree," Keynes wrote, "where we devote our intelligences to anticipating what average opinion expects the average opinion to be."

While the stock market's performance is loosely tied to verifiable economic benchmarks—earnings reports, job numbers, consumer spending—it's mainly a funhouse mirror of past and present expectations, reflecting a hopeful or gloomy outlook on what's next.

In 2011, two economists combed through thousands of news stories between 2005 and 2010, measuring the frequency of negative phrases, such as "financial crisis" and "credit crunch." They measured the ups and downs of bank stocks over the same period. As expected, the two measures moved in tandem. However, rather than the mood of news coverage reflecting negative stock performance, as one might anticipate, mood drove the market. Downbeat news coverage sapped investor confidence, the study's authors concluded, and the pessimism was self-fulfilling.

Likewise, in 2011, computer scientists crafted an algorithm that distills Twitter feeds into an index of the nation's collective mood and thereby predicts short-term stock market changes with nearly 90 percent accuracy. A London-based hedge fund quickly snapped up exclusive use of the algorithm for $40 million.

Indeed, there is money to be made by anticipating what average opinion expects average opinion to be. Stock markets are primed by what professional investors call "the dumb money," by which they mean me, and probably you, too. The dumb money can be counted on to buy the stocks that everybody else is buying, to overreact, to sell winners too soon, and to hold on tenaciously to losers.

Few people understand these tendencies as well as finance professors Terrance Odean and Brad Barber, who have studied average investor behavior for more than a decade. It's a problem of too many choices and too much information, according to Odean, which gets solved by default.

"Investors wait for a stock to catch their attention," Odean says. "Then, if they like it, they buy it."

What do we like? Rising stocks. "There can be a feedback loop," Odean says. "When I buy a stock believing it will go up, that drives the stock up, and then you buy it, which drives the stock up even more."

A few years ago, Odean and Barber analyzed thousands of accounts at a large discount broker during a five-year period when the market grew 17.9 percent overall. The average account earned just 16.4 percent. Tellingly, the more account holders bought and sold stock, the worse they did, with the highest quintile of accounts in terms of trading earning just 11.4 percent.

Still, the dumb money deserves respect from the suits on Wall Street. Without us, their profits would be a lot harder to come by. Every winning deal needs a loser.

This doesn't mean that amateurs can't make smart, prescient

investments, or that financial professionals have all the answers.* In fact, up to 70 percent of U.S. stock trades are now triggered by computers owned by investment firms that scour the markets and gobble up every useful bit of public information in real time. The algorithms initiate millions of trades a day, buying and selling the same stocks in milliseconds and pouncing on the tiniest sliver of opportunity.

The real trouble isn't that we dumb-moneys don't know what we're doing, it's that so many of us think that we do. In a study of about 1,600 investors who had recently switched from phone-based to online trading, Odean and Barber found that investors tended to jump into online trading after a period of unusually strong trading performance. Once online, they traded "more actively, more speculatively, and less profitably." Prior to going online, these investors had outperformed the market by more than 4 percent annually. Over five years investing online, they lagged the market by more than 3 percent.

"Overconfidence gives you the courage to act on your misguided convictions," says Odean.

THE SHIFTING SANDS OF TRUST

On September 13, 2007, economists gathered for a conference at the Bank of England. They were seated at a formal dinner, awaiting their host—the bank's governor, Mervyn King. The conference overflowed with optimism. It focused on competing theories of how the economies of the developed world had managed to remain so steady and generally prosperous over the previous quarter century.

---

* Recently, Duke economists studied the stock market forecasts of chief financial officers. Specifically, the CFOs were asked to name a range of growth rates for the S&P 500 stock index that they believed had an 80 percent chance of including the actual market return for the following year. Obviously, one could game this challenge by giving a ridiculously wide spread (somewhere between economic Armageddon and investor Nirvana), but these were professionals with years of experience. They gave much more reasonable, informed forecasts for the year ahead. Two thirds of them were wrong.

King never showed up for dinner. He'd been called away to ne-
gotiate the first bailout of the Great Recession, for Northern Rock,
one of England's largest banks. It was an attempt to bolster confidence that instead sparked panic and the first major bank run in
the U.K. since the 1930s.

Northern Rock bank was heavily invested in the American
mortgage market. In the summer of 2007, people began losing
their faith in ever-rising home prices and banks tightened their
grip on their money. They suddenly stopped lending, including to
one another. This led Northern Rock to ask for an emergency loan
from the Bank of England, which was granted on September 14.

At the time, deposits in British banks were fully insured only
up to 2,000 pounds. The details of the emergency loan weren't revealed. Northern Rock's phone lines jammed, and its Web site
crashed under the crush of inquiries. Northern Rock depositors
streamed to their local branches to take out their money. Some
came just for information or for a personal reassurance that their
money was safe. Others saw the queues stretching down the sidewalk, and the panic spread.

As one man waiting for hours to close out his account put it,
even if the risk was small, "I don't want to be the mug left without
my savings."

In their book *Animal Spirits* (2009), economists George Akerlof
and Robert Shiller describe the credit crisis that followed collapsing home prices as a bursting trust bubble. Credit, they point out,
derives from the Latin *credo,* meaning "I believe." In a bubble,
trust and optimism feed off each other, because more optimistic
people are more likely to trust each other, and that very trust facil-
itates optimism's spread.

"In good times, people trust. They make decisions spontane-
ously. They know instinctively that they will be successful. They
suspend their suspicions," write Akerlof and Shiller. "As long as
people remain trusting, their impulsiveness will not be evident.
But then, when the confidence disappears, the tide goes out. The
nakedness of their decisions stands revealed."

A bank run is the quintessential self-fulfilling prophecy of fearful expectations. It lays bare the importance of trust and the consequences of its loss. Why are we so willing to trust one moment, and so quick to abandon it the next?

For one thing, reciprocated trust feels good. It lights up our brain's reward system. Violated trust, meanwhile, registers in the same brain areas as physical pain. In 2002, anthropologist James Rilling showed both effects while scanning the brains of people playing a "prisoner's dilemma" game for money with an assortment of trustworthy people, rogue knaves, and computer algorithms.

In each round, players chose to cooperate or defect from their partner. A subject earned the most money, $3, if she defected and her partner chose to cooperate. By contrast, if she decided to cooperate and her partner defected, then she got nothing. Mutual cooperation won both players $2. Mutual defection earned both players just $1.

Notably, the real reward wasn't the money, but trust itself. Reactions in the brain's reward and pain-sensitive regions occurred only when Rilling's subjects thought they were playing with a human partner (in reality, it was always a computer). When they knew they were playing with a computer, activity in these brain areas didn't budge, no matter the outcome. People uphold trust. Computers just run programs. The brain knows the difference.

Our brains assess the value of fairness in the same way. In studies using the "ultimatum game," people reject grossly unfair splits of money, thereby killing the deal and ensuring that nobody gets a dime. When offered the same uneven split by a computer, however, they happily accept. Brain scans suggest that the first instinct is to take whatever money is offered, because, after all, something is more than nothing. Yet there's more at stake than our rational self-interest when a human being is on the other end of the deal—specifically, upholding the collective value of fairness.

Of course, valuing trust makes sense in these games. I scratch your back and you scratch mine. However, the value of trust also rises and falls outside the bounds of strategy and immediate reciprocity. Much like a publicly traded stock or home values, our valuation of trust changes according to our expectations of how much *others* value it.

For a 2010 study, social network gurus James Fowler and Nicholas Christakis had people play a series of "public goods" games with different groups of strangers. In these games, subjects staked with a modest amount of money can give whatever they want to a communal pot of money that is then tripled in value and split evenly. After each round, everybody learns who gave what. Usually in these games, people start off trusting each other to some degree. Then some players inevitably try to get something for nothing, or next to nothing, and their free riding eventually kills trust and drives donations into the ground.

In Fowler and Christakis's study, however, subjects dealt with a new group of players every time. Each round was a fresh start and a one-shot deal, so neither reputation nor reciprocity had any pull. Nevertheless, the players' contributions in any given round rose and fell according to how generous their fellow players had been in *earlier* rounds.

The more those previous partners had given—indeed, the more that previous partners of those previous partners had given—the more trusting and generous subjects would be with their new group. Even without concern over developing a reputation, or an opportunity to reciprocate, trust ripples out.

Trust can evaporate just as easily. Ironically, punishments for not cooperating can backfire precisely because they imply low expectations for trustworthy behavior. If people could be trusted, after all, then no sanctions would be necessary. In one recent experiment, people played two rounds of a trust game. Some initially played with punishments for violating trust and then played a second round without these sanctions. Everyone else played both rounds without sanctions. After each game, players rated how much they trusted their fellow group members on a sliding scale.

People who played under the threat of sanctions cooperated more, but trusted each other less than those who played without sanctions. When the sanctions were removed, the value of trust dropped even further and cooperation among these players took a nosedive.

WHY WE NEVER THINK ALONE

We are constantly recalibrating the value of social norms—including trust, fairness, and honesty—based on how much they seem to be valued by others, especially others with whom we identify.

In one study, for instance, college students taking a math exam were more likely to cheat when a fellow test taker (actually a confederate of the researchers) obviously cheated. The effect was much bigger when the cheater wore a T-shirt identifying his allegiance to the university where the experiments took place, rather than a T-shirt representing the school's bitter rival.

Lest this invite the "T-shirt defense" for every moral lapse, it's important to note that these studies suggest that choices can be influenced, not explained, by implicit shifts in behavioral expectations that we neither recognize as externally generated, nor even notice as shifts.

Indeed, our brains seem preoccupied with social expectations, and research increasingly suggests that navigating them is a centerpiece of conscious thought. We split from our closest primate relative around five or six million years ago. Our brains have since tripled in size. A lot of the extra thinking power is geared toward reckoning with "theory of mind," the understanding that other individuals have their own thoughts and desires, and the related expectations of social norms.

A few years ago, anthropologists compared chimpanzees, orangutans, and toddlers on a range of cognitive skills. Could they remember a toy's hiding place? Could they use a tool to snag an out-of-reach treat? Could they follow pointing or find other ways to explain what they wanted? Would they understand somebody else's intentions? Would they help?

The apes were just as good as the kids at understanding and manipulating the physical world. But the toddlers dominated in the social domain.

The brain areas most involved in social cognition are found in the brain's so-called default network, which had long puzzled neuroscientists because it consumed so much energy but was most active when the mind didn't seem to be doing anything in particular. The default network came alive when the mind wandered. By contrast, during intense, goal-directed, conscious thinking, it seemed to doze off. However, scientists increasingly believe this default network is actually hard at work formulating expectations and exploring social scenarios based on theory of mind.

In 2010, Harvard and MIT researchers partnered in a study in which people judged characters in vignettes who inflicted grievous harm on one another, either intentionally or by accident. For example, Grace gives her friend sugar for her coffee that is actually poison. Or a character's malevolence is foiled by chance, such as when Grace means to poison her friend's coffee but, whoops, gives her plain old sugar by mistake. The researchers used magnetic pulses to disrupt a portion of the default network—specifically the junction of the brain's parietal and temporal lobes—that had been particularly active in brain scan studies of people making moral judgments. Compared to control subjects, people with a disrupted default network gave much less weight to the motivations of these killers and would-be killers when evaluating their misdeeds.

HARNESSING SOCIAL EXPECTATIONS

All in all, much of this research seems to suggest that collective expectations hum along quietly in the background, creating value in ways that are largely unnoticed and beyond our control or leading us by the nose into all sorts of blunders. Can we use the power of social expectations in a positive way? Indeed we can.

Social expectations are powerful motivators. For instance, consider the finding that hotel guests are much more likely to reuse their towels when the placard explaining the program notes that most guests take part, rather than touting the environmental benefits. This isn't just a question of numbers, or majority rules. It's more than guilt and being mindful of one's image. Social expectations can turn traditional business models upside down by changing the perception of value. For centuries, fixed prices have been the measure of value for both businesses and their customers, and the trick has always been to price one's widgets just right, even though it never really was *just right*. The aggregated actions of a market made up of rational consumers should (and often does) help businesses solve this pricing puzzle. But in many situations, the market's answer to pricing is less than perfect. Inevitably, for some would-be customers, the widget's value falls just short of the asking price, and so sales are lost, while other customers would no doubt have paid much more.

Recently, sparked by some high-profile success stories, a growing number of businesses have sprung up that thrive despite allowing customers to pay whatever they want, including nothing, for the product or service being provided.

The "pay what you wish" idea isn't exactly new—street musicians, public broadcasting, and anybody who works for tips all depend on people reaching into their wallets and pulling out whatever they choose. It's always been considered marginal, however. A business might survive that way, but it was no way to turn a real profit.

Then, in October 2007, the British alt-rock band Radiohead let fans download their latest release, *In Rainbows*, and pay whatever they wanted for it.

On the checkout page, customers saw only a box with a question mark in it. When they clicked it, up popped this message: "It's up to you." Another click: "No, really. It's up to you."

One of the band's managers, Chris Hufford, who helped come up with the idea, called it "virtual busking," riffing on the street entertainer model. Others called it bat-shit crazy. Regardless, it worked. About 1.8 million people downloaded the album, and 40 percent of them paid for it. It averaged out to $2.26 per download, which made In Rainbows the biggest moneymaker in the band's history.

There was no study done of who paid, who didn't, and why, but the general idea, first pushed by Dan Ariely and fellow behavioral economist James Heyman, is that transactions can be governed by two sets of expectations—market-based and social norms. Giving people control over what they pay dissolves the expectations of a business transaction and replaces them with social expectations, such as trust, cooperation, and reciprocity.

Of course, Radiohead's success could be a fluke, and just another perk of being internationally famous. The band has millions of fans. They can sell more concert tickets and T-shirts to those they woo with their pay-what-you-wish publicity. Most businesses just have customers, along with competitors offering nearly the same products and services. To be fair, Radiohead kept a close watch on their pricing experiment. They made it clear that they could pull the plug on the deal at any moment, and they did so about three weeks later as the more ardent fans gave way to customers with a so-so commitment to the band who were just free riding for some free tunes.

Could pay-what-you-wish work for less glamorous businesses? Economists at the University of California, San Diego, had the same question. They partnered with an amusement park concession stand to test a hypothesis about what might make pay-what-you-wish work.

The business operated in the shadow of the park's biggest roller coaster and sold people photographs of themselves as they screamed their way through the ride. Normally these souvenirs went for $13. The researchers convinced the concessionaire to offer a deal—Pay what you want! Oh, and we'll give half of our revenue to a children's charity.

As with the Radiohead downloads, customers could pay nothing for their photos. Yet nobody did. In fact, over the two days of the deal, the concession made twice their normal profit while raising several thousand dollars for the charity. "Nobody could see what the customer paid except maybe their spouse and the cashier," says researcher Ayelet Gneezy. "But there's this notion of, 'I can't go cheap on a charity.'"

It wasn't just about the charity. In a different version of the experiment, when the concession offered half its revenue to charity but charged the regular price, sales and revenue did not increase from baseline. The difference, according to Gneezy, was consumer expectations—specifically the assumption that a business is concerned about profit first, and everything else second, including children's charities.

The researchers asserted that while customers applaud good corporate citizenship, they may also discount it as a roundabout form of marketing. They speculated that by letting customers name their price, the concession made itself vulnerable to big losses—the antithesis of profit—so the wary expectations of a business transaction gave way to expectations of what the researchers dubbed "shared social responsibility," which increased the perceived value of the souvenir photos.

It's not that pay-what-you-wish will always work. In many parts of the economy, it would likely be a disaster. The point is that it *can* work in more places than one might expect, and in some cases works best—both for the business and the community it serves.

With that said, it's legitimate to ask whether pay-what-you-wish only works thanks to the endless supply of suckers in this world. Are customers who pay more than they need to for a

Radiohead album being duped in a sense? Are they getting real value for the extra money?

You could ask a similar question about paying for fashion or the trappings of dinner at an expensive restaurant. The scenarios are laced with subjectivity and unique circumstances, which make them difficult to study. In 2009, Ariely and Michael Norton, a professor at Harvard Business School, published a review paper proposing the idea of "conceptual consumption," which pushed for an expanded definition of expected value in consumer choice.

Modern humans, in the industrialized world no longer worry about scarcity or focus consumption on meeting basic needs, they argued. We are free to spend more and more time and mental energy consuming ideas, including expectations, goals, social norms, and variety. Rather than framing these motivators as distractions or deviations from rational decisions, Ariely and Norton argued that consuming concepts offers genuine pleasure and utility. The value is real, in other words.

For instance, people often choose a cell phone or other electronic gizmo loaded with features that they'll never master, which makes the phone less usable, possibly even frustrating, in addition to more expensive.

"They're making a mistake in some sense," says Norton. They buy a more complicated, feature-rich product, despite its usability challenges, because they think people will think more highly of them. The thing is, Norton says, they're right.

Working with Georgetown University marketing professor Debora Thompson, Norton showed that customers choose more expensive, feature-filled electronics when they believe that their choices will be seen and judged by others. Then the researchers asked a separate group of people to evaluate two hypothetical consumers based on the cell phone or digital camera they chose—either the one with fifteen features, or the one with thirty features. People judged customers who sprang for the feature-rich phones and cameras more favorably overall, and saw them as more technologically savvy and open to new experiences.

The customers who opted for feature-rich phones and cameras may have busted their budget on products that they won't fully utilize, but they *may* still come out ahead when social utility is weighed in the balance of their expectations.

"They do get an extra source of positive social feedback from people that might make it worth not being able to use those features," Norton says. "It's not just in their heads."

THE POWERS THAT BELIEVE

So much of our economy depends on shared expectations. If people lose that faith, a ton of value vanishes. The consequences can be dire. J. S. G. Boggs and his drawings of money pulled on the threads of those shared expectations. No wonder people got touchy about it.

In 1993, Boggs was a fellow for art and ethics at Carnegie Mellon University in Pittsburgh. Early one morning, Secret Service agents and local police raided Boggs's home, studio, and office, confiscating every money drawing they could find.

The authorities had swooped in to stop "Project Pittsburgh," Boggs's scheme to spread a million dollars of his currency around town. It wasn't just the sheer quantity of Boggs Bills that spooked the Secret Service. It was the fact that he had plans to keep the money in circulation, to spread the faith well beyond the small circle of folks who usually played along when Boggs spent his drawings one at a time. To the authorities, Project Pittsburgh wasn't whimsical. It was plain dangerous.

Boggs's inspiration for his Pittsburgh money was the old five-dollar greenback note from the nineteenth century. Pictured on its back was a row of five silver dollars to reinforce the comforting expectation that the bill could be swapped for silver at any time. On the back of every Boggs Bill used in Project Pittsburgh were five empty circles reserved for the thumbprint of every person willing to accept the drawing as payment. In the creation of value, we are all complicit.

YOU ARE ALWAYS ON MY MIND

6] THE FINE LINE BETWEEN YOU AND ME

We've seen how our expectations can bolster or sa-
botage our best efforts—such as the weight lifters
strengthened by imaginary steroids and the tangled feet of English penalty shooters—and how the expectations of wanting
hold sway over what we like and value. Let's dig a little deeper
and explore how our fast-forward brains help determine who we
are and who we may become.

This process begins with the brain's need to find meaning in
the daily deluge of sensory input. The late Richard Gregory, a British neuroscientist, claimed sensation was a bunch of "predictive
hypotheses." The brain learns to expect small things to be lighter
than larger ones. It expects objects to appear smaller as they move
away from us and to grow larger as they draw near. Our brains
use these expectations to find patterns, identify objects, and fill in
gaps.

Gregory proved his point with illusions, such as the famous
Müller-Lyer line segments bracketed by inward- or outward-
facing arrows. The lines are the same length, but the arrows suggest perspective—that one is more distant than the other. The brain
concludes that the "distant" one must be longer.

"Though seeing and hearing and touch seem simple and direct,
they are not. They are fallible inferences based on knowledge and
assumptions which may or may not be appropriate to the situation," Gregory wrote. "Listen to a tape recording of an audience
clapping. In the kitchen, it sounds like bacon frying. In the garden
on a dull day, it sounds like rain."

The person you think you are is likewise a bundle of predictive hypotheses. Your brain starts with a basic mental model of a human body that is continuously refined over the years. It lumps everything into two categories: *This is you* and, nearly as important, *That is not you.*

The assumptions of self-perception range beyond our corporal selves. Are we old or young? Ugly or beautiful? Are we the same as everybody else in this room, at this school, or on this street, or are we different? And if so, how should we act? The answers are awash in self-fulfilling prophecies that can both enrich us and hold us back. By tweaking the expectations of self-perception, we can stretch the boundaries of who we are.

HAUNTED BY A PHANTOM LIMB

Lieutenant John Pucillo lay in his hospital bed and screamed. The pain came from everywhere, but mostly from his left leg, which felt like it was twisted up behind his back. It didn't matter that Pucillo didn't have a left leg anymore, not since a roadside bomb in Baghdad gutted his armored truck. Logic couldn't kill this pain. Neither could drugs. Pucillo had pressed the button on his morphine drip so often that it locked him out.

Any soldier knows the risks, and Pucillo served in an explosive ordnance disposal (EOD) unit—clearing mines and defusing bombs. In EOD, Pucillo says, "you either get the bomb, or the bomb gets you." On May 19, 2006, while shepherding a convoy along a Baghdad highway, the bomb got Pucillo.

He knew something was wrong within seconds of the blast, but to avoid going into shock he didn't look down. Pucillo was evacuated to a Baghdad casualty center and taken immediately to an operating room where a surgeon leaned over and gave him the news. "Dude, your left leg is gone, but you're going to live."

That was the deal, and Pucillo accepted it. Subconsciously, though, some part of his brain still expected his leg to be there and to move when commanded. When it didn't, the neural confusion translated into pain that made him scream.

Pucillo is among more than 1,100 American soldiers who have come home from Iraq or Afghanistan missing a leg or an arm. About 90 percent of amputees feel their lost limb re-form on occasion—sometimes too long or too short, other times itchy, or wet, or stuck in a strange position, and often in severe pain.

The pain of "phantom limbs" offers a glimpse into the expectations of self-perception. We don't usually notice until something goes wrong, but our brains expect us to have two arms and two legs. When one seems to be missing, our brains go searching for answers.

In one famous experiment, a subject sat with his left arm resting on a table but hidden by a small screen while a life-sized rubber hand and arm sat on the table in full view. For the next few minutes, an experimenter stroked the rubber hand and the subject's hidden hand with two small paintbrushes, synchronizing each stroke. Amazingly, the subject eventually reported feeling the brushstrokes on the visible rubber hand rather than on his actual hand. In order to reconcile what it saw and felt, the brain made a best guess and took ownership of the rubber hand. It didn't matter that the subject knew this could not be so.

The brain expects an intact body, and it will bend reality to meet this expectation, even if that means creating limbs out of thin air. The first physician to name these sensations "phantom limbs" was Silas Weir Mitchell, a military surgeon who worked at Philadelphia's "Stump Hospital" after the Civil War. For more than a century, nobody knew what to do about phantom limb pain. Physicians tried everything—heavy doses of painkillers, snipping the remaining nerves in the stump, cutting the pathways for sensory input in the spinal cord. None of these approaches really worked, because the brain didn't need any peripheral sensation to conjure the ghost limb and feel the terrible pain. It did both all on its own.

In the early 1990s, the neuroscientist Vilayanur (V. S.) Ramachandran made a breakthrough in combating this strange, yet excruciating sensation. He found a way to trick an amputee's brain

out of feeling phantom limb pain. If the pain resulted from a mis-
match of motor commands and visual feedback, he figured, then
why not simulate what the brain expects to see.

It was a long shot, but Ramachandran tried out the idea with a
man who'd lost an arm and was desperate to relieve the constant,
painful sensations of it re-forming. He wedged a large mirror into
a box and told the man to move his intact arm in front of it while
imagining that he was moving both arms in tandem—raising and
lowering them, opening and closing both hands, wiggling all ten
fingers.

Over the next two weeks, the man did these mirror exercises for
ten minutes a day. To everyone's surprise, including Ramachandran's, it worked. While watching the reflection, the man felt his
arm re-form and return to his control. With the brain's expectations of an intact body thus satisfied, the phantom pain subsided,
although it didn't vanish completely. The researchers tried the
mirror therapy with ten more amputees, and it worked for six of
them. A few other amputees were given mirror therapy in the
years that followed, but it took another decade, and two major
wars, for doctors to push the idea into clinical care.

In 2004, Commander Jack Tsao, a U.S. Navy neurologist, began
treating patients at Walter Reed Medical Center. The fighting in
Iraq was escalating and more soldiers were coming home missing
limbs. Tsao had read about Ramachandran's work in graduate
school, and he was surprised to learn that there had never been a
clinical trial of mirror therapy. In 2006, he led a study of eighteen
veterans who had recently lost a leg or a foot and had phantom
limb pain, and divided them into three random groups. One group
did mirror therapy. Another did the same leg movements in front
of a covered mirror. The third group simply visualized the movement of their lost limb.

Lieutenant Pucillo was transferred to Walter Reed that summer
and landed in Tsao's mirror therapy group. Every day, for four
weeks, he watched his intact leg and its reflection as he flexed
his calves, rolled his feet, and wiggled his toes. The leg would

re-form during these exercises, but without the pain. Indeed, all the patients in the mirror therapy group reported a significant decrease in phantom pain after four weeks, but only two of the patients in the mental visualization and only one patient in the covered mirror group did likewise.

Soon Pucillo felt strong enough to quit the heavy doses of pain medication he'd been taking, a necessary step in his quest to return to active duty. By 2007, he had checked out of Walter Reed and was exercising regularly with a variety of prosthetic legs— one for biking, one for swimming, one for running, and so on. He returned to active duty and was promoted to lieutenant commander.

In a world of multimillion-dollar brain scanners and machines that can induce virtual brain lesions with magnetic pulses, there's something romantic about neuroscience practiced with nothing more than a $15 mirror from Target. From a research perspective, however, it's somewhat restrictive. Wiggling fingers and toes taps into a limited range of bodily expectations. Confined to the mirror, it's hard to act natural and move as a whole person does.

Researchers have responded to this challenge by expanding mirror therapy into the virtual world. Donning a head-mounted visual display, amputees look out on a virtual lab room from a first-person perspective with all their limbs intact. As they imagine moving both arms through a range of motions, infrared sensors track the intact limb in three dimensions, and the computer generates two perfect, real-time virtual mimics.

In a 2009 study, five out of eight amputees who regained their lost limb in virtual reality experienced a significant reduction in phantom limb pain. The subjects who felt the most pain relief also reported the most vivid sensory illusion in the virtual world—the sensation of touching surfaces, feeling objects, and contact between phantom fingers.

That same year, the Defense Department began developing a prosthetic limb that could talk to the brain. The first step is

building algorithms that can translate brain signals—from electrodes on the skull or from implanted sensors—into limb movements. Initial testing for brain-responsive prosthetics has been
done in a series of virtual worlds dubbed "virtual integration environments" in which subjects use their minds to control virtual
limbs doing basic tasks, such as grasping an object, pulling a lever,
or kicking a ball. In 2011, Commander Tsao began collaborating in
this research. Perhaps the virtual arms and legs used to help develop a brain-responsive prosthetic could, at the same time, help
amputees overcome their phantom pain. As of this writing, no results have been published.

CREATING A NEW YOU FROM THE TOP DOWN

The same neural trickery that can reanimate a lost limb also has
the potential to change who we think we are. The rubber hand illusion, for instance, offers more than a creepy sensation. At some
level, people adopt it as part of themselves. They start to care
about what happens to it.

When an experimenter suddenly grabs a finger of the rubber
hand and bends it backward, the subject starts to sweat. This is
not the kind of secondhand fear that comes with watching blood
spray in a horror movie. It's personal.

"What is most surprising about this illusion," wrote Ramachandran in a 2003 review of these effects, "is that a lifetime of experience should be negated by just a few minutes of the right kind
of sensory stimulation. One's body image, despite its appearance
of durability, is a transitory internal construct that can be easily
and profoundly modified."

In 2007, British neuroscientists led by H. Henrik Ehrsson did
the rubber hand illusion with people in a brain scanner. In a variation on the original study, the brushstrokes on the rubber hand
and the real hand were done slightly out of sync for half the
subjects, dubbed the "nonownership group." Ehrsson figured
that without synchronized visual and tactile stimuli, the illusion

wouldn't take, and the brain would not take ownership of the rubber hand.

Every so often, the experimenter would stop stroking the rubber hand, reach for a sharp needle, and pretend to stab it, while never actually touching it. As expected, people in the nonownership group, whose hidden hands had been brushed out of sync with the rubber hand, weren't alarmed by the stabbing threat. People whose hands were brushed in sync with the rubber hand, however, did not like it at all. Their anxiety levels spiked, as did activity in brain areas associated with the anticipation of pain, including the insula and the anterior cingulate cortex. These were the same brain regions that lit up when experimenters threatened to stab the subjects' actual hands with the needle.

The next year, Ehrsson was able to transfer ownership of a subject's entire body to a mannequin viewed through closed-circuit video in a head-mounted display. After brushing the torso of the mannequin and the subject for a few minutes, the researchers would lunge at the mannequin with a knife. Once again, the illusion was thwarted by out-of-sync brushstrokes, and these folks were unmoved by the attempted stabbing. By contrast, anxiety measured by skin conductance went through the roof for subjects in the body-swap condition induced by synchronous touch.

"The effect is so robust, that the person can face his or her biological body and shake hands with it without breaking the illusion," Ehrsson noted.

Other researchers have conjured similar body-transfer illusions with virtual reality. No synchronous touching needed. In these studies, people explore virtual worlds, usually one with a large mirror, from the first-person perspective of an avatar that mimics their every move thanks to infrared tracking. It doesn't take long for people to accept the avatar as themselves at some level, and treat the virtual world as real-ish. In virtual reality circles, they call it "presence."

This may seem like a bunch of parlor tricks, but the implications are huge. A few lines of code can change who you think you are and the expectations that go along with it.

A NEW YOU

I'm standing in Stanford University's Virtual Human Interaction Lab when the floor shudders and springs open before me. I lean over and look down—way down—into a deep pit, spanned by one remaining sliver of floor. The lab's director, psychologist Jeremy Bailenson, tells me to cross it.

Other than the pit, this virtual lab is an exact replica of the real lab that I entered a couple of minutes ago. A closet hides the two dozen servers that update the world displayed in my headgear sixty times a second.

As I shuffle along the narrow bridge, I feel queasy and my palms sweat. One third of Bailenson's subjects refuse to make the attempt. Many people fall into the pit. The bravest ones jump. I fall. The walls fly by, and I land with a jolt that rushes up my legs thanks to a burst of bass from huge speakers called butt-kickers hidden beneath the lab's flooring. Occasionally subjects who fall in the virtual world crumble to the floor in the real one.

In Bailenson's studies, people "wear" avatars of every size, shape, age, and ethnicity. Sometimes they're on their own. More often, they meet computer-controlled "agents" whose identities are equally interchangeable, as well as other avatars worn either by subjects or by a researcher separated in physical space. As an added twist, avatars need not look the same to any two people in the virtual world. You may see your virtual self as African American, for instance, but everybody else sees you as white.

Bailenson immerses these avatars in virtual cities, casinos, offices, forests, and crime scenes in order to hack the expectations of self-perception and see what shakes loose. Can we rewire ourselves to be somewhat more friendly, or ambitious, or tolerant souls? At the same time, Bailenson is sneaking a peek into a fast-approaching future of online identities that are digitally dispersed.

In a flash, the lab vanishes, and I'm in the middle of a two-lane country road. There's a rickety farmhouse on my left. Cows graze behind its stockade fence. The pit is now a sinkhole with exposed sewer pipes, spanned by a plank of wood. Across the sinkhole is a jackknifed tractor-trailer. The driver's okay. In fact, he's over there, beckoning me to cross.

A few seconds later, I'm at a busy intersection in what looks like a European metropolis. Cars race past, and people amble down the sidewalks enjoying a sunny day. I people-watch for a minute before the sky darkens, and it starts raining. Then it starts snowing. And just when my virtual European vacation couldn't get any worse, the butt-kickers trigger an earthquake. The whole city shakes violently, threatening collapse.

My world changes once more, and I'm back in the virtual lab, looking at myself in a mirror. I'm better looking than usual, but it doesn't last. Bailenson tells me to bend down low for a few seconds so I can't see the mirror. When I straighten up again, I'm considerably less handsome, with a huge forehead, no upper lip, a piggish nose, and a bulbous chin.

I still feel like myself. I know I'm staring at a computer-generated avatar. Yet Bailenson's research suggests that I have indeed changed. The tall, handsome me will think, feel, and act differently from the short, pig-faced me.

The idea flows from "self-perception theory," which says that in addition to observing, perceiving, and interpreting the rest of the world, part of your brain is busy observing, perceiving, and interpreting you. The expectations of self-perception sway your attitudes and behaviors so they match the assumptions you've made about yourself. As a speculative example, getting a military haircut *might* make you slightly more disciplined, or a little more gung ho!

A few years ago, Cornell psychologist Thomas Gilovich, he of the hot hand research, led a famous study of this theory. Gilovich had learned that the much penalized Oakland Raiders of the National Football League were flagged more in the black uniforms they wore for home games than in the white uniforms they wore as the visiting team. Did black uniforms make the Raiders play more aggressively?

Gilovich combed through National Football League and National Hockey League archival data and found that teams wearing black uniforms were indeed penalized more. This difference held between teams and within the same team when they wore their black uniforms, usually at home, as opposed to another color.

In Gilovich's lab, subjects judged football and hockey players in photographs to be more "bad," "mean," and "aggressive" when their uniforms were at least half black. That finding could indicate that the Raiders were simply the victims of biased refs. However, a follow-up experiment by Gilovich suggested otherwise.

Teams of subjects chose five games from a long list, supposedly for an upcoming competition with another team waiting in a nearby room. The games ranged from the über-tame "putting contest" and "block stacking" to the blood-curdling "chicken fight" and "dart gun duel." The study was rigged so that team members chose games both before and after being given black or white uniforms.

Without uniforms, teams chose equally aggressive games. After people put on black uniforms, however, they chose more aggressive games compared with teams who put on white. There's an expectation that badasses wear black, and badasses don't stack blocks. In the movies, Gilovich noted, the bad guys dress in black. Maybe it's a choice, reflecting their sinister nature, he wrote. Or maybe, as this study suggested, "some people become bad guys *because* they wear black."

Games are games, though. Could the expectations of self-perception change something more serious about who we are, such as our moral code? In 2010, a large group of women tried on sunglasses for what was billed as a marketing study. Some wore designer sunglasses while others wore sunglasses marked as "counterfeit." In reality, everybody wore the same name brand sunglasses. Nevertheless, in cognitive tasks given during the experiment, women wearing the "counterfeit" sunglasses cheated more. They also expected that people in written vignettes would more likely lie to an insurance agent, inflate an expense report, and steal office supplies. The researchers speculated that knowingly wearing knockoff sunglasses subconsciously triggered a less authentic, "counterfeit self." This changed the wearer's moral expectations of both herself and others, and she acted accordingly.

Rather than sunglasses or uniforms, subjects in Bailenson's self-perception research wear avatars. And a changed virtual self can have surprising effects on people. For instance, college students of all sizes who wore obese avatars during six weeks of exploring the multiplayer online world *Second Life,* where everyone is impossibly thin and beautiful, reported feeling very alone and spent hours trying to work off the computer-generated flab in a virtual gym.

Meanwhile, among the 77,000 *World of Warcraft* players tracked by Bailenson and his team, those with taller and better looking* avatars bested the shorter, uglier ones, even though appearance confers no actual functional advantages in the game—taller characters can't move faster, for example, or jump higher than shorter ones.

Bailenson isn't simply adding a virtual chapter to a long tradition of self-perception studies. He makes an even bolder claim. Not only do handsome avatars act differently than pig-faced avatars in the virtual world, but these changes in attitudes and behaviors carry over into people's offline selves. Bailenson observed this transference in several studies he did with doctoral student Nick Yee, who is now a staff scientist at the Palo Alto Research Center. They called it the Proteus Effect.

For example, wearing better-looking avatars gave college student subjects the confidence to contact more attractive potential dates in a follow-up study that was ostensibly about online dating. As a side note, people given ugly avatars were more likely to exaggerate their height in the dating profile.† Meanwhile, people

---

* They established this with a separate group of people rating the attractiveness of each character type during pilot testing.

† Their actual height was covertly measured by the lab's optical tracking system.

assigned taller avatars offered more aggressive, unfair splits of money in a virtual ultimatum game, played with a researcher confederate blind to the subjects' appearance. This effect carried over into an offline face-to-face negotiation.

"We thought baseline measures of self-esteem would be a very big mediator, but they didn't matter," Bailenson says of these results. The subject's actual height didn't matter, either.

The expectations of the Proteus Effect aren't monolithic. Gender, for instance, made a key difference in a study of virtual eating. Women whose avatars visibly pudged after eating virtual Reese's Cups, or slimmed down after opting for virtual carrots, ate fewer real chocolates when casually offered a bowl of them at the end of the experiment than did women whose avatars did not change after eating. For men, the effect was just the opposite. Women, apparently, became more body conscious while watching their avatar gain and lose weight during a virtual snack. Men just got hungry.

A NEW ME

Presence makes all the difference. A gut-level switch is flipped when you accept an avatar as yourself. It can change attitudes and behaviors in ways that reasoning and mental imagery cannot.

Witness the recent rise of cybertherapy. Phobic patients are exposed to virtual snakes, heights, and unfriendly crowds. Soldiers with post-traumatic stress encounter virtual war zones. In 2008, a group of Italian researchers created Eureka, an island in *Second Life* where addicts' avatars can go for online therapy sessions and, under a therapist's supervision, strengthen their resolve to stay on the wagon with visits to virtual bars, malls, and casinos.

Presence can also take the empathetic ideal of walking a mile in another's shoes to a new level of verisimilitude. A few decades of virtual aging, for instance, spurs young adults to care more about saving for retirement. According to a recent McKinsey report, the average American family is nearly 40 percent short of what they'll need for a secure retirement, and a third of households have no retirement savings at all. Not surprisingly, young people save the least. More than half of Americans aged eighteen to twenty-seven have not begun saving for retirement, according to a national survey done in 2011, and nearly two thirds of them said they never even thought about retirement.

Part of the issue is that we don't think of our future selves as, well, ourselves. Instead, we treat our future selves like other people entirely. This psychological distance undercuts the impact of delayed rewards and consequences and skews our decisions. We know we should pocket our credit cards and save more, but we just can't deny our current selves a splurge or two, or three, especially when our future selves are picking up the tab.

Psychologist Emily Pronin showed this future-self estrangement in a 2008 study. Participants made choices for their current selves, their next-semester selves, and anonymous others, some presented as real choices and others as pure hypotheticals. How much of a disgusting liquid, specifically water mixed with ketchup and soy sauce, should subjects drink for an upcoming scientific study? How much time would they like to devote to volunteer tutoring? In general, people went easier on their current selves without distinguishing between their next-semester selves and strangers.

Pyschologists and behavioral economists call our tendency to favor smaller immediate rewards over larger future rewards "delay discounting." For years, they've puzzled over this impatient quirk that leads us into one bad decision after another. Why is it so habitual? What might be a remedy?

In 2009, the psychologist Hal Ersner-Hershfield used a variety of questionnaires to measure how close people felt to their future selves ten years down the road. It turned out that the more people identified with their future selves the less likely they were to engage in delay discounting when offered a choice between two monetary rewards. In fact, another study found that delay discounting evaporated when researchers coaxed greater closeness between a subject's current and future selves by having them imagine using a future cash reward in a specific scenario based on actual plans.

Bailenson's research offered another way to reconcile the current and future selves. For a 2011 study, he and Ersner-Hershfield created seventy-year-old versions of their college student subjects using a photo-morphing algorithm. They stuck the elderly faces onto subjects' avatars. Control subjects, meanwhile, wore unaltered, current-self avatars. Once in the virtual world, participants checked their avatars out in a virtual mirror and then met a confederate avatar of the researchers for some perfunctory small talk. As in Bailenson's previous studies, all avatars looked the same to the confederates.

Once outside of the virtual world, subjects filled out numerous surveys, including one on retirement savings. After spending just a few minutes as a septuagenarian, students said they'd allocate more than twice the amount of money to retirement, compared to controls.

Not only can virtual reality change who we think we are, it can lead us to see more of ourselves in others, which increases empathy, even when we're not aware of the resemblance. Real-world research supporting this includes the "chameleon effect," demonstrated in the late 1990s by psychologist Tanya Chartrand. Simply put, we like and trust people more when they covertly mimic us, particularly our gestures and other nonverbal tics.

More recent work by psychologists David DeSteno and Piercarlo Valdesolo shows how deep this effect can go and how inadvertently it can be triggered. For a 2011 study, they let subjects eavesdrop via closed-circuit television on an interaction between two actors pretending to be fellow subjects. One of the fake subjects took an opportunity to cheat and thereby get out of helping the other guy with a tedious task.

A few minutes earlier, during a supposedly separate experiment, the subject and the soon-to-be victim had been seated together at a table. They were told to tap along to musical beats, heard through headphones, that played either the same or a slightly different rhythm. After witnessing the unfairness, subjects who'd tapped in unison with the victim showed more sympathy and compassion for him, and they were also much more likely to offer help with his task.

The computer-generated agents in Bailenson's virtual worlds can be programmed to mimic a subject's every move, making them perfect chameleons. In one study, an agent approached student avatars and pitched a new campus security policy that would require them to carry university identification at all times. While making their case, some agents mirrored participants' head movements after a few seconds delay.* Others did not.

People found chameleon agents to be more persuasive, credible, trustworthy, and intelligent. More than 95 percent of them had no idea they were being copied. No doubt, that worked in the agent's favor. Mimicry loses its charm when it becomes obvious, as anybody with a sibling can attest. *Stop copying me!* Indeed, in companion studies, when the mimicry was too blatant it backfired, and support for the new security policy plummeted.

Yet what if more was at stake than campus security? What if we were choosing the next president of the United States? Bailenson and colleagues used an algorithm to blend a candidate's face with the participant's face. According to random assignment, subjects looked at photos of candidates that had either been morphed with that subject's face or with the face of another participant. Then they rated the candidates in several ways, including personal traits, such as honesty, intelligence, and leadership ability. They also indicated how likely they were to vote for each candidate.

Remarkably, even when staring at a face that contained 60 percent candidate and 40 percent themselves, nobody guessed that the faces had been altered. When subjects viewed unfamiliar candidates, such as those contesting an out-of-state governor's race, likely votes tilted significantly to candidates whose faces were self-morphed rather than other-morphed. When candidates were

*The ideal delay for the most effective mimicry was four seconds.

known, partisan agreement prevailed, but only among the strongly partisan. Among weak partisans and independents, people favored the candidate in whom they, quite literally, saw themselves.

LESSONS OF A LOST LEG

Before Pucillo joined the navy and traveled the world clearing mines and defusing bombs, he was a kid growing up in Marlboro, Massachusetts. The eldest son of Italian immigrants, Pucillo was kind of a wild child, breaking curfews and bucking restrictions. At eighteen, he says, "I was a typical kid who wasn't sure what he wanted to do with his life."

He found his calling in the navy. His work in EOD, and the guys he led, meant everything to him. Aside from the pain, the thought of not being able to return to his unit was one of the worst things about losing his leg.

Phantom limbs are painful reminders that while we are who we are, we are also who we expect to be. The simplicity of mirror therapy suggests that those expectations are surprisingly easy to manipulate and change.

That's good news for guys like Pucillo, because it offers a remarkably simple way to ease the pain that drugs and surgery can't touch. For the rest of us, it suggests that the boundary between ourselves and everyone else is more porous than we think. Our minds size us up and best-guess who we are and what we're experiencing in the same ways they size up people we don't know nearly so intimately. Spending time in the digital skin of an avatar who is taller, uglier, or older than we are can change who we think we are, and what we expect of ourselves. The ease with which this shift occurs may be a little disconcerting. It can also be liberating.

In the second half of 2006, Pucillo had to rebuild his expectations about who he was, while enduring the pain of rehabilitation and the frustration of relearning basic tasks like how to walk.

"I crumbled," he says. "People have a bad day. I had a bad year.

I thought to myself that it was over. I was done. I just couldn't do any more."

He kept at it, though, and the part of his brain devoted to self-perception took notice. When he walked out of Walter Reed in early 2007, he was missing a leg, but he'd gained a new sense of himself. When Pucillo thought about the challenges he might face from here on out, he expected to overcome them. This determination not only brought him back to active duty, but led him to parachute jump training, which he completed in the summer of 2008. He started running and swimming again, and his goal is to compete in a triathlon. In the fall of 2008, he began a master's degree program in National Strategic Decision Making at the U.S. Naval War College.

"I didn't know where the navy was going to lead me seventeen years ago, and I still don't," says Pucillo. "To me, the next goal is whatever I want. I'm going to keep my plate open and see what life throws at me."

7] YOU THINK, THEREFORE I AM

In November 2009, Fernando Bermudez walked out of Sing Sing prison. He was driven home to Danbury, Connecticut, where his wife and three kids were waiting for him. It was a home he'd never seen.

Bermudez had been in a maximum-security prison for eighteen years, nearly half his life. On August 4, 1991, five teenagers told the cops they saw him walk up to Raymond Blount outside a Greenwich Village nightclub and shoot him in the gut. Blount was dragged a few blocks by his friends before he died on the sidewalk. At the trial, all five witnesses pointed out Bermudez. All of them got it wrong.

The sentence was twenty-three years to life, and Bermudez spent every minute of his incarceration working to clear his name. Within two years of the trial, all the witnesses recanted in sworn affidavits. It wasn't enough, not nearly. It would take many more years of work by private investigators and pro bono lawyers before a judge overturned the conviction and declared Bermudez innocent of the killing.

Bermudez was free, but his mind was not. Aside from family, almost everyone he knew was behind bars. He'd grown used to prison's routines and even the confinement. The hubbub of a house full of kids overwhelmed him. He was nervous and easily spooked. When he walked the dog, he felt like guards were watching from unseen towers, and that he'd be arrested if he ventured too far. Crowds made him anxious. So did busy streets. He'd forgotten how to drive. When Bermudez couldn't sleep, he'd curl up in his son's bedroom, because it was small like his cell.

Bermudez won his freedom without DNA evidence, which makes his case fairly unique among nearly three hundred violent crime convictions overturned in the past two decades. Otherwise, it's tragically typical. Three quarters of people wrongfully imprisoned are there because an eyewitness pointed out the wrong guy. Most of these mistaken witnesses aren't malicious. Often they simply pick the person they are expected to pick.

We are awash in expectations of one another, and try as we might, we can't keep them to ourselves. Some form in an instant, signaled by glances or subtle expressions, and disappear just as quickly, while others build slowly or hover in the cultural ether. They can fly harmlessly through our thoughts. Or, as Bermudez discovered, they can change the course of a life.

PLUGGING THE LEAKY MIND

How do unspoken expectations become self-fulfilling prophecies? The scientific story begins with a horse named Hans who amazed audiences in Berlin at the dawn of the twentieth century by solving equations and answering trivia questions. Hans shook his head and nodded for yes/no questions. Mostly he answered by tapping his right hoof.*

The horse's owner, Wilhelm von Osten, was a former math teacher and an avid hunter known for his piercing gaze, woolly white beard, and wide-rimmed black slouch hat. Every day at noon, Osten would walk Hans onto a paved courtyard in Berlin and start the show, which was always free, even after the fame of "Clever Hans" spread worldwide.

It was an era of "thinking" animal acts—the clever dog of Utrecht, the reading pig of London, Don the talking English setter,

---

* For numeric answers as well as spelling out answers by tapping once for A, twice for B, etc.

and Rosa, a mare who did many Hans-like tricks in a vaude-ville act. Those others were highly trained animals, however, obeying smooth yet obvious signals by their human handlers. Hans was special. If Osten was signaling him, nobody could say how.

In 1904, a commission of zoologists, veterinarians, schoolmas-ters, psychologists, and circus managers looked into Hans's act. Confident in his horse, Osten welcomed the investigation, and the experts eventually concluded that however Hans did what he did, there wasn't any "cheating" by Osten.

Maybe "The Horse Actually Reasons," a *New York Times* head-line suggested. The educators studying Hans thought as much, comparing his intellect to that of a thirteen-year-old child. An-other idea was that Osten and Hans communicated telepathically. Or maybe Osten had mesmerized his horse and was controlling him through the force of his will.

It took a follow-up investigation led by a young scientist named Oskar Pfungst to unravel the mystery of Hans's cleverness. Pfungst found two big clues: First, while Hans routinely answered questions asked by people other than Osten, he had a much tougher time when his owner was out of sight. Second, the horse did even worse when the person asking him a question didn't know the answer.

Pfungst and his team didn't accuse Osten of fraud. But they did conclude that he was unintentionally signaling the horse. Indeed, the fact that Osten was unaware of these cues is likely what made them so effective.

When awaiting an answer from Hans, Osten's head or body leaned slightly forward. As the horse neared the correct answer, Osten would straighten up, just a touch, and Hans's tapping would slow down. Hans was sensitive to the tiniest "stop" signals by a human questioner—a nearly imperceptible upward tick of the head, slightly raised eyebrows, or dilating nostrils.

Pfungst tested these unintentional cues in his lab by putting himself in the role of Hans. He would try to guess a number that another person was thinking of by tapping out the answer while scrutinizing the person's posture and expression. Pfungst did 350 of these tests on unwitting subjects. He guessed correctly nearly three quarters of the time, according to his own records.

What made these hints work? Belief, according to Pfungst. When a questioner expected Hans, or Pfungst in the lab, to somehow know the correct response, it created a palpable tension, released at the correct number of taps, that a believer could not help but reveal.

Osten believed in his horse's ability to think. He routinely scolded Hans for mistakes. The report by Pfungst and his team hurt Osten deeply. He refused to accept the findings and kept performing with Hans until his death in 1907.

In 1965, Pfungst's report was republished with an extended introduction by the psychologist Robert Rosenthal, who believed that similar unspoken expectations might be contaminating research by his fellow psychologists.

"Many experimenters over the years may have fulfilled their experimental prophecies by unintentionally communicating information to their subjects," Rosenthal wrote. For more than five decades, Rosenthal has rooted out expectancy effects, and the power of unintended, nonverbal communication. It all began when he ruined his dissertation.

In the 1950s, Rosenthal was a doctoral student at UCLA, heavily influenced by Sigmund Freud. He was studying "projection," in which a person deflects his or her shameful thoughts and feelings by suspecting that others are harboring them. It is the mind's "I know you are, but what am I?" defense against threats to self-image. For his dissertation research, he wanted to see how recent success or failure influenced the traits that a person read into the face of another. Guided by Rosenthal, subjects judged faces in photographs before and after taking a quick IQ test at which they would either "succeed" or "fail" via false feedback. As Rosenthal had expected, subjects in the success condition saw the people in the photos as more successful, while those in the failure group saw more failure. The trouble was that the effect showed up in ratings done *before* the IQ test.

"There were already treatment effects from treatments they had yet to receive, which should not be possible," says Rosenthal. He puzzled over his results. Prior to the IQ test, subjects had no way of knowing whether they were going to succeed or fail. Rosenthal knew, however. Not only that. He also knew what he expected his subjects to see in the faces he showed them as a result. Could his expectations really have changed what people perceived? After all, they were just thoughts.

Rosenthal set up more photo-judging experiments, but he gave alternate hypotheses to the research assistants leading subjects through the task. One group of assistants was told that subjects would likely see more failure in the photos; the others were told that subjects would see more success. Either way, subjects rated their photos just as the experimenters expected.

Our brains are abuzz with expectations about one another. And in the decades since his photo-judging experiments, Rosenthal has been cracking the unspoken, unintentional code in which we communicate them—the patterns of subtle, unconscious hints we give in courtrooms, classrooms, doctor's offices, and job interviews about who we think is guilty, competent, or intelligent. In some cases, such as detecting deception, it takes real expertise to pick up on the clues. In other cases, any fool (or horse) can do it.

These expectations aren't marching orders. In some of Rosenthal's photo-judging experiments, for instance, research confederates masquerading as the first few subjects deliberately disconfirmed the experimenter's hypothesis. After that, the balance of expectations tipped, and the real subjects who followed likewise tended to disconfirm the original hypothesis.

All it takes for one of these expectations to become a self-fulfilling prophecy is a little momentum. That's how Fernando Bermudez got sent "up north" for nearly two decades. Bermudez wasn't framed by a rogue villain. He wasn't buried by one huge police or prosecutorial blunder, but rather by an avalanche of small ones, all triggered by a teenage girl picking his photo out of a folder.

SEEING A MAN WHO ISN'T THERE

More than a year after his release from prison, on a sweltering day in July 2011, Bermudez was in Manhattan. Even though the sky threatened rain, he decided to take a long walk up Broadway, starting near Wall Street and heading north. When he reached 13th Street, he suddenly hooked a left and went one block to University Place.

Bermudez had never been to this intersection before in his life. Twenty years earlier, however, a teenager named Raymond Blount was shot and killed here in the wee hours of a summer night. Blount had punched another kid inside a nearby nightclub. Later the fight spilled out onto the street, with crowds of teenagers punching each other, breaking bottles, and jumping on cars. That's when somebody went up to Blount and shot him at close range—one of 2,154 murders in New York City that year, after 2,245 the year before. It was bloody chaos, and city authorities were desperate to regain control. They needed convictions.

Bermudez had spent most of that night, including around three in the morning when Blount was shot, cruising Manhattan with three friends. They drove a green BMW 325 that Bermudez and his dad had salvaged and rebuilt. They were celebrating Bermudez's upcoming enrollment in Bronx Community College. Mainly, they were trying to pick up girls.

After the shooting, the cops rounded up several of the victim's friends and acquaintances who witnessed the crime. They said they saw the kid who got punched talking to a Hispanic man who then ran up and murdered their friend. They said the shooter was just under six feet tall and about 165 pounds, with a fade haircut. The detectives put all the witnesses in the same room at the precinct and gave them files of photos to search through. It wasn't long before a girl picked out Bermudez's photo, which was taken a year prior when he was arrested for marijuana possession.

"Look at this one!" she said and passed it around. She wasn't certain Bermudez was the killer, but he looked familiar. Plus, she liked the look of him. "What a cutie!" she said. Standing six foot one and weighing 215 pounds, Bermudez was bigger than the initial suspect descriptions, but that didn't matter. The cops had an eyewitness identification. Courtroom gold. Bermudez became their man, and nothing could get in the way of that belief.

Two hours later, the detectives showed the witnesses Bermudez's photo again in a photo lineup with five other Hispanic males. Bermudez was number two. He was the only one with a fade haircut.

"I want you to look at these six photos here in front of you and to decide *which one* you think is responsible," the detectives told them.* They all picked number two.

The next day, police swarmed Bermudez's home in Washington Heights and arrested him. They stuck him in a live lineup with five other guys. All the witnesses—who had just seen Bermudez's mug shot, passed it around, and then picked it out of a photo array—again identified him as the shooter.

In the meantime, the police found the kid that the victim had punched before he got shot. Efraim "Shorty" Lopez was only sixteen, but he already had a long rap sheet. In fact, he'd just been busted for stealing cars and he had violated the curfew of a five-day work release from Rikers Island by being at the nightclub. Now the cops had Lopez on the hook as an accessory to murder. He would become their star witness.

The detectives interrogated Lopez for more than twenty-four hours, asking repeatedly about the shooter. Lopez admitted he knew the guy from around the neighborhood (Lopez lived on West 92nd Street; Bermudez lived on 204th Street, more than six

---

* Italics mine. Telling a witness that a lineup contains the suspect is suggestive, because it encourages the witness to pick *somebody*, even if it's just a guess.

miles north), but said he didn't know him well. Lopez said the shooter's name was Lou, known on the street as Wool Lou, because he sold "wools," which were cigarettes rolled up with crack cocaine.

In fact, a guy named Luis "Wool Lou" did live in Lopez's neighborhood, sold drugs, stole cars, and was actually Lopez's good friend. Wool Lou looked a lot like Bermudez, too, except he was shorter and slimmer. None of this was discovered until years later, however, by a private detective.* The cops interrogating Lopez never investigated. Instead, they always called the shooter "Woolou," never Lou. In the prosecution's case, Woolou became Bermudez's street name. Lopez, meanwhile, received immunity from prosecution for his testimony.

Bermudez was identified by a group of young eyewitnesses, "who sat together and discussed his photograph," noted the judge who finally declared Bermudez innocent. "Together, they all decided the defendant resembled the shooter. Before long, he became the shooter."

Last fall, Bermudez gave a lecture at John Jay College of Criminal Justice in New York City, one of many talks he's given about wrongful convictions.

"My story today is a provocation," Bermudez told the students at John Jay. In his case, mistaken identification was compounded by shoddy police work. However, suggestive lineups are a problem even when everything is done by the book. In the first multisite field study of eyewitness identification techniques, published in 2011, 42 percent of witnesses in traditional lineups got it wrong.

Bermudez was introduced by Professor Jennifer Dysart, an eyewitness identification expert who testified at the 2009 hearing that set Bermudez free. Dysart is also a leading advocate for lineup reform, which aims to minimize the influence of expectations on eyewitness picks.

* The detective not only found Wool Lou (Luis Munoz), but located his extended family and was given a picture of him by his grandmother. Munoz has not been charged in the killing of Raymond Blount.

There are two main ideas for lineup reform. First, make them double-blind, so that the police officer in charge doesn't know who the suspect is, or even if the suspect is present. Second, show witnesses one person at a time and have them say yes, no, or not sure, before moving on. This is known as a sequential lineup. A few states and local jurisdictions have adopted these reforms in recent years, but most police departments still handle eyewitness identifications the old-fashioned way—simultaneous lineups overseen by somebody in the know.

The stories of wrongful convictions are peppered with bits of suggestion guiding witnesses to a suspect—a lone photo repeated in multiple arrays, one photo handled more deliberately than the rest, quick remarks such as, "take your time," or, "you did great" after an identification. The tip-offs need not be blatant or intentional. The subconscious motivation may be sympathy for witnesses who want justice done, or who may be victims themselves, Dysart speculates.

How much do identifications change when the person running the lineup knows who the suspect is? According to one study, witnesses to mock crimes who knew that a lineup included the suspect identified that person 86 percent of the time when the lineup administrator knew who the suspect was, but only 64 percent of the time when the lineup was double-blind. When trained observers later coded videos of these lineups, they found that administrators who knew who the suspect was gave all sorts of subtle hints—such as telling witnesses to take another look when they failed to identify somebody, handling photos of the suspect more slowly, and "placing pressure on the witness to choose."

Wait a minute. Doesn't a higher rate of suspect identifications indicate a better procedure? Not if the advantage is based on guesswork and the kind of self-fulfilling prophecies that can turn innocent guys like Bermudez into convicted murderers.

In the aforementioned study, for instance, the lineup administrator's knowledge led to more suspect identifications, but it didn't affect how often a witness picked nobody from the lineup.

In other words, the nonverbal hints only swayed witnesses who weren't sure, directing their best guess to the suspect. The tendency for motivated witnesses to guess and pick *somebody* is compounded by traditional, simultaneous lineups. Instead of asking whether any of the individuals match their memory of the culprit, witnesses ask themselves a much more loaded question: which of these guys looks the *most like* the guy who did it? That's more of a choice than a true identification, Dysart contends.

Even when suspects are indeed guilty, double-blind and sequential lineups outperform the old-fashioned kind on a crucial measure: diagnosticity. That's the ratio of suspect identifications over obviously incorrect filler picks, and the higher that ratio goes, the less likely it is that any identification is a guess and the more likely it is that the prosecution will get reliable witnesses making confident, accurate identifications in court. In lab studies, double-blind and sequential lineups tend to lower the rate of suspect identification, but they lower filler identifications even more, which gives double-blind and sequential lineups a big advantage in diagnosticity.

In 2011, Dysart coauthored a meta-analysis of studies comparing simultaneous and sequential lineups. Sequential lineups averaged an 8 percent drop in suspect identifications, but a 22 percent reduction in false identifications.

"There's a clear difference between eyewitness choices and eyewitness identifications," she says. "Having a person in the room who knows the right answer can't help a witness with true recognition. It just can't. And if we want to present this evidence to the jury as a true identification, then we have to remove the suggestion."

Still, studies comparing these techniques in real cases with actual witnesses to violent crimes were lacking until late in 2011, when Dysart and colleagues published the initial results of the first multisite field study of lineups, with the cooperation of police departments in Charlotte, Tucson, San Diego, and Austin.

The study's focus was simultaneous versus sequential lineups, so all the photo arrays were done with computer software that theoretically made all of them double-blind. Nevertheless, for about a quarter of these lineups, an officer who knew who the suspect was oversaw the procedure. The researchers set these aside for a separate analysis and focused on about five hundred identifications that were truly double-blind to isolate the differences between simultaneous and sequential lineups.

Unlike in lab studies, witnesses in real cases identified suspects at the same rate with either procedure. The real difference was in the rate of known misidentifications. Witnesses who identified somebody picked a filler 42 percent of the time from simultaneous lineups compared to just 31 percent in sequential lineups.

Until DNA exonerations started to mount in the 1990s, including several innocent people plucked from death row, the scattered warnings of eyewitness fallibility were lost in the clamor for law and order, harsher sentences, and safer streets. Then, in 1999, the National Institute of Justice recommended double-blind, sequential police lineups. Following that, New Jersey (2001), Wisconsin (2005), North Carolina (2008), and Texas (2011), as well as a number of local jurisdictions, such as Minneapolis, Denver, and Dallas, have adopted double-blind, sequential lineups. As of this writing, the vast majority of police departments still handle eyewitness identifications in the traditional way.

BE ALL THEY THINK YOU CAN BE

Eyewitness misidentifications are the central ingredient in an alchemy that can turn innocent people into convicted criminals. The beliefs and behaviors of the accused matter little in this process. The wrongfully convicted feel and act no more guilty after sentencing than they did before being wrongfully accused. In other cases, however, it's precisely our responses to the expectations of others that give their assumptions the ring of truth.

In 1890, the United States Census Bureau introduced a new

gadget called the Hollerith Tabulating Machine that coded demographic data sheets into punch cards. The cards made number crunching a lot easier, but the machine itself was an intimidating behemoth. Its inventor, Herman Hollerith, estimated that a trained operator could process about 550 cards per day. That benchmark was passed on to the Census Bureau workers. They were performing at about that level within two weeks. Some managed to go a little faster, but the effort exhausted them.

Then a new group of workers were trained on the machine with no mention of the 550-card expectation. These folks were soon punching out more than two thousand cards a day without breaking a sweat. Performance doesn't just follow expectations wherever they lead, however. Some people are more likely to respond to certain expectations in particular circumstances. The complexity of this relationship is nowhere more evident than the research into teacher expectations, which began with Rosenthal's *Pygmalion in the Classroom* (1968) a book-length treatment of his two-year study at a South San Francisco elementary school.

The school's principal, Lenore Jacobson, was Rosenthal's coauthor and helped him put one over on the teachers. In the spring of 1964, all the students at Jacobson's school took an IQ test that she and Rosenthal dressed up as the "Harvard Test of Inflected Acquisition," which could supposedly identify students who were about to bloom academically.

Regardless of how they scored, some students were randomly deemed likely to bloom. At the beginning of the next school year the names of the bloomers were quietly passed on to their new teachers. Over the next two years, Rosenthal and Jacobson compared the bloomers to the rest of the students. The results, dubbed the Pygmalion Effect, are often summed up as follows: the kids who were expected to bloom, did.

That's an oversimplification of what actually happened. Across the entire school, expectations boosted reading grades and IQ scores of the bloomers in a modest, but statistically significant

154 MIND OVER MIND

way. At year's end, teachers also rated bloomers as happier, more curious, more interesting, and more likely to succeed in the future. Behind the averages, however, things got messy.

In year one, first and second grade bloomers made impressive gains in IQ scores and reading. There were no big IQ advantages for bloomers in other grades, however. Meanwhile, boy bloomers made most of the gains in verbal scores compared to their peers, while the bloomers' reasoning advantages existed mostly among the girls. These results and the similarly mixed findings of replications have fueled decades of debate. The heart of the argument isn't whether teachers have different expectations for different students—of course they do—it's whether these expectations simply reflect student potential, or actively shape it.

In recent years, researchers have abandoned the either-or approach and examined the possibility that teacher expectations may be powerful in certain circumstances and toothless in others. What these studies have found is that the self-fulfilling effects of teacher expectations are usually small, and even disappear, when averaged across large heterogeneous groups of students. But they can be major influences, both good and bad, on poorer kids, minorities, students with a history of underachieving, students just entering a new class, or those starting at a new school.*

"There's an expectation in scientific research that if a phenomenon exists, then you should be able to see it everywhere and the effects are universal," says social psychologist Rhona Weinstein. She and her collaborators spent many years observing classrooms and looking at expectations from a fairly neglected perspective: the students'.

They created an index of differential teacher treatment toward high and low achievers, against which students rated their own

---

*While most of the follow-up work on the Pygmalion Effect has focused on children in the classroom, researchers over the years have induced self-fulfilling prophecies of adult performance by manipulating expectations of occupational trainees, officer candidates, and employees at different bank branches, among others.

classrooms. At the beginning of the school year, the researchers asked students to rank their expected academic achievement relative to their classmates' and also had the teachers rank their students. Finally, they observed the classrooms and kept tabs on the students' progress.

Every class had high and low achievers, and the kids generally knew where they stood. These distinctions meant very different things from one teacher to the next, however. Some teachers grouped students by ability, often by reading level, and made much of these distinctions by seating them at separate tables, for example, or calling one group the "stars" and another the "clowns." In these classrooms, challenges were for top students while remediation and repetition was the rule for those who fell behind. In other classrooms, by contrast, students reported more equitable treatment by teachers who often mixed high and low achievers into "teams" that changed frequently.

In one study, for example, teacher expectations in classrooms with "high differential treatment," accounted for up to 18 percent of the differences in student achievement at year's end, compared to 5 percent in classrooms with "low differential treatment." This effect was independent of any prior achievement differences between students.

These students didn't just measure their own abilities differently, they had different expectations about ability itself. Students whose teachers made strong distinctions between the high and low achievers often defined smartness as finishing work quickly and correctly. In these classrooms, there was a stigma to working too hard, and an extra one for making mistakes. Being smart meant easy mastery.

For Weinstein, changing these expectations for the "smart" and "talented" and the resulting differences in learning opportunities are top priorities. She opposes things like tracking students by ability and keeping material easy and repetitive for kids who have early trouble.

"The question is, do we focus on identifying the star talents and giving them the best opportunities, or are we focused on expecting the best for all, and developing talent," she says.

In 2005, Weinstein and colleagues at the University of California, Berkeley, cofounded a high school in Berkeley with the Aspire charter school network. It's called California College Preparatory Academy, aka CAL Prep. Nearly all of the students at CAL Prep are African American or Hispanic, and more than half get free or reduced-priced lunch, paid for by the federal government. While nearly three quarters of the students' parents never made it to college, high expectations are part of the school's charter. Every CAL Prep student is expected to complete college coursework before graduating.

How have they done so far? California measures the quality of its public schools using an index pegged to student improvement on standardized tests covering math, science, English, history, and other subjects, as well as the required high school graduation exam. The index runs from 200 to 1,000, and a score of 800 or above means a school is "high-performing." In 2011, CAL Prep graduated its first class and earned an 825, ranking it in the top 15 percent of all California public high schools and the top 15 percent of the state's charter high schools as well. Every student in this graduating class was accepted to college.

THE FEAR OF PROVING THEM RIGHT

Teachers are far from the only source of student expectations. Parents, siblings, friends, and neighborhoods all contribute to the mix. How do your parents react to a C grade? Do you have a lot of books in the house? Are you ostracized for being studious?

Then there's what "they" expect—the expectations of stereotypes that can clutter our brains and muck up performance both inside and outside the classroom. Psychologists Claude Steele and Joshua Aronson coined the term "stereotype threat" in the mid-1990s. Stereotype threat lurks at the intersection of personal and group expectations. You may think you'll do well on an upcoming math test, but based on your race, or gender, or where you grew up, "they" don't think much of your chances. Some of the more prevalent stereotyped academic expectations include: Girls are better at reading and social skills. Boys, especially Asians, are better at spatial and quantitative reasoning, and therefore make better scientists and mathematicians. African American and Hispanic students struggle academically. It doesn't matter if students believe in these stereotypes. Students can be hobbled by the worry that they will confirm these negative expectations when it counts the most, and so they often do.

In Steele and Aronson's initial research, a large group of black and white Stanford University students took a difficult verbal exam. The researchers varied the test's written instructions—describing it as either a measure of intelligence or part of a nondiagnostic study. Black and white students performed equally when the test was described as nondiagnostic. When this same test supposedly measured intelligence, however, blacks did significantly worse than whites. Steele and Aronson concluded that the performance of black students suffered on the "intelligence" test because their brains were cluttered with worry over the stereotype that blacks are less intelligent than whites.

Any student can be hurt by stereotype threat, not just members of traditionally disadvantaged groups. Subsequent research shows that these negative expectations don't need an ugly history, or any history at all, to get inside a student's head and wreak havoc. For example, the math scores of white male Stanford students with high math SATs took a nosedive in a study when experimenters said that they were investigating why Asians seem to crush everybody else in math. These were high-achieving kids who knew they were good at math and had a history of math success to back it up. These students never confronted a stereotype that white men can't add, or a talking Ken doll whining about math being hard. All it took to make these math stars stumble was a stereotype putting them in the "loser" category.

In short, it doesn't matter who you are. Stereotype threat can find you. Fortunately, despite how entrenched many stereotypes are, our identities are impressively multiple and malleable, sometimes shifting minute by minute.

In one study, Asian American female college students took a math test. Asians are stereotypically superior in math, while females stereotypically struggle in math. So for these students' performance, the stereotyped expectations about math ability could cut either way. Before taking the test, the students filled out a demographic survey meant to prime either their Asian identity or their female identity. The survey geared to ethnicity asked questions such as, "How many generations has your family lived in America?" When aimed at gender, it asked things like, "Do you live in co-ed or single sex housing?" A control group's survey included only neutral questions, such as whether the subject lived on or off campus.

The results confirmed the expectations of the stereotypes. Students primed to think about being Asian did better on the math test than the control group. Those primed to think of their gender did worse. A few questions were enough to juggle identity and trigger loads of associations and expectations, of which math ability was surely just one. Not only that, the results suggested a possible "stereotype boost." If negative stereotypes could trip us up, might positive stereotypes occasionally give us a lift?

Another group of researchers tested that possibility using a similar experiment with Asian American women taking a math test. This time, however, the women were asked to rate their agreement with explicit statements about ethnic or gender stereotypes, such as, "Overall, my race is considered good by others." This time, subjects primed to think of their Asian heritage did *worse* on the math test than the other two groups.

Why the difference? When expectations for success are held privately, "they are likely to provide a confidence boost that contributes to successful performance," the researchers concluded. "However, when a positive performance is anticipated by an external audience, an individual may experience apprehension about meeting those high expectations."

The researchers had a name for this boost gone bust: choking under pressure. If anxiety is the main culprit, then maybe stereotype threat can be countered much like any other sources of worry, from a large audience to a lost lucky charm. It's not necessary to wipe negative stereotypes off the face of the earth, as noble as that goal may be. If the anxiety can be isolated and defused, then who cares what "they" expect?

Choking researcher Sian Beilock, whom we met in Chapter 2, tried out the idea by recruiting expert male golfers for a test of putting skill. Before stepping onto the putting green in Beilock's lab, the golfers read one of two descriptions of the experiment. It was either a simple putting task or a study about why women seem to be better at putting than men. The guys who read the stereotyped instructions indicating that women were superior at putting had a bad day on the green. They putted much less accurately than the control group golfers whose instructions made no mention of gender.

Beilock then tried a simple remedy that had worked for skilled athletes in the grip of anxiety—distraction. In a follow-up experiment, some of the golfers were told to putt while listening to a series of recorded words, and to repeat a certain target word out loud every time they heard it. In pretest putts, before the golfers read about women out-putting men, this distraction had no real impact on their performance, compared to control group golfers who putted without distraction. After reading the stereotype-laden instructions, however, the distracted golfers putted best.

The threat of negative stereotypes may even be thwarted simply by acknowledging the anxiety these expectations cause, as a study in 2009 showed. Psychologists gave math word problems to male and female students recruited from an introductory statistics class. The researchers told one group that the word problems were a math test and they were looking into gender differences in math performance. They told a second group that they were studying general cognitive processes. A third group was also told it was a math test, but before beginning, a researcher discussed stereotype threat and noted that the anxiety women sometimes felt during these tests might be a result of these negative stereotypes that "have nothing to do with your actual ability to do well on the test."

When the word problems were described as a math test, women did much worse than men. Women did just as well as men when negative stereotypes were either sidestepped by not calling the study a math test *or* when these stereotypes were discussed at length. In the latter case, the researchers concluded, the women were able to externalize their anxiety and thereby make the threat much less personal.

In 2011, Beilock used a similar approach for a real-world intervention with high school kids. Students given the opportunity to write for ten minutes about their test-related worries before taking a high-stakes math exam scored better than they did on a low-stakes pretest. By contrast, students who wrote nothing or who wrote on an unrelated emotional topic did much worse when the pressure was on. Writing about anxieties kept them from bouncing around the students' heads and cluttering up working memory, the researchers concluded.

In fact, anxiety can even be turned to a student's advantage when given the right spin. In a 2010 study, a group of college students taking a practice Graduate Record Exam (GRE) were told that pretest jitters—sweaty palms and stomach butterflies—had actually been shown to improve performance. On the subsequent test, they averaged 739 on the math section, compared to 684 for the controls, while there were no significant differences in verbal scores between the groups. The researchers took saliva samples from test takers to get a hormonal reading on their arousal. Among the test takers given the positive spin, more arousal correlated with better math scores. Oh, and the nervous ones did better on the actual GRE, too.

A similar tactic worked in another study from 2010 aimed at

stereotype threat. The researchers encouraged students to interpret their worries over confirming negative stereotypes as positive motivational energy. They found that reframing a math test as
a "challenge" rather than a "true measure of their ability" was
enough to ward off stereotype threat among black middle school
students in North Carolina. The same technique worked with
white Princeton University students taking a math test who had
just been reminded that they'd graduated from a high school not
known to send many students to Princeton.

"It's not just removing the anxiety, it's turning that arousal into
a motivator, rather than a debilitator," says Aronson. "With those
students in North Carolina, it turned out that writing down their
race was actually helpful. Maybe you can't remove the threat, but
you can give the person a lens through which to view it that actually improves performance."

WHEN HIGH SELF-ESTEEM FALLS SHORT

When psychologist Carol Dweck was growing up in the 1950s,
her sixth grade teacher seated the class in order of IQ. Dweck sat
in the first seat of the front row. Instead of pride and confidence,
however, she felt dread. Now that she was officially the smartest
kid in the class, there was no place to go but down. If she faltered,
that failure would be as obvious and tangible as her new seat.

Dweck has since made a lifelong study of how people deal with
failure. She has found that having the right expectations about
failure can be crucial to ultimate success. In her research, Dweck
contrasts "entity theory," which says success is largely determined by the extent of one's natural talents, and "incremental theory," which says people define their abilities and limitations
through effort. For lay audiences, Dweck uses the friendlier terms,
"fixed mindset" and "growth mindset."

If you have a fixed mindset, then you believe people are born
with a certain mix of strengths and weaknesses. These talents
can be spotted in instances of early success, and cultivated to

ever-greater levels of achievement. Failure and success don't mix easily in the fixed mindset. You might try your hand at basketball, guitar, or a second language, but if you have a hard time of it, then you should seriously consider seeking excellence elsewhere.

The growth mindset gives far less weight to natural strengths and weaknesses and instead focuses on learning. People with a growth mindset expect, even appreciate, failure as an opportunity to improve. In essence, the growth mindset sees most attributes, including intelligence, as a constant work in progress.

How do these two mindsets impact achievement? In one of Dweck's landmark studies, she and fellow psychologist Claudia Mueller gave fifth graders logic puzzles. The first puzzles were relatively easy, and the kids did well. When researchers went over the scores individually with students, they praised some of them for being smart, others for working hard, and gave no feedback to kids in the control group. Then they gave the students some harder puzzles. The students were all told that they did "a lot worse" on these. In other words, they failed. How would they respond?

In a final round, the researchers asked the students individually whether they wanted to do more easy puzzles or try more of the harder puzzles.

Independent of their actual puzzle performance, the kids praised for their intelligence tended to duck the challenge, while the kids praised for their effort were the most likely to go for it. In follow-up experiments where the kids didn't have a choice and everyone was given another round of harder puzzles after their initial failure, the students who were praised for being smart did worse and gave up sooner than those praised for their effort. They were also more likely to inflate their scores when given the chance, and they were more interested in finding out how other kids scored than learning tips for solving the problems they missed. The "smart" kids became image-conscious, while praising effort stoked an eagerness to keep learning.

The results suggest why America's decades-long focus on bolstering children's self-esteem has had mixed results in schools. Young people definitely feel better about themselves than they did a few decades ago. Between the early 1950s and the late 1980s, the percentage of American teenagers who agreed with the statement "I am an important person" on a long-standing adolescent survey jumped from 12 percent to about 80 percent. Meanwhile, psychologists Jean Twenge and W. Keith Campbell found that between 1979 and 2006, college student scores on the Narcissistic Personality Inventory rose by 30 percent.

All this good feeling has not translated into better test scores. Quite the opposite. A 2006 study of the quadrennial Trends in International Mathematics and Science Study (TIMSS) found that a nation's math performance was inversely related to the math self-confidence of that nation's students. In a 2009 follow-up, the same trends were found with science—the more confident students were, the worse they did. Finally, the performance of American fifteen-year-olds on another oft-cited test, the Programme for International Student Assessment (PISA), is consistently mediocre, although the American students are tops in academic self-confidence.

When the lackluster PISA results were released in December 2010, Education Secretary Arne Duncan called the gap between self-confidence and performance a "stunning finding" and said ego stroking was to blame. "Students here are being commended for work that would not be acceptable in high-performing education systems," he said.

Overcommending does seem evident in American universities where "grade inflation" is steadily making every student's work above average. The problem is especially acute at private colleges and universities where 86 percent of all grades are As and Bs, according to a 2010 study. Quite a lot of a grade's value depends on expectations. If everybody's outstanding, what does outstanding mean, and why work to obtain the label? There's a similar trend in

American high schools, particularly in wealthy suburbs, where so many students earn straight A plusses that graduation ceremonies must accommodate dozens of valedictorians.

While low expectations may be poisonous to student achievement, inflating self-esteem isn't necessarily the antidote. In 2007, psychologist Don Forsyth led a self-esteem intervention in which weekly e-mails were sent to students in an introductory psychology class who earned a D or an F on their first exam. The e-mails had practice questions that could be used to prep for the next exam. Some of the e-mails also included a little pep talk, usually a few words about staying positive and believing in yourself.

The practice questions by themselves didn't help most students. Their grades on the final remained dismal. But students who also received a self-esteem boost did *worse*. Their average score went from 57 percent on the first test to 38 percent on the final. It's not that the self-esteem didn't take. A survey done after the final showed that the students given e-pep-talks did feel better about themselves than the other subjects did, even as they crashed and burned.

High self-esteem makes us overestimate the role our talents and intelligence play in our accomplishments. The bias can disrupt the balance between our expectations for success and our ability to achieve it, as Harvard and Duke University researchers recently demonstrated. They recruited undergraduates to take a math quiz or a test of general knowledge that asked questions such as, How many U.S. states border Mexico? Some of the tests had an answer key at the bottom in small print, ostensibly so the students could score their own exams. Students taking the test without an answer key turned in their exams to a proctor who checked their work and told them their scores.

Not surprisingly, students who took the tests with an answer key did much better. More important, the answer key students didn't think that having the answers made any difference in their performance. They certainly didn't think they'd "cheated." When asked how well they thought they'd do on a subsequent test, one with no answer key provided, they had much higher score expectations than the control students. Again, not surprisingly, when they actually took the second test with no answer key, they did no better than controls.

There's an important distinction between high expectations, which usually come along with concrete plans and intentions to carry them out, and fantasies, which are all about basking in the pleasure of imagined accomplishments and illusory achievement. They can have opposite effects on motivation. In a recent study, German researchers tried to pry apart expectations and fantasies. Their subjects included students at the start of a psychology course, students about to graduate and enter the job market, and older people about to undergo hip replacement surgery. They asked everybody about their goals—the psychology students were after high grades, the soon-to-graduate wanted a job in their field, and the hip surgery patients wanted a speedy recovery. The expectations questions were about the likelihood of reaching their goals and how important the goal was to the subject. As a measure of fantasies, subjects wrote vignettes on topics related to their goals, such as a typical day in the months after graduation, or taking a walk with friends three months after surgery. The vignettes were later coded for positive and negative thoughts.

Over the following months and years, the researchers measured everyone's success. They checked the final grades of the psychology students. Two years after graduation, they asked the graduating students about job offers and current salary. They reviewed detailed reports about every hip replacement patient's range of motion, stair-climbing ability, and other progress measures in physical therapy. In each case, those who'd had higher expectations had more success. The trend line of results was just the opposite when it came to positive fantasies.

"As positive expectations reflect past successes, they signal that investment in the future will pay off," the researchers concluded. "Positive fantasies, to the contrary, lead people to mentally enjoy the desired future in the here and now, and thus curb investment and future success."

To have high expectations is not to deny the possibility of failure. In fact, when the late Reverend Peter J. Gomes, longtime pastor of Harvard's Memorial Church, addressed graduating seniors, failure was a favorite theme. In a sermon titled, "Failure: What's Good About It?" Gomes noted, "Most of the students have been led to believe that, for the amount of money their parents are paying, failure is impossible."

On a day set aside for congratulations and high hopes, Gomes felt obliged to disabuse the graduates of this notion by reminding them, "Most of you will know more of failure than of success, and if you can learn from your failures, you will have learned much."

There's a critical difference between believing everyone can succeed and declaring everyone a winner before the starting gun is fired. Recall that the students in the Pygmalion study were described as *poised* to bloom, not already in full flower. Likewise, the key to student achievement in the classrooms studied by Rhona Weinstein wasn't teachers who lavished their charges with praise, but those who instilled a growth mindset. In these classrooms, effort, including periods of struggle, was the cornerstone of potential, rather than a telltale sign of its absence.

"Self-esteem should grow naturally from overcoming challenges and learning," says Weinstein. "Self-esteem without true competence is worthless."

The sort of self-esteem that benefits students isn't focused on who they are but on who they may become. That dilutes the importance of any single grade or test score, be it superb or subpar. It keeps the focus on what's next. This self-esteem is bolstered when students face challenges and overcome setbacks. To deny failure and flee from struggle would undermine its foundations.

In 2007, Dweck and her colleagues tried teaching a growth mindset to low-achieving middle school math students as part of eight weekly meetings with a student adviser. Other low-achieving students in a control group were instead given a lesson on memory during these sessions and then engaged in discussions of whatever academic issues interested them.

Over a year and a half, the researchers checked the students' math grades three times—a year before, just prior to the intervention, and after the intervention. The average grades of each group dipped to the same level between the first two time periods. After the intervention, the grades of the control group continued to slide, but grades rebounded for the growth mindset group.

Middle school is a hothouse of expectations. Both physically and psychologically, middle school students are tiptoeing up to their adult selves. The self-scrutiny in these years is excruciating. So it's noteworthy that this intervention wasn't about shining up individual self-worth. Rather, the whole idea was to keep things in flux, which means that getting an A doesn't make you "smart" any more than getting a D makes you "stupid." The growth mindset is a bulwark against premature self-definition, a spur for those inclined to think too little, or too much, of themselves.

8] WHAT IT TAKES

On February 13, 2008, New York governor Eliot Spitzer checked in to room 871 at the Mayflower Renaissance Hotel in Washington, D.C. At the time, Spitzer's star was on the rise. In his years as a top prosecutor, he'd taken on the mob and won. Then he'd gone after Internet scammers, polluters, and shady corporate dealers. Married, with three daughters, he exuded an image of the upright citizen, fighting for fair play.

The press loved Spitzer's brawling approach to white-collar crime. His face graced front pages and magazine covers. In the late 1990s, he had jumped into politics and he hadn't lost yet. According to well-connected people in a position to know, he seemed destined for even bigger things. How big? There were whispers that he might one day be president of the United States.

What the presidential whisperers didn't know, however, was that despite all his success, Spitzer was actually incredibly and tragically weak. That weakness was about to be caught on tape.

Before arriving at the Mayflower, Spitzer made several calls to arrange for a high-priced prostitute. A federal wiretap of the escort service captured every sordid detail. This wasn't Spitzer's first time hiring a hooker. He was a regular customer. In two years, he'd spent more than $100,000 on illicit liaisons.

Before his rise to governor, Spitzer spent nearly a decade as New York state attorney general, where he earned a national reputation as the scourge of Wall Street. He was the new sheriff who was ready and eager to ride against the Masters of the Universe. He excoriated the executives of high finance as greedy and corrupt. He littered their posh offices with subpoenas. He came after them for price fixing, insider trading, and cooking the books. Along the way, people began to sense that Spitzer wasn't just fighting the good fight against white-collar criminals, but bullying and grandstanding. Most famously, he sued Richard Grasso, the former chairman of the New York Stock Exchange* for earning too much money—in 2003, Grasso took home about $140 million in a deferred compensation package. As governor, Spitzer tangled openly with Republican legislators, allegedly telling the top Republican in the State Assembly, "I'm a fucking steamroller, and I'll roll over you."

The world of entitlement and privilege with which Spitzer clashed so fiercely happened to be where he was born and bred. He came from money and attended the best schools. He'd never had to struggle. Still, Spitzer believed in the ideals he preached, and he worked hard to reach a position where he could fight for them. Once he had that power, he used it with great relish, but he had no power over himself.

On March 10, 2008, after the *New York Times* broke the news of Spitzer's D.C. dalliance and outed him as "Client 9" in a federal investigation of Emperors Club VIP, the governor walked up to a podium with his wife, Silda, and admitted his guilt.

"I have acted in a way that violates my obligation to my family and violates my, or any, sense of right or wrong," Spitzer said. Two days later, when he resigned in disgrace, cheers erupted on the floor of the New York Stock Exchange. Just a few months later, the market would be in free fall thanks, in part, to the excesses against which Spitzer railed.

Eliot Spitzer had many enemies, but his wounds were self-inflicted, as he admitted in a 2010 documentary about the scandal. "There are all sorts of rumors about bringing me down," he said. "I brought myself down."

The story of powerful people undone by a glaring, unconscionable loss of self-control is so common that it's cliché. Why are

---

* At the time, NYSE was a not-for-profit exchange.

powerful people so prone to self-destruction? Let's start with a closer look at power itself.

Its obvious sources include physical strength, superior intelligence, money, and influence. Power over others is a trapping of success. Its outward effects are easy to spot. Powerful people win arguments. They tell other people what to do and then sit in judgment of their performance. When they speak, people listen.

What's harder to see is how power makes its presence known in the brains of the powerful. Power changes us. It alters the body's balance of hormones, buffers stress, and affects how we think and behave. We associate power with hierarchy, strength, and control, but we can feel powerful without any of those things. To a surprising extent, we can think up our own power and summon its effects—both good and bad—as readily as we can trigger pain relief with a sugar pill disguised as aspirin.

POWER IS AS POWER DOES

Folks in Washington called it the "Johnson Treatment." It was the mixture of flattery and threats that Lyndon Johnson used to get his way, often while leaning into others with his six-foot-four frame. There's an iconic photo of the Johnson Treatment being inflicted on Georgia senator Richard Russell, who opposed the 1964 Civil Rights Act. In another, Johnson's target is newly appointed Supreme Court Justice Abe Fortas. There's even a four-photo Johnson Treatment series in which Senator Theodore Green of Rhode Island bends like a wet noodle in a suit.

The photos all convey one thing with crystal clarity: power. All the men had it, but Johnson had more. Even if you had no idea who the men in these pictures were, the power dynamic would still be apparent at a glance. In fact, studies suggest that if you put any two people in that pose, the one standing in for LBJ would actually get a boost of placebo power. This person would be increasingly ready to speak up and eager to take charge. And when this person spoke, other people would be more likely to listen.

Physiologically, the effects of this placebo power would be the same as power derived from actual authority—lower stress hormones, increased testosterone, and changes in brain function that promote risk taking and action over deliberation. What's more, unlike traditional power, placebo power doesn't require anybody to agree that you're in charge. Yank that poor, browbeaten senator out of the tableau, and the towering LBJ stand-in still gets a power surge.

How so? It's another trick of our fast-forward brains. We typically think that our minds control our bodies, but our bodies control our minds, too. Psychologists call it embodied cognition. The details of sensory perception trigger a constantly unfolding world of associations and expectations that, in turn, alter our perception of subsequent sensory details. A metaphor is much more than a literary device. It is also a cognitive reflex.

For instance, people who are given a warm drink at the outset of an experiment are more likely to judge a stranger's personality as warm than are those given a cold beverage. People think job candidates are more substantially qualified when reviewing their résumés on a heavier clipboard. They drive harder bargains when seated in uncushioned chairs. And so it goes.

This seems a little crazy, until you consider the mind in evolutionary terms. In a recent essay, the biologist Robert Sapolsky noted that the same brain areas—the insula in particular—light up when people think about viscerally disgusting things, such as eating a cockroach, as when thinking about villainous people doing morally disgusting things such as kicking an old lady with failing kidneys out on the street because she's a few days late with the rent.

"When we evolved the capacity to be disgusted by moral failures, we didn't evolve a new brain region to handle it," Sapolsky writes. "Instead, the insula expanded its portfolio."

The ideas of embodied cognition are rooted in a theory developed by two founding fathers of modern psychology, William James and Carl Lange, which posits that emotions are the brain's interpretation of the body's automatic reactions. Accordingly, rather than anxiety causing our heart to race and palms to sweat, we feel our racing heart and sweating palms and conclude that we're anxious.

"We feel sorry because we cry, angry because we strike, afraid because we tremble," James wrote. "Without the bodily states following on the perception, the latter would be purely cognitive in form, pale, colorless, destitute of emotional warmth."

Some interesting possibilities follow, many of which have been validated in research, such as smiling increases happiness, tilting the head upward induces pride, and hunching over invites the blues. What physical pose might spark feelings of power? Psychologists Dana Carney, Amy Cuddy, and Andy Yap started with something obvious—looking big.

Both people and animals display dominance by spreading out and taking up as much space as possible. Think of two people at a conference table. One is seated with his head slightly bowed, his hands in his lap, and his shoulders hunched. The other has his hands laced behind his head and his feet propped on the table. Who's the boss?

The message is self-evident and is everywhere you look—from Superman standing with his chest thrust out, his hands on his hips, and his cape billowing, to Jack Donaghy, Alec Baldwin's caricature of a corporate shark, seating people in tiny chairs during contract negotiations.

Of course, we often dismiss looking big as nonverbal trash talk—fake-it-till-you-make-it huff and puff that's easily deflated. Yet, what if looking big is more than a display of power by those who already have it or a hopeful bluff by those who don't? What if showing off is secondary and audiences unnecessary, because the main effects of looking big and the power assumptions it conveys are internal?

For a 2010 study, Carney, Cuddy, and Yap randomly assigned subjects to hold expansive or hunched poses, one seated and one standing, for one minute each. Importantly, subjects in these experiments weren't told that these poses were meant to convey power, or the lack thereof. Before and after the posing, they took saliva samples for hormonal analysis. Cortisol is a stress hormone. Other studies have found that cortisol levels spike in people put in situations where they feel powerless or subordinate—such as being told to follow the orders of a fellow subject. Testosterone levels, by contrast, usually increase along with power.

After participants in this study finished posing, they sat down and answered some questions, including how powerful and "in charge" they felt and whether they'd rather get a sure $2 or take a 50/50 chance of getting either $4 or nothing. The expansive posers felt more powerful than the hunchers, and they had a bigger appetite for risk. Their hormones also changed, with cortisol dropping and testosterone spiking. It was the exact opposite of the hormonal shift in the hunchers. Consider that there were no social interactions whatsoever in this research, and no titles, assessments, or other indications of rank. There was nobody to impress or to be intimidated by. These effects mirrored those found in people given "real" power, and they were all from sitting and standing a certain way for two minutes with nobody else in the room.

We implicitly expect power and authority from people in expansive poses, *including from ourselves*. Nevertheless, power in our society revolves around roles and hierarchies. The boss feels powerful at the meeting because she's the boss, not because she's resting her feet on the table. Right? Yes and no.

In 2011, psychologists at Stanford and Northwestern put people into high and lower power poses by pretending that they were market testing ergonomic chairs. They also randomly assigned everybody roles, specifically managers or subordinates in a two-person puzzle challenge that was followed by several individual tasks.

The managers in the puzzle challenge reported feeling more

powerful than the subordinates, no matter how they'd been posed. The opposite was true, however, in an implicit measure of power,* where the people who sat in expansive poses scored higher regardless of their role as manager or subordinate. And in the tasks, body poses dominated hierarchy when it came to eliciting two behaviors associated with powerful people—taking action and thinking abstractly. People may have consciously associated their recent role as a manager or subordinate with different levels of power, the researchers concluded, but part of their brains interpreted their bodies' expansive or hunched pose as "the appropriate cue for behavior."

The brain expects power from a pose much as it expects pain relief from a sugar pill. And like placebo pain relief, placebo power has real effects. To test the strength of these effects, Carney and Cuddy set people in high or low power poses and shortly thereafter had them give an impromptu speech as part of a mock interview for their "dream job." Their audience: two stone-faced experimenters who were evaluating their performance.

The speeches were videotaped and later coded for content and delivery by research assistants who didn't know the hypothesis or how the people giving speeches had been posed. In yet-to-be-published results, those subjects who'd posed expansively before the speech were rated as performing much better and were more likely to be "hired." The advantage had nothing to do with what they said.

The ratings for speech content were fairly equal, says Cuddy, "It was all about how engaging and captivating people were when delivering them."

In this case, audience reaction mattered. But the audience wasn't impressed by seeing people look big. Indeed, they never saw anybody pose. They were reacting to the aftermath of those poses, the placebo power, and how it had changed the speakers

---

*Subjects completed word fragments with "the first word that comes to mind." Each of these could become a word related to power or unrelated to power (e.g., L_AD could be LEAD or LOAD).

themselves. In other words, this wasn't like a peacock strutting by the lovely peahens in full fan. It was more like a peacock wandering off by himself, puffing out his plumage then folding it back, and still impressing the ladies on his return.

This was more than show. When it comes to power, faking it and making it are sometimes one and the same. Carney and her colleagues think the feeling of power and the accompanying hormonal changes are essentially an all-purpose stress buffer that anybody can tap into, regardless of rank, title, wealth, or the usual prerogatives of authority. Their research suggests that a few minutes of looking big before an exam, presentation, interview, or any stressful event can ease our anxiety via the feeling of placebo power.

EVEN PLACEBO POWER CORRUPTS

The potential of placebo power doesn't mean that it's an unalloyed good. Indeed, one of the anxieties that power soothes is the stress of lying and cheating (see Eliot Spitzer). When we're dishonest, our thoughts get weighed down with worries over concealing the truth, violating social norms and our own moral code, hurting others, and, of course, getting caught. This cognitive and emotional friction sparks the subtle nonverbal tics known as tells.

When we consider whether to lie, we are singed by the emotional anticipation of potential negative outcomes. We pre-feel a touch of the resulting distress, which can take the shine off a lie's potential upside. Power may blunt the sting of stressful pre-feeling.

In another study, Carney found that feeling powerful made it much easier for people to lie about stealing money. After undergoing a power manipulation in which some subjects were bosses and others were underlings, subjects were individually brought to a room and left there alone to answer questions on a computer. Eventually, the computer would tell the subject to steal $100 hidden in the room and to keep it a secret or else to just stay put and await the experimenter's return. Granted, this was just a study, but the thieves were motivated to lie and lie well. They were told they could keep the money and be entered into a lottery for $500 if they escaped detection.

When the experimenter came back to the room, the subject was put under the hot lights of a scripted interrogation: *Did you steal the money? Why should I believe you? Are you lying to me now?* Videos of the interrogation were later scoured for the physical tells of deception, such as quick, one-sided shrugs and halting or overly rapid speech.

The results told a tale of power, hormones, and easy lies. According to follow-up questions, the bosses didn't think theft and lying were any less wrong than the underlings did, but they were much better at both. Saliva samples showed that bosses who lied had the same hormonal profile as truth tellers, with no signs of stress. After the interrogation, only the lowly subordinate liars showed a spike in the stress hormone cortisol. Likewise, only the low-powered liars reported negative moral emotions, such as bashfulness, guilt, or scorn, and they were also the only ones to be caught leaking their deception via nonverbal tells.

Does power work the same way outside the controlled environment of a lab? So far, the data says yes. In a yet-to-be-published study led by Yap, researchers approached people on the streets of Boston and New York and asked them if they'd take a couple minutes for a study on stretching. It was a ruse to get them into a high or low power pose.

Here was the deal: get $4 for completing a short survey after standing expansively (with chin up, feet apart, and hands on hips) or contracted (hunched shoulders with both arms and legs crossed) for one minute. After subjects finished the survey, however, the researcher would get distracted and hand them $8—three one-dollar bills and a five-dollar bill—slightly fanned out so the overpayment would be obvious to anyone who was paying attention.

Everybody was overpaid. The question was, who would fess

up and who would simply pocket the extra cash? More than three quarters of the people who stood in an expansive power pose kept the money and walked away, compared to just a third of those who'd held the hunched pose.

This scenario may seem a little far-fetched. We don't spend a lot of time holding poses on the sidewalk. We do, however, spend a lot of time in spaces that foster expansive or contracted postures. Consider the many hours you sit at your desk, for instance, or on your daily commute. Could spreading out at a big desk or in a larger car make people feel powerful and, subsequently, make it slightly easier for them to lie and cheat?

In a follow-up lab experiment, participants worked on collages. Their paper, glue, scissors, crayons, and glitter were either spread over an executive-sized workspace or were crammed into something about the size of an airplane tray table. After creating their collages, subjects unscrambled anagrams while still at their workspaces and were paid a few extra bucks for every one they solved. People who got to spread out were much more likely to cheat by inflating their scores on the anagram task when the opportunity arose.

Finally, the researchers scoured Manhattan for double-parked cars and found that every cubic foot of extra cockpit space increased the likelihood of illegal parking by about 50 percent. Of course, bigger cars are harder to wedge into the rare legal parking spots in Manhattan. Nevertheless, the link between cockpit expansiveness and illegal parking remained significant even after controlling for the exterior size of the cars.

Carney thinks power alters decisions about risk and morality by changing the brain's balance of expectations. As cortisol dips, testosterone surges and disrupts the medial prefrontal cortex. In doing so, power disables the brain's anticipatory alarm bells at the same time that it juices the reward system.

"Power is an intoxicant," says Carney. "It basically green-lights everything."

Thus, it's possible that the same hormonal cocktail that gave

Eliot Spitzer the boldness to go after Wall Street titans, made even more potent by his rise to the governor's office, also led to his recklessness and self-destruction.

Power (even the placebo variety) can become its own worst enemy by undermining willpower, which many people now believe to be the true handmaiden of success.

THE IMPORTANCE OF POWER OVER OURSELVES

What psychologists call "self-regulation" and the rest of us call willpower is increasingly hailed as the key to reaching goals and accomplishing great things. In studies of winners and what makes them tick, willpower is leaving both natural talent and smarts choking on its determined dust.

Willpower is rooted in expectations, specifically the ability to stay focused on distant goals and avoid the temptation of shortcuts and the diversion of immediate gratification. It gives us the strength to keep at it when the going gets tough. In both short- and long-term studies, tests of willpower and self-control have proven to be excellent indicators of eventual success, beating IQ and SAT scores and even specially crafted measures, such as West Point's Whole Candidate Score.

In short, it takes a whole lot of willpower to pursue success to the highest levels, and boatloads more to resist the high that often follows, which begs the question: where does willpower come from?

According to some researchers, it is willpower with a capital P—a strength fueled by the same energy resources used by our muscles. We have only so much. It can be augmented by regular exercise, but also drained by overuse. If we're not careful, our willpower may be all used up when we need it the most. Without gas, the car won't start.

Is that the end of the story? Some of the latest self-control research suggests that we can fill our tank with placebo willpower. Practicing self-control may indeed tap the body's energy supply, but as with physical exercise, expectations may ultimately rule our willpower endurance.

IS WILLPOWER A RENEWABLE RESOURCE?

The biggest willpower theory these days is "ego depletion," developed by the psychologist Roy Baumeister (whom we met in Chapter 2). In a series of studies, Baumeister showed that when people use their willpower for one thing, such as resisting chocolate chip cookies or holding back tears during a sad movie, they quit subsequent tasks, such as solving difficult geometric puzzles, sooner than control subjects.

Baumeister and colleagues have linked this limited supply of willpower to glucose, the body's main energy source. Thinking actually uses up a surprising amount of energy. Studies suggest that the brain accounts for up to 20 percent of the body's daily glucose consumption. In Baumeister's research, subjects who drank sugar-sweetened lemonade held up better over a series of willpower tasks than did subjects whose lemonade contained no-calorie sweetener.

Measures of glucose in blood samples taken before and after willpower tests confirm that self-control is an energy hog. Baumeister and colleagues found that while the willpower muscle tires after strenuous use, it can also be strengthened over the long term with exercise.

The difference seems to be all about timing. Try to quit smoking, ease up on alcohol, start your diet, stop procrastinating, and exercise more all at once, and you are likely to fall off every single wagon. Whereas gradually increasing willpower stamina in one area of your life can improve self-discipline all over the place.

Still, none of that changes the basic arithmetic of ego depletion: in the short term, using willpower for one thing leaves less in the tank for the next task, unless it's replenished with nutrients. It's as simple as that. The notion of placebo willpower would seem to toss this critical strength back into the murky realm of pure mind from which Baumeister and his team so recently dragged it. Or would it? Such a conclusion relies on the old stigma that placebo effects are distinct from everything "real."

Repeatedly, we see that distinction blurred if not erased entirely. Painkilling expectations release opioids that act just like morphine; the expectations of an energy drink free up actual carbohydrates; simply looking powerful drops cortisol and raises testosterone as much as actually being in charge, and sometimes more. Time and again, the effects of expectations and assumptions mimic at least some of the changes triggered by more conventional means. Why not with self-control, our newly rediscovered secret to success?

One of the first researchers to give it a shot was Veronika Job, a psychologist at the University of Zurich. In 2010, Job was a postdoctoral researcher working with Carol Dweck, whose work on fixed and growth mindsets we covered in the previous chapter. In a series of experiments, Job, Dweck, and fellow Stanford psychologist Gregory Walton, found that believing willpower was actually an unlimited resource could fend off its depletion. Instead of resisting chocolate chip cookies and holding back tears, the researchers told some subjects to cross out every letter "e" on multiple pages of boring typewritten text. They made it harder for other subjects by giving them complex rules for crossing out the "e," such as only when at least two letters separated it from another vowel. Then everybody was given a follow-up "Stroop test" in which subjects are shown color words (red, green, blue, etc.) written in either the same or a different color font. For example, they may see the word "red" written in a red or blue font. It's a classic self-control task, because the instructions are to name the color of the font aloud, which means that subjects must control the urge to simply read the word.

Overall, people given the more taxing "e" task went slower and made more errors on the Stroop test. Score one for ego depletion. However, at the outset of the experiment, subjects took a survey on personality and intelligence that asked whether they thought willpower and "mental stamina" were limited or unlimited resources. It turned out that only people who thought their mental stamina was *limited* did worse on the follow-up self-control task. Those who thought that self-control was an *unlimited* resource showed no ill effects of the complicated "e" task and did just as well on the Stroop.

The researchers then tried manipulating people's willpower expectations. In a second experiment, they biased the initial questionnaire toward a belief in limited or unlimited willpower. They were testing the effects of willpower suggestion, and there was something else they wanted to check. Was it possible that people who believed in unlimited willpower did better on follow-up tasks only because they threw caution to the wind and burned up energy reserves that a more prudent person would have safeguarded for an emergency? If so, then these folks might do okay on the first follow-up task but would likely do horribly on a third challenge, which is what the researchers added.

In the end, the number of tasks didn't matter. People who did the complicated "e" task did worse on the next two tasks, but only if they'd initially been led to believe that their mental stamina was limited and readily depleted. If they believed in unlimited mental stamina, they did well on all three tasks.

What did seem to matter, the researchers would discover in a final experiment, was stress. The more energy-sapping stress people were under, the more their willpower expectations seemed to influence their ability to resist temptation and stay focused. In this experiment, undergraduates completed a survey about their willpower and also described a long-term personal goal. The students then checked in with the researchers three times during the semester via an online questionnaire—at the beginning, midway through, and during finals—to confess their willpower sins. They reported how much junk food they were eating, how much time they spent zoning out in front of the TV or poking around Facebook instead of studying, and whether they had made any progress toward their goals.

At the beginning and midway through the semester, the students were all eating about the same amount of junk, procrastinating about the same, and progressing toward their long-term goals at similar rates, no matter what they believed about willpower. When stress ramped up during finals, however, students who believed that they had only so much willpower were having a lot harder time laying off the chips, sticking to their studies, and working toward their goals.

Although these effects followed a belief in *unlimited* willpower, Job and her team were careful to note that, "we do not question that biological resources contribute to successful self-control." As with physical endurance, the fact that limits exist and the notion that beliefs could push and pull them need not be incompatible.

Meanwhile, researchers at Indiana University decided to see if placebos could replenish willpower as reliably as the carbohydrates of sugary lemonade did in Baumeister's studies. First, they depleted some subjects' willpower with a task borrowed from Baumeister's work: seated before a plate of freshly baked chocolate chip cookies and a bowl of radishes, people in the willpower-depletion group were told not to eat the cookies and instead to munch on radishes. Other subjects, by contrast, were free to eat as many cookies as they pleased.

Before their snack, participants read a short fact sheet about where the food was produced, including information on potential allergens and nutrition. This gave the researchers cover for their next trick—serving a lemon drink prefaced by its own fact sheet that mentioned its tendency to either sap or boost mental stamina. For a control group, the drink's fact sheet offered no suggestions about its cognitive effects. In reality, everybody drank the same calorie-free, artificially sweetened lemonade. Finally, subjects were given a series of challenging numerical matrix puzzles to solve, a task they were told they could quit at any time. The question being investigated was how long people would keep trying.

People who didn't expect anything from their lemon drink quit the puzzles just as the theory of ego depletion said they would.

Specifically, those who had to resist delicious cookies quit the puzzles faster than cookie eaters. The results were very different, however, among people who had expectations for their lemonade. When it came to quitting time, those expectations outweighed the effects of resisting or indulging in the cookies.

Cookie eaters who expected the lemonade to sap their mental stamina quit the puzzles just as quickly as radish eaters from the control group. Meanwhile, radish eaters who expected the lemonade to replenish their mental resources persisted just as long on the puzzles as cookie eaters from the control group.

In follow-ups, the researchers upped the ante. They switched the replenishment expectations from lemonade to something more ephemeral—mood. First, they asked subjects to write about an intensely positive or negative personal memory, to put them in a good or bad mood. Then they used biased questionnaires to slyly suggest that either positive mood or negative mood boosted mental stamina. A control group wasn't given any suggestions about mood's cognitive effects. Subjects then moved on to a series of depletion tasks, finishing up with extremely difficult anagrams.

Once again, the researchers wanted to see who persisted on the anagrams and who gave up in a hurry, and once again people who were not expecting anything from their mood changes followed the usual pattern. The ones who'd been given the more depleting tasks up front quit the anagrams earlier, and they made the most mistakes.

By contrast, people put in a positive mood did just as well as anybody on the anagrams and tried just as hard, no matter how depleting their initial tasks were, *if* they'd been told that positive mood was mentally refreshing. If they'd been told that negative mood was invigorating, then happiness did nothing for them. The anagram performance of subjects who had dredged up unhappy memories followed an equal and opposite pattern. If they were told that a little negative mood could bolster mental stamina, then they did just as well as anybody on the anagrams, despite their initial depletion.

These findings suggested that whatever you expect to refresh your willpower will do so. "Any mental reprieve," the researchers concluded, "whether in the form of a snack, social interaction, perusing the Internet, a catnap, or a vacation—will be most effective when people believe the experience will restore their mental capacities." In other words, wherever your beliefs lead, your willpower will follow.

As in the studies led by Job, these researchers suggested that the strength and endurance of our willpower is ultimately the result of expectations stretching real limits. Lead researcher Josh Clarkson suspects that expectations don't create new willpower resources, but instead guide their allocation and allow broader access to what we already have on board, akin to the central governor theory of exercise endurance. Indeed, a 2012 study on willpower found that swishing and spitting a glucose solution protected people from ego depletion, just as carbohydrate swishing had increased the endurance of long-distance cyclists, while having no effect on blood glucose levels.

It's likely possible to reach the end of our willpower rope, to literally have no more strength for focused mental effort, says Clarkson. Nevertheless, we spend most of our time under more ambiguous circumstances—How fatiguing was that task? How depleted do I really feel? Did I get enough sleep or have a decent breakfast? In these gray areas, he surmises, perceptions play a huge role.

"You could say our results are contradictory to the strength model of self-control, because mere perception leads to these effects," says Clarkson, alluding to Baumeister's theory of limited willpower energy. "We just think we're redefining strength."

REDEFINING STRENGTH

Conventional wisdom holds that a person's power and willpower are easily measured. The divisions are clear. You either sit in the corner office or you don't. You either resist that extra slice of pie, or you chow down.

The research covered in this chapter suggests it's not that simple. To a certain degree, both power and willpower are also a state of mind, responsive to our expectations.

They both swirl around success and achievement, but sometimes they pull in opposite directions. It is fun to consider placebo power and what we might gain just by standing a little taller or taking up a bit more space in the world. In the end, though, it may help us more to have high expectations for our willpower—the extra strength to keep plugging away and the ability to resist the temptations that power invites. These enhanced willpower expectations may be even more critical to our ultimate success.

(YOU WILL) GET WELL SOON

9] FAITH IN A BOTTLE

The biggest turning point in placebo history since the mesmerism trials occurred on Christmas Eve 1955. On that day, the *Journal of the American Medical Association* published an article by Henry Beecher, a Harvard anesthesiologist, called "The Powerful Placebo." It would define the placebo's role in medicine for decades as a chimera to be vanquished in the name of good science seeking real therapeutic effects.

Beecher had witnessed placebo power as an army doctor serving with American troops fighting their way off the beaches of southern Italy in 1944. The Germans were raining down artillery, and Beecher's field hospital was running out of morphine. Desperate, he gave some of the injured shots of saline (the injected equivalent of a sugar pill) along with assurances that their pain would soon subside. The ruse worked well enough, relieving the soldiers' pain and preventing the onset of potentially fatal shock.

Beecher took up the study of placebos when he returned to his Harvard Medical School professorship after the war. His landmark 1955 paper analyzed more than a dozen drug studies that used placebo control groups, involving conditions ranging from postoperative pain to seasickness to the common cold. Beecher concluded that about one third of patients given a placebo will improve due simply to their expectations of relief.

The problem, Beecher argued, was that most medical research didn't account for the effects of expectations, which made it impossible to determine the true efficacy of any given treatment. The solution was to randomly give some subjects placebos alongside those getting the real therapy, with neither subjects nor clinicians knowing who was getting what treatment. What Beecher proposed was the "double-blind, randomized placebo-controlled trial," which is now ubiquitous in medical research.

Beecher was the first physician to treat the healing potential of expectations with respect, but his attitude really wasn't much different from those expressed by Mesmer's investigators in 1784—imagination and expectations had real power, but it was only the power to deceive. Placebos were essential to good research precisely because they were everything science was not—based in myth, sustained by faith, and dependent on lies.

"They have two real functions," he wrote of placebos. "One of which is to distinguish pharmacological effects from the effects of suggestion, and the other is to obtain an unbiased assessment of the results of experiment."

Researchers needed to account for, and quarantine, the effects of these mendacious fantasies before they ruined the scientific understanding of medical therapies and the true course of disease.

Beecher played pretty fast and loose in his case for scientific rigor. Nearly half of the studies he analyzed were his own, and almost none of them had a no-treatment group. This matters, because people recover from illnesses all the time due to the natural course of disease. Without a measure of "spontaneous recovery"—often done by keeping people on the study's waiting list—it's impossible to distinguish the patients who responded to placebo treatment from those who would have improved just as much by staying at home.

Thus, Beecher's anti-bias mission ended up biasing his analysis. "He felt that medicine was out of control, which it was," says Ted Kaptchuk, a placebo researcher at Harvard Medical School. "He had an ethical motive, but he wasn't objective."

The bottom line is that Beecher's one third placebo response rate is bogus. A more accurate measure is this: it depends. Placebos work wonders with certain ailments, but can't seem to touch others. The source of placebo expectations also matters. It matters if the sham treatment is a pill, or an injection, or a topical cream. If it's a pill, the color makes a difference. So does the name. It even matters whether the placebo was given in America, France, Germany, or Brazil. Finally, the placebo response rate to the same drug can change from year to year.

Beecher's slanted case for objectivity largely succeeded. The rise of the double-blind placebo-controlled trial followed the publication of his paper, and that's been the placebo's main role ever since—an acknowledged, but not very well known or admired, player in the search for scientific truth. If patients taking a drug do significantly* better than those taking a placebo, then the researchers claim to have isolated the *real* drug effect. In truth, even real drugs often benefit from a placebo lift, but more on that later.

Placebos today still struggle with the twin stigmas of unreality and deception articulated in 1784. While their use in clinical trials has been critical to the safe advance of medical research, these stigmas have kept an even larger potential at bay.

PLACEBOS GET REAL

Fittingly, before "placebo" entered medical parlance, it was a prayer. The word is Latin for "I shall please," dating to Psalm 116: "Placebo Domino in regione vivorum," or, "I shall please the Lord in the land of the living."† Accordingly, in the Middle Ages, placebos were a disparaging nickname for the hired mourners at funerals who chanted the psalm through their fake tears and phony lamentations. When "placebo" first appeared in medical dictionaries a few years after Franklin's commission, it was defined as a way to amuse or mollify difficult patients.

It would be nearly two centuries before anyone dared suggest that placebo responders weren't simply being duped. One of the

---

*"Significantly" meaning that the results have at most a 5 percent chance of happening by chance.

† Actually, the Latin Psalm is a fourth-century mistranslation of the original Hebrew. Translated correctly, that line from Psalm 116 reads, "I shall *walk with* the Lord in the land of the living," which seems more upstanding in every way, or at least more upright.

first to do so was Stewart Wolf, a contemporary of Beecher and a gastroenterologist at Cornell University. Wolf had a patient called Tom whose esophagus closed up with scarring after he took an overzealous swig of scalding clam chowder as a boy. From then on, Tom fed himself by spitting chewed food into a tube inserted through a hole in his belly.

This misfortune gave Wolf a peephole directly into Tom's stomach where he could watch the aftermath of eating, drinking, stress, and various drugs. Some of the drugs caused abdominal cramping and diarrhea, and in experiments, Wolf watched placebo versions cause the exact same gastrointestinal gymnastics.

"Placebo effects which modify the pharmacologic action of drugs or endow inert agents with potency are not imaginary," Wolf asserted.

Individual case studies are low on the scientific totem pole, however, and like Beecher, Wolf was more interested in warning researchers about placebos than in exploring their healing potential. Most importantly, nobody knew *how* something as ephemeral as an expectation might work its way into the body. To be taken seriously any medical treatment needs a plausible mechanism. With placebos, there was only mystery.

This started to change in the 1970s. First, scientists discovered that our brains make their own painkillers, opioids known as endorphins and enkephalins. Might these be at work in placebos? Two neurologists, Jon Levine and Howard Fields, teamed up with an oral surgeon named Newton Gordon to test the idea by giving people recovering from dental surgery a placebo shot they said was painkiller, while also secretly injecting some patients with naloxone, a drug that disrupts opioids. The placebo painkiller worked, except in the naloxone patients. If placebo pain relief was just a figment of patient imagination, then an opioid blocker should make no difference among those given fake drugs. Yet it did, which suggested that the pain relief from expectations was real enough to be blocked biochemically.

The second big placebo discovery of the decade was that they don't need a doctor's suggestion to work. The body can generate powerful placebo expectations all on its own via conditioning, the anticipatory reflex made famous by Pavlov's hungry dogs. In classical conditioning a stimulus (a bell in the case of Pavlov's dogs) is repeatedly paired with an unconditioned stimulus (dog chow) that triggers a biological response (the dogs salivate). After a while, the dogs start salivating at the sound of the bell, even when no food arrives.

In the mid 1970s, the psychologist Robert Ader was researching the strength of conditioning effects on rats. Placebos were the furthest thing from his mind. He conditioned rats to fear a deliciously sweet saccharin solution that they normally loved by pairing it with a drug that gave the rats a stomachache. Ader wanted to know how long it would take the rats to get over their newly learned fear of saccharin after the drug was removed and get back to their instinctive love of sweetness. The longest holdouts were eventually force-fed pure saccharin solution with eyedroppers in order to complete the experiment's protocols. That's when things got weird. Inexplicably, the rats kept dying. The rats that had initially consumed the most saccharin solution during the conditioning trials tended to avoid it the longest, and these were the same rats that were meeting an untimely and mysterious end.

What was going on? Ader knew that the drug he chose to give the rats stomach trouble also suppressed the immune system. It was typically used to treat autoimmune diseases such as lupus. Even though the rats had no conscious expectations about what was ruining their sweet drink, maybe on some level their little brains learned to anticipate and mimic some of the drug effects from the saccharin flavor. If so, the most drastic immunosuppression would happen in the most strongly conditioned holdouts, the ones force-fed by eyedropper. Indeed, follow-up studies Ader did with the immunologist Nicholas Cohen confirmed the existence of a conditioned placebo response. Even without the drug, saccharin triggered automatic expectations that weakened the rats' immune systems and left the door open to all sorts of diseases that kept claiming the rats' lives.

These findings were tantalizing, but they left plenty of unknowns. For instance, could placebo effects caused by conditioned responses be triggered for ailments that weren't specific to the immune system? Would they work in humans? How would placebos induced by verbal suggestion stack up against a conditioned placebo effect? Most of these questions went unexplored until the 1990s, when scientists began unraveling how placebos really work, and when they don't.

PROPHECIES FOLLOW MANY PATHS

In his lab at the University of Turin Medical School, the neuroscientist Fabrizio Benedetti zaps people with lasers, squeezes them with tourniquets, and burns them with the essence of chili peppers. His subjects' suffering is not without purpose, however. By trying different combinations of painkilling drugs, along with placebos induced by conditioning and verbal suggestion, Benedetti has shown that our brains have more than one way to think away pain.

In one multiday study, Benedetti gave every subject's arm a painful tourniquet squeeze without any analgesic treatment in order to establish a baseline pain tolerance. On two subsequent days, he injected subjects with one of two potent pain relievers prior to the tourniquet pain. The subjects weren't told what they were being injected with, but some were given the opiate morphine while the others were given ketorolac, a drug that kills pain by fighting inflammation, similar to how aspirin works. On the final day, subjects were again injected prior to the tourniquet, but instead of the usual painkiller, they were secretly given either saline or the opioid blocker naloxone.

As it had in dental surgery patients whose placebo pain relief followed verbal suggestion, naloxone blocked conditioned placebo effects—but not in every case. It thwarted the pain relief only in people conditioned with the opiate morphine. Naloxone had no effect on placebo pain relief for patients conditioned with the anti-inflammatory ketorolac. Apparently, opioids weren't causing this particular placebo effect. As they had in Ader's rats, conditioned placebos seemed to follow the physiological path of the drugs they mimicked.

Just as the efficacy of placebo steroids may dissuade athletes from using chemical performance boosters, the power of placebos might help lessen the use, and abuse, of prescription pain relievers. In another Benedetti pain study, patients recovering from surgery in the hospital were told they could ask for as many painkiller pills as they needed. They were also hooked up to an intravenous saline drip. Some patients were told nothing about the drip. Others were told it was a potent analgesic. A third group was told it could be either painkiller or saline.

Patients who believed they *might* be getting painkiller through the IV asked for 20 percent fewer pain pills than those who knew nothing. Meanwhile, patients assured that the drip was painkiller cut their pill intake by more than a third. That's impressive, given the serious side effects of heavy-duty painkillers, including liver damage, long-term chronic pain, and recent surges in prescription drug addiction, much of which begins in postoperative settings.

Meanwhile, the mix of conditioning and verbal suggestion has allowed researchers to explore the healing reach of expectations well beyond pain relief. In many cases, such as treating Parkinson's patients with placebo dopamine drugs or sham stimulation of motor neurons, both verbal suggestion and conditioning are effective, and they are most powerful when combined. Sometimes, conditioned placebos are stronger than those caused by verbal suggestion, but they can still be wiped out if the patient is told the truth. In other cases, such as the placebo treatment of hormonal deficiencies, conditioned placebos get the job done no matter what a patient thinks.

"There are some placebo responses that are completely unconscious," Benedetti says. "You don't need to believe in the therapy. You don't need to trust your doctor."

Benedetti has also been among the few researchers to begin exploring another, darker route to the placebo response, one that may turn out to be among the most promising. Specifically, if expectations can heal, they can harm, too. Enter the nocebo, Latin for "I shall harm," the placebo's sinister cousin.

Some allergies, for instance, are thought to have a strong nocebo component. Allergies are the result of a hyperactive immune response, and the immune system doesn't like to be caught flat-footed. It tries to anticipate danger and cut it off at the pass. When the brain expects trouble—a suspected toxin or pathogen, for instance—it instigates a flurry of neural messages that are converted into hormones and signaling proteins that crank up our immune system here and dial it down a little there. In studies, fake allergens of all sorts, from artificial plants to phantom chemicals, have triggered rashes, red eyes, and asthma attacks.

The term nocebo was coined in 1961, but few researchers have dared to explore the phenomenon in research. It's one thing to hoodwink people into feeling better but quite another to trick them into even more misery. Nevertheless, both illness and recovery are riddled with nocebos. If we can avoid nocebos or block their mechanisms, then we create a placebo through the back door.

For instance, Benedetti and fellow researchers secretly cut the morphine drips to a group of postoperative patients who'd been getting the painkiller for two hours. These patients had agreed to participate in a study where their morphine might be interrupted at some point. They just didn't know if, or when, this might happen. Meanwhile, a second group of patients knew exactly when the morphine stopped flowing, because they were told by a doctor or a nurse. Over the next four hours, the pain ratings of patients who knew they'd been cut off more than doubled while the pain sensation of the blissfully ignorant barely budged. More pain came only to those who expected it.

Benedetti has also been able to block nocebo effects biochemically. He used a computerized infusion pump to secretly dose subjects with a chemical called proglumide that disrupts the neu-rotransmitter CCK (cholecystokinin) known for spreading pulses of fear and anxiety through the brain. The same study also used secret infusions of the opioid blocker naloxone. On their own, nei-ther chemical had any effect on the pain, *unless* a subject was also given a shot of saline and the suggestion that it was a painkiller. Among these folks, the placebo pain relief was blocked by hidden naloxone, and *enhanced* by the hidden proglumide. The results suggest that both positive and negative expectations can become biochemical realities that change the balance of experienced pain. Push one side down and the other goes up, a seesaw of pain per-ception.

As with placebos, nocebo expectations go well beyond pain. About one cancer patient in four feels "anticipatory nausea" be-fore chemotherapy, for instance. It can be caused just by seeing the hospital room or hearing the voices of the clinicians who give the treatments.

Likewise, drug side effect warnings can be self-fulfilling proph-ecies. In one study, Italian doctors gave a drug to men with en-larged prostates. Half the men were simply given a prescription. The others were also counseled at length on the potential side ef-fects: erectile dysfunction, decreased libido, and "problems of ejaculation." Real downers for any man to hear. Lo and behold, when patients evaluated the drug several months later, those who'd been warned reported about three times the rate of sexual side effects.

Disclosure of possible side effects is an ethical must, and the dangers of downplaying them are more serious than inducing them via nocebo suggestion. Still, it's easy to cause patients a lot of unnecessary trouble with careless wording.

Sometimes, nocebo side effects are so severe that people in the placebo groups of clinical trials drop out. A 2009 review of trials for different types of migraine drugs found a high rate of side effects in the subjects taking placebos, ranging from dry mouth to nausea to numbness. These side effects mimicked those of the active medication. Nocebo anorexia and memory loss, for example, occurred only in the placebo arms of anticonvulsant trials in which patients were warned of these specific drug risks.

While researchers go to great lengths to isolate the links between a drug and patient side effects in clinical trials of new therapies, many of the warnings on well-established drugs are from postmarketing surveillance—basically whatever users report to their doctors—with little control over alternative causation.

CONTAGIOUS EXPECTATIONS

Despite the lack of clinical scrutiny, nocebos lurk behind some of the most visible influences of expectations on our health. These powerful effects are not triggered by a doctor's claims or by the rigors of conditioning, but by each other.

For example, early in 1962, fear swept the shores of Lake Victoria, from northern Tanzania to southern Uganda. The menace was an unusual one, particularly for a region long accustomed to hardship: in village after village, children couldn't stop laughing. The epidemic started in a girls boarding school near the Tanzanian town of Bukoba, with just three girls at first. Within six weeks, most of the students were cackling, and sometimes crying, uncontrollably.

According to a report by regional health authorities, these fits of laughter and tears could last for hours. There weren't many other symptoms—no fever, no tremors, no fainting. Eventually the school closed, and the girls were sent home to neighboring villages where they infected hundreds of other teenagers throughout the region.

"Many of the patients say that they are frightened of something, but do not give any further information," the authorities noted. Villagers called it "a spreading madness."

As the laughing fits spread, doctors took blood from affected teenagers and sent it to the Virus Research Institute in the Ugandan city of Entebbe. They did spinal taps in search of bacterial infection. They tested the air and water in villages hit by the laughing disease, and they checked their stocks of plantains, beans, meat, and maize flour. They found nothing. The contagious laughter continued for more than a year before dying out.

When an epidemic strikes without any known viral, bacterial, or chemical trigger, it may be a socially spread nocebo of fearful expectations that researchers call mass psychogenic illness (MPI).

Among the most dramatic examples of MPI were the dancing plagues of the late Middle Ages and early Renaissance that swept through cities in Germany, the Low Countries, and northeastern France. These epidemics often began with a single person dancing in public, unable to stop, often for days. Soon enough, others joined in, just as compulsively, with more writhing than rhythm. They danced for days on swollen legs and bruised and bloodied feet. They screamed for help and begged for God's mercy. Some danced themselves to death.

The largest wave of compulsive dancing hit Strasbourg in the summer of 1518. By the end of August, hundreds of people were dancing wildly throughout the city. Town officials overruled local physicians who said the dancers should be bled, but their chosen prescription was just as alarming: more dancing! They gathered the stricken into guildhalls and even built a stage for them in the public square. They hired dancers to keep up the energy and musicians to play a lively accompaniment. Not surprisingly, the dancers kept going and kept dying. Eventually the town leaders changed their minds and deemed the dancing a curse from an angry Saint Vitus, an early Christian whom the Romans tossed into a cauldron of boiling oil and then to the lions for refusing to renounce his faith. By the fourteenth century, the Vatican declared Saint Vitus a "holy helper" who could answer the prayers of people who had epilepsy or trouble conceiving. On his feast day, it was customary to dance at his shrine. However, saints who could heal when venerated could afflict when angered, so the town's next remedy for the dancing was civic contrition—which meant cracking down on gambling and prostitution, and the banishment of those known to traffic in vice.

Mass psychogenic illnesses are fueled by stress and flow from expectations. According to John Waller, author of *A Time to Dance, a Time to Die* (2008), there were at least ten dancing outbreaks in towns along the Rhine and Mosel rivers, and most of them followed periods of tremendous hardship, such as the waves of crop-killing weather and famine that preceded the 1518 epidemic in Strasbourg.

A hungry and fearful populace was primed for a freak-out, but the loss of control that followed was scripted by cultural expectations. The region's pious citizens knew well the story of Saint Vitus, and some of the first of these dancing plagues began on or near June 15, Saint Vitus' Day.

Today's versions of MPI follow more modern expectations—including fears of environmental toxins and terrorist attacks. In November 1998, for example, a teacher in a Tennessee high school came down with a headache, nausea, and shortness of breath after complaining of a "gasoline-like" smell. Soon her students began to feel sick, too. Eventually more than a hundred staff and students were taken to the emergency room. The school was evacuated and closed for two days while extensive tests were done to locate the source of toxicity. Nothing was ever found. Sometime later, questionnaires revealed that people who reported symptoms were more likely to have known or seen somebody else get sick.

Certainly, MPI should be a designation of last resort. In addition to the risk of neglecting a dangerous toxin or infection, there's the unfortunate implication that those with symptoms are either lemmings or liars. In 2011, more than a dozen teenagers, mostly girls, in Le Roy, a town outside Rochester, New York, were hit with a mysterious outbreak of uncontrollable facial tics and muscle spasms. Investigations by public health authorities found no evidence of environmental or infectious causes, leading many to suspect MPI. That suspicion didn't sit well with many of the girls and their families. They took it as a suggestion that they were faking, that there was no pill they could take to get better, and there was no one to blame but themselves. It's the same stigma that's followed placebos for centuries, of course, only applied to the nocebo in this case. If the mind causes it, then it can't be real.

As we've seen, however, the brain has many ways to make good on our expectations, both good and bad. In response to a clinician's promise, the brain releases painkillers as strong as morphine. Anxiety short-circuits anticipation and the athlete's worst fears come true. The embodied expectations of looking powerful can send our hormones racing. As Ader's saccharin-slurping rats demonstrated, the immune system can be ratcheted up and down without a word being said.

We saw in Chapters 6 and 8 how readily we take cues for our own behavior from watching others. Why couldn't placebo and nocebo effects spread socially, too? In 2007, for a rare lab study of nocebo contagion, psychologists at the University of Hull (UK) somehow recruited 120 people to test "individual reactions to environmental substances." The researchers gave everybody an inhaler that supposedly contained a toxin known to cause headaches, nausea, itchy skin, and drowsiness. In reality, the inhalers contained nothing but plain old air.

Each subject was paired with another subject who was actually an actor in cahoots with the researchers. Sometimes the actor would show symptoms, either by answering the researchers' questions or by wincing, yawning, or throat clearing, and so on. In other cases, they'd stay symptom free.

Isolated in a room, the pairs of participants were told to inhale the toxin and then to hold their breath for three seconds. Over the next hour, a researcher checked in every ten minutes to see how they were feeling. They always spoke to the confederate first, and asked about the four symptoms mentioned up front and four other unexpected symptoms—watery eyes, scratchy throat, tightening chest, and difficulty breathing. Subjects whose partners displayed phony symptoms felt sicker and reported significantly more symptoms than subjects whose partners seemed unaffected by the "toxin."

Placebos can also be contagious, as Benedetti and his colleague Luana Colloca demonstrated in 2009. Subjects enduring painful electric shocks to their hand experienced placebo pain relief when a green light on the machine delivering the shocks was illuminated and felt more pain when the light was red. They weren't told what these lights meant—in reality, they meant nothing—but they'd watched another subject, actually a confederate of the researchers, faking his way through the red and green light shocks. Notably, the placebo pain relief was much stronger for these folks than it was for another group of subjects who were told up front what the lights meant but were given no demonstration.

ARE WE HARDWIRED TO HEAL OURSELVES?

If placebo effects are real and powerful and caused by everything under the sun, then why do they seem so capricious? Why are some people so responsive to placebos in clinical trials while others are unaffected? The same could be asked about most drugs, none of which work for everybody. Be that as it may, researchers have long tried to identify personality traits that could predict placebo responders—in order to keep them out of clinical trials. If we could spot these impressionable weirdos, the thinking goes, then we could keep their troublesome self-healing tendencies from mucking up our serious biomedical science.

Thus far, such studies have revealed nothing in particular. Findings that a certain personality type leads to an enhanced placebo response are usually balanced by contradictory evidence. In addition, there are crossover studies in which people who do not respond at all to a placebo pill respond strongly to a different kind of placebo, such as a saline injection.

Indeed, the contours of a general placebo response are so shaky that few who study it claim that it's part of our common human wiring or delve into another big why of placebos: why did we evolve an ability to heal ourselves that is so mysterious and conditional?

Rather than peering back through evolution for an answer, some scientists have started looking to the brain for a unifying explanation of placebos. Increasingly, they've linked placebos with the brain's dopamine-fueled reward circuitry.

Remember that dopamine doesn't spike *during* the enjoyment of a reward, but rather in *anticipation* of it. "A reward is coming! A reward is coming!"* In the case of medical treatment, that anticipated reward is symptom relief.

The theory is that when a person expects relief from a placebo, the brain stem pumps out an anticipatory blast of dopamine, and when it hits a more cognitive part of the brain, namely the orbitofrontal cortex, this anticipatory signal is made specific, something like, "don't worry, here comes pain relief," or, "relax, this asthma attack will soon subside." Among placebo responders, that cognitive signal then triggers the neurotransmitters or hormones that fulfill the specific expectation, such as more opioids and reduced CCK for painkilling, more dopamine for Parkinson's relief, or more serotonin to lift your mood.

Most of the evidence for this comes from brain scans of people getting placebos. A 2007 study at the University of Michigan, for instance, showed that people whose reward circuits were more active when expecting money were also more likely to respond to a placebo pain reliever.

Again, dopamine in the brain's reward system is a measure of wanting, and study subjects who express more desire to avoid pain or have other symptom relief also tend to experience stronger placebo effects. One study pinned nearly two thirds of the variation in placebo responses to how much fear and distress subjects reported while anticipating pain.

---

* Dopamine activity is also known to spike or dip *after* the reward is received, but only if the reward is better or worse than was expected.

Pain is a complex stew of sensory stimuli selected by attention, stirred up with memory and associations, and then heated by emotion and motivation. Two studies in 2010 showed the link between emotional and physical pain quite clearly. In one of these, young men and women who were recently dumped by a romantic partner endured two painful experiences while in a brain scanner. First, their arms were singed with heat. Then they had to look at photos of their lost love and recall memories of the defunct relationship. In both cases, the brains did the same painful dance. Meanwhile, another group of researchers asked their young subjects to bring in photos of a new love, along with a picture of an "equally attractive" acquaintance. Inside the brain scanner, they gazed at their beloved while painful heat was applied to their hands. Love's pain relief was comparable to morphine, and far more powerful than the relief people felt when they looked at the attractive acquaintance.

By identifying brain areas activated by both physical and emotional pain, and the threat of such pain, the neuroscientist Tor Wager hopes to find more objective means of measuring and predicting placebo pain relief. For a 2011 study, Wager and his lab analyzed the brain scans of people who were about to get a painful shock to a wrist where the researchers had just slathered a placebo painkilling cream. They wanted to see if the degree of placebo response could be *predicted* by activity levels in specific brain networks as subjects lay there awaiting the pain.

Brain activity is not a neat division of labor. There's a lot of messy overlap. Still, some brain areas are more closely associated with certain tasks than others, and Wager's team focused on activity in the regions most associated with cognitive control, pain processing, and what's known as emotional appraisal—sorting through the constant barrage of sensory stimuli to decide what matters and whether it bodes well or ill for us in the immediate future. In Wager's study, only the activity in the brain's emotional appraisal network predicted the degree of placebo pain relief that a person experienced.

"I think the fundamental placebo process is really a decision your brain makes, and it may be unconscious or partly conscious, based on what the situation is and what's important and valuable right now," Wager says.

He suggests that the placebo response is part of a neural system focused on what's next. Our brains combine what we've learned about our world with internally generated signals about how we're doing emotionally and physically, in order to evaluate how everything in our immediate environment will affect us in the near future. With each assessment, our brain calibrates a finely tuned physiological response.

For more than two centuries, medical science has done its best to quarantine placebo effects in research and banish them from patient care. It hasn't succeeded in either endeavor. There's mounting evidence that the sources of our expectations for both sickness and recovery are more widespread and pervasive than any lab can replicate. The evolving contagions of mass psychogenic illness—from the dancing curse of Saint Vitus to suspected environmental toxins—offer one hint to how sensitive our bodies are to our specific beliefs, hopes, and fears. As the next chapter will argue, placebo power isn't based in lies but rather in everything we think of as true.

10] HEALING REDEFINED

In 1784, the king's investigators saw the potential of imagination, but Mesmer's insistence that he healed by controlling cosmic magnetic forces made imagination easy to dismiss. More than a century and a half later, Beecher's warnings defined the placebo's role in clinical research by again insisting that deception was at the heart of its effects. In the decades that followed, doctors, patients, and medical ethicists considered placebos inherently dishonest, because even if their effects weren't a mirage, you still had to lie to achieve them.

Using placebo effects to enhance health and healing remains ethically treacherous. Today's medical minds may no longer see armed revolt and moral decay swirling in the imagination of their patients as they did in Mesmer's day, but placebo remains a dirty word in their ranks. Every major medical association forbids the use of placebos in patient care, counting it as an ethics violation. Most of these associations also place heavy restrictions on the use of placebos in clinical trials.

Tapping expectations for the sake of healing is still equated with ignorance, quackery, and lawsuits. Suggesting that a medical intervention works, even partly, by engaging the placebo response is the worst kind of slander against its practitioners. Trust is the bedrock of any therapeutic relationship, and the bottom line is that the placebo is considered a lie. Yet what if there were ways to enhance healing expectations without deception? Increasingly, this seems possible.

Researchers are starting to seek out the true sources of placebo potency. While placebos are still commonly thought of only as sugar pills and saline shots, expectations are naturally at work everywhere along the continuum of health, illness, and recovery, with lies playing no role at all.

PLACEBOS BEYOND SUGAR PILLS

In 2000, the *New York Times Magazine* published a remarkable account of Dr. J. Bruce Moseley's arthroscopic surgery on an elderly World War II veteran with a bad right knee. The patient was anesthetized but awake on the operating table. Moseley, who was also the team doctor for the NBA's Houston Rockets, was on the other side of the surgical drape. He fished a sealed envelope from his pocket, opened it, and scanned the contents before returning it and reaching for the scalpel. He wasn't going to operate. He was going to fake it.

To be convincing, Moseley opened up the patient's knee with three incisions. He asked the nurse for various instruments and manipulated the joint. He splashed saline to simulate the usual rinsing. Then he stitched the knee up, and the old man was wheeled into the recovery room none the wiser.

The patient, Sylvester Colligan, was one of about 180 people whom Moseley recruited to test the efficacy of arthroscopic knee surgery, which at the time was performed hundreds of thousands of times a year. One third of these patients would have the full procedure, which involved rinsing and scraping out the knee joint. Another third would have their knee joints rinsed, but not scraped. The rest would get the same treatment Colligan did—nothing. In order to avoid inadvertently tipping off patients, Moseley didn't learn who was getting the real surgery until he opened that envelope in the operating room.

Turns out, the sham surgery actually worked *better* than the real procedure. Two weeks after the operation, placebo patients had less pain and more improvement on tests of walking and stair climbing. One year later, they still did better than those who underwent the full procedure. After two years, there were no significant differences in knee pain or overall mobility between the groups.

A couple of years after Colligan's "operation," even after learning that he'd undergone placebo surgery, he told the *New York Times* reporter that his knee never felt better. "It's just like my other knee now. I give a whole lot of credit to Dr. Moseley," he said. "Whenever I see him on the TV during a basketball game, I call the wife in and say, 'Hey, there's the doctor that fixed my knee!'"

What should we make of results like this? Do they tell a story of unnecessary surgery debunked, or one of potential self-healing discovered? Or both? Moseley hadn't set out to do either. Originally, he had simply wanted to know if scraping and rinsing the joint during surgery was better than just rinsing. When a colleague proposed the sham operation, he was skeptical. Placebo effects were for sugar pills, after all, not for surgery. Ironically, it's exactly this sort of assumption that makes the placebo response so potentially powerful in surgery. We believe in our pills. But we believe in surgery even more.

Sham surgery as a placebo control is rare, for good reasons. The ethical line for deceiving people in medical care is much bolder and brighter for a patient population, particularly if that deception involves anesthesia and scalpels. In fact, prior to Moseley's investigation, the most well known use of sham surgery dated from four decades earlier. It was used to test the first widely performed operation to treat angina, the chest pain of clogged arteries. The procedure, developed by Italian physicians in the 1950s, was known as "mammary artery ligation." The mammary arteries were tied off below the point where they branched to the heart. Presumably, this enhanced the coronary blood flow.

About two thirds of patients who first underwent the surgery reported symptomatic improvement, and the procedure became quite popular. A number of cardiologists were skeptical, however, based on the basic anatomy of what connects to what near the heart. In 1959 and 1960, two independent groups of doctors pitted the surgery against a placebo operation. Overall, 67 percent of the patients getting the real surgery showed substantial improvement, but so did 83 percent of those whose surgery was a figment of their imagination, aside from the scars.

More recently, studies have found that pacemakers need not be turned on to help patients with certain conditions, including vasovagal syncope, which basically causes people to faint a lot, and the more serious hypertrophic cardiomyopathy, an abnormal thickening of the heart muscle that can be fatal. Sham surgery also helped people with severe heart disease just as much as a newfangled surgery called transmyocardial laser revascularization, in which a laser is used to make a few dozen tiny holes in the heart, presumably to create more channels for the blood.

The fact that placebo operations work as well as some medical procedures doesn't mean that surgery is useless, just as the fact that expectations can dull pain doesn't mean we should abandon aspirin. Acknowledging the power of expectations on health is not an argument that medical interventions are beside the point. The two approaches are not mutually exclusive. Indeed, they are completely tangled up—placebos are enhanced by the effectiveness of the "real" treatments they mimic, and in turn, these treatments owe some of their efficacy to our multilayered expectations.

Every procedure or consultation with a doctor, even a visit to the drugstore, is laden with expectations and assumptions. A lifetime of prior experiences with doctors and other caregivers is just the start. Expectations also accumulate outside of health care settings gradually, like stalagmites, drip by drip. They grow as the news anchors warn us about this year's killer flu and list its symptoms, and they keep growing during commercial breaks when drug ads suggest that we may have low testosterone, malfunctioning serotonin, an overactive bladder, or overactive nerves. The same ads helpfully offer prescription fixes, although the listed side effects are alarming—strange dreams, suicidal thoughts, erections that last for days. For a moment, we consider trying that new insomnia pill, until we remember that a co-worker took it and sleep-drove into the bushes. Instead, when we can't sleep we pass the time searching online for some clues about our rash and read all about Lyme disease.

These expectations aren't easily isolated by clinical trials. They go even deeper, to our cultural beliefs about childhood and old age, our notions about what "healthy" feels like, our superstitions, and even our associations with different colors.

This is partly why, more than two centuries after Mesmer, some of our biggest, or at least most lucrative, medical advances are sustained by the power of what's in our heads. The *good* news is that the ubiquity of these assumptions means that we may be able to harness their power without lying to others or fooling ourselves. Instead of tricking patients with sugar pills and saline shots masquerading as "real" medicine, the most promising placebos tap the layers of expectations woven into our notions of health and healing.

WHEN THE POWER OF NOTHING IS ALMOST EVERYTHING

Hard-nosed medical science has accomplished amazing things in the past century. It has eradicated smallpox and very nearly defeated polio, developed an arsenal of antibiotics, successfully transplanted almost every major organ, increased life expectancy by decades, and sequenced the three billion bits of DNA that make up the human genome. Often, however, our faith in science leads to therapies that rely as much on faith as they do on science.

Consider a clinical trial in which 75 percent of the people taking a medication are healed versus just 50 percent taking a placebo. Voilà! The drug effect can be seen in that 25 percent difference. Pretty good, right? Not necessarily. In 2005, Benedetti demonstrated how easily apparent drug effects could be inflated by the power of expectations.

Under the guise of testing a new painkiller in a clinical trial, Benedetti injected participants with either saline or proglumide, the drug that blocks the neurotransmitter CCK. Some of the subjects were injected openly while others received hidden doses of either the proglumide or saline from a computerized infusion pump. With open injections, typical of a clinical trial, the proglumide had a clear painkilling advantage over the saline. If this had been an actual clinical trial, the results would certainly help the drug be approved, marketed, and widely prescribed.

The problem was that when the shots were given covertly, there was *no difference* in pain relief between proglumide and placebo. On its own, without the expectations of pain relief brought on by the open injection, this new "painkiller" was actually powerless.

In 2007, a real-world version of this scenario unfolded. The German national health care system decided to study acupuncture as a treatment for chronic back pain, which was becoming a staggering expense for taxpayers due to physical therapy and disability payments.

The German clinical trials tested acupuncture against well-established and already covered treatments, including anti-inflammatory drugs, physical therapy, and a combination of the two. Acupuncture beat them all. These were promising results, except that the researchers also tested sham acupuncture, and that beat the conventional therapies, too. In a final twist, sham acupuncture did just as well as real acupuncture. So what exactly was easing German back pain, and what treatment should the taxpayer cover?

In fact, many drugmakers are now confronting a placebo crisis. William Potter, a former drug company researcher and executive, was among the first to realize it. Reviewing clinical trial results in the late 1990s while at Eli Lilly, Potter saw that dummy pills were gaining on established drugs such as Prozac. Meanwhile, newer antidepressants, an industry cash cow, were also having a tough time besting placebos.

Eager to find out why, Potter teamed up with David DeBrota, a physician colleague with experience in the drugmaker's IT department, to search through Lilly's published and unpublished drug trials. What they found was alarming. Over the decades, placebo responses had been increasing. Even more striking was the tremendous unpredictability of placebo response across studies of the same drugs. Among the baffling variables was geography. Prozac, for instance, beat placebo by a much wider margin in American clinical trials than it did in Europe or South Africa.

Could decades of pharmaceutical advances be largely smoke and mirrors? If so, a generation of industry investment was in peril. Speaking before a congressional oversight committee in the fall of 2010, Potter explained how so much time and money had been spent on pills that were being drowned out by placebo effects. In the late 1980s and early 1990s, neuroscience labs were identifying hundreds of potential drug targets and therapeutic pathways for diseases such as depression, schizophrenia, and Parkinson's. Excited by the rapid pace of discovery, the drug industry focused on the central nervous system as the next frontier for high-impact, high-profit products. They poured money and human resources into their development.

As it turned out, the central nervous system was where new drugs went to die, often after a futile slog against placebos. "The brain is so complex and there are many homeostatic protective mechanisms," Potter says in an interview. "Sooner or later, it started to hit everybody that there was no viable business model for developing novel psychiatric drugs."

The advent of truly new drugs, made of novel chemical compounds, slowed to a trickle. According to Potter's testimony, only one out of twenty central nervous system targets selected for development led to a viable drug approved by the FDA, and the pipeline for the lucky few averaged more than thirteen years and cost about $1.8 billion.

The solution was "me too" drugs—slight alterations of existing compounds, presented with the fanfare of new clinical trials and a blizzard of ads. Another strategy was relicensing a drug for marginal disorders, such as testing antidepressants to treat shopaholics. The "me too" drugs and relicensing made tons of money for drug companies and their advertisers.

"You could get rich on those, and everybody did," says Potter. "But then what becomes most important is not the science, it's the marketing. And that's the simple story of how everything went south."

While central nervous system drugs in development were foundering against sugar pills, researchers were also uncovering the true placebo component of drugs that were already widely prescribed. In the mid-1990s, psychologists Irving Kirsch and Guy Sapirstein pooled a number of published antidepressant studies that included a no-treatment group. While patients in these trials routinely got better, Kirsch and Sapirstein noticed that the difference in improvement between placebo and no treatment was *twice as big* as the difference between placebos and real pills. Only a quarter of the total benefit from antidepressants could be attributed to the drugs, while half was due to the placebo dose of expectations.

In 2008, Kirsch and a new group of collaborators expanded their analysis to also include unpublished antidepressant studies, which they obtained from the FDA. This time, the results were even more striking: 82 percent of the antidepressant benefit could be reproduced by a placebo, leaving just 18 percent for the drug.

That same year, another group of researchers wrote a review of antidepressant trials in the *New England Journal of Medicine* indicating that selective publication of positive results "conveyed an effect size [for the drugs] nearly one third larger than the effect size derived from the FDA data."

Finally, Kirsch noted that drug advantages over placebos grew in line with the severity of a patient's initial depression. It reached clinical significance only after baseline depression scores hit 28 on the Hamilton Scale, which indicates very severe depression. Remarkably, according to his analysis, this wasn't because the drugs worked any better for the most severely depressed. Instead, it was due almost entirely to a dip in placebo response among the most dejected subjects. A 2010 follow-up on Kirsch's meta-analysis largely corroborated his findings, concluding that the benefit of antidepressants for people with mild to moderate depression was "minimal or nonexistent, on average," although these researchers did note that antidepressants had a "substantial" benefit over placebos for patients with very severe depression.

A brain scan study of men hospitalized for depression observed similar changes in the brains of men who felt better after several weeks of taking a pill, no matter whether that pill was Prozac or a placebo. Granted, in this study led by Emory psychiatrist Helen Mayberg, the common brain changes were bigger in the active drug group, and there were a few effects that were unique to the brains of men taking Prozac. Mayberg concluded that these differences might be relevant to separate findings that antidepressants beat placebos more handily when it came to preventing relapse in severely depressed people.

By the time Kirsch and others began to question antidepressant efficacy, doctors were writing 147 million prescriptions for these pills every year in the United States, even after studies linked them to increased suicidal thoughts and behaviors in teenagers and young adults. In 2004, the state of New York sued Glaxo-SmithKline for deliberately hiding such "adverse events" from trials of its SSRI, Paxil. The case was settled when the company agreed to pay $2.5 million and establish a public registry of all clinical trial results.

Part of the solution advocated by Potter is an honest assessment of the placebo's power in the central nervous system. This includes industry-funded research of the placebo itself, which a few companies have now tentatively and anonymously begun. The centerpiece of these efforts is a massive data-sharing initiative on placebo effects in clinical trials that Potter began developing in 2009 and that is now being spearheaded by the industry-sponsored Foundation for the National Institutes of Health, an organization that creates public-private medical research efforts.

The project's initial focus is on antidepressant placebo response. For more than half a century, depression has been evaluated with the Hamilton Scale, a rangy, symptom-based, 51-point rating system. The idea is to go beyond the Hamilton by marrying the shared placebo data with new research aimed at finding actual biomarkers for depression. Ultimately, the goal is to separate the disease subtypes that respond much better to drug treatment versus placebos from those that don't. This distinction would allow more targeted drug development while reducing unnecessary prescriptions.

For the subtypes of depression that respond overwhelmingly to placebos, Potter says, "the best intervention is probably time, structure, and support," not another pill.

WE ARE NOT DECEIVED. WE DECEIVE OURSELVES.

In the late 1970s and early 1980s, French and Brazilian patients with ulcers enrolled in separate clinical trials of the acid reflux drug Tagamet. The protocols weren't exactly the same, but they were pretty close. Ulcers were healed in 76 percent of the French and 60 percent of the Brazilians taking the drug. That's a big difference, but the real head-scratcher was that 59 percent of the French who took placebos also got better compared to only 10 percent of Brazilians.

After Dan Moerman, a medical anthropologist at the University of Michigan, spotted this oddity, he dug up more than one hundred other trials of ulcer treatments. In those studies, the rate of placebo healing was all over the place. The highest was 60 percent, in German patients. Why? Cultural stereotypes spring to mind. For instance, was this some northern European obedience to medical authority? *Nein!* Moerman points out that placebo healing of ulcers in neighboring Denmark and the Netherlands reached only about 20 percent. And by the way, Germans had among the *lowest* rates of placebo response for high blood pressure treatments.

It's fun to make silly speculations about cross-cultural ulcer attitudes, but the implications of such differences in placebo efficacy
are much more basic. Just as Potter discovered, placebo effects are
not easy to separate from the healing process. Often they *are* the
healing process, and their sources are deeply rooted in our most
basic beliefs about the world.

Take our assumptions about color, for instance. In American
studies, pink placebo stimulants beat out blue ones and patients
felt more effects from red and black pills, which they perceived
to be stronger than white pills. Green pills reduced anxiety more
than yellow pills in a British study, but yellow pills were better at
cheering up the depressed. These associations aren't news to
drugmakers. A Dutch study found that stimulants sold in Holland tend to be red, orange, or yellow, while depressants or tran-
quilizers are typically blue, green, or purple. Numbers matter, too.
In studies where dosage varies, subjects who take more placebos
experience stronger effects.

Moving up from these fundamentals, marketing can also influence drug efficacy. In 2010, drug companies spent more than $4.3
billion to push their prescription medications directly to consumers, more than triple what they spent in 1997 when the FDA first
allowed such advertising. All that cash doesn't just sell medicine,
it changes how well it works.

For decades, drugmakers have puzzled over the inexplicable
loss of efficacy in established drugs after "new and improved"
treatments burst on the scene. For example, when Tagamet first
came on the market, it could heal ulcers in 72 percent of patients,
averaged across clinical trials. After Zantac was introduced a few
years later, Tagamet could heal only 64 percent of ulcers.

In the 1980s, British researchers found that aspirin soothed
headaches better when patients believed it was a popular brand
rather than generic. In the same study, placebos also provided
more pain relief when given the brand name label.

Even price matters. In 2006, MIT and Stanford researchers
zapped study participants with a series of electric shocks, and

then gave them a new "painkiller" pill—a placebo, of course—before delivering more shocks of the same intensity. They told some people that the drug would be sold at $2.50 per pill. They told the others that the drug had been discounted from $2.50 to just 10 cents per pill. No reason was given for the price cut, but what it apparently meant to study subjects was that the pills were of lesser quality. Only about 60 percent of the discount group felt pain relief from their pills, compared to about 85 percent of people given full-priced placebos.

"This may help explain the popularity of high-cost medical therapies . . . over inexpensive, widely available alternatives," the researchers concluded, "and why patients switching from branded medications may report that their generic equivalents are less effective."

If you push this kind of thinking far enough, as Moerman did in his book *Meaning, Medicine and the "Placebo Effect"* (2002), then you start to realize just how unfortunate the phrase "placebo effect" really is. For years, but without much luck, Moerman has advocated a new term, one that could encompass the woeful dancers at Strasbourg, the renewal of Sylvester Colligan's knee, and the sleepy eyes of study subjects taking an inert blue pill: "meaning response."

This is not just semantics. It frees expectation effects from the sugar pill and the saline injection posing as "real" treatments. It lets their self-healing potential loose in the much larger context surrounding our encounters with sickness and healing. Potentially, it also lifts the stigma of trickery and deception.

BEING MINDFUL OF MEANING

In 1981, two groups of men in their late seventies and early eighties shuffled aboard a bus in Cambridge, Massachusetts, that drove them about sixty miles north and more than two decades into the past.

The men were going to spend a week at an old New Hampshire

monastery that Harvard psychologist Ellen Langer and her lab team had transformed into an inn set in 1959—first one group and then the other. The researchers had filled the monastery with furnishings and mementos to evoke the 1950s, such as *Life* magazine and the *Saturday Evening Post,* a black-and-white television, and a vintage radio.

Before the men spent their week in 1959, they took a battery of tests, checking vision, dexterity, strength, memory, intelligence, and so forth. The researchers also snapped Polaroids of the men's faces. They told them not to bring anything in their luggage that would disturb the "Nifty Fifties" vibe—no recent magazines and no current books or family photos.

The men in the control group spent their week reminiscing and recalling their younger days. Those in the experimental group, however, were told to imagine that the year was actually 1959— that they were twenty-two years younger, Eisenhower was president, and *Ben-Hur* had just been released. All week, they talked about 1959 in the present tense. Whether they were introducing themselves to the other men or speaking with one of the researchers, they were to be their 1959 selves. This began immediately upon arrival when these men, several of whom had trouble getting onto the bus unassisted, were told to carry their own bags to their rooms. They were surprised. Some protested—*Impossible!* Yet they all did it, in some cases just inches at a time.

When the men in the experimental group met for their daily discussions of "current" affairs, such as Castro's takeover of Cuba, the space race with the Soviets, and the Baltimore Colts victory over the New York Giants in the NFL championship game, the conversations were spirited, sometimes even heated. For entertainment, they watched Sgt. Bilko, Jack Benny, and Ed Sullivan on the black-and-white television. During card games, the radio played Perry Como, Rosemary Clooney, and Nat "King" Cole. On movie nights, they watched *North by Northwest* and *Some Like It Hot.* The men helped serve the meals and clean up afterward. They made their way up and down the stairs without assistance.

When the bus returned these men to present-day Cambridge, the researchers gave them another battery of mental and physical tests and took a second Polaroid. Men from both groups showed improvements. They stood taller and walked with a steadier gait. They were more flexible, and their arthritis diminished so they had stronger grips and better manual dexterity. Many of them bettered their performance on the intelligence and memory tests, too. On all these metrics, the men who'd spent the week pretending to be two decades younger did significantly better. To top it off, they looked younger, too, according to outside observers who later reviewed their before-and-after photographs.

Langer's goal was to probe the connections between mind and body and to see if countering the expectations of aging could alter its physical manifestations. It was one of Langer's first tests of what she calls "mindfulness"—the rejection of certainty, labels, and sameness. She contrasts it with the absolutes and inevitability of "mindlessness." For example, does vision worsen with age? A mindless answer is yes. So is the blissfully defiant no! The mindful answer is maybe.

Making better use of expectations in health requires us to reconcile with maybe. This isn't easy. We want to know our prognosis. We crave definitive answers. Is red wine good for us or bad for us? Exactly how many eggs can I safely eat every week? If Germans can heal their own ulcers, then tell us how, so we can bottle it like the miracle water from the rocky spring in Lourdes, France.

Actually, those who make pilgrimages to Lourdes, where the Virgin Mary is said to have appeared in 1858, embody the power of maybe. Via a webcam, you can watch them complete their journey to the rocky grotto and its freshwater spring. All day they come, from 5:30 A.M., when the sanctuary opens, until midnight. The Vatican designated Lourdes a holy place of healing in 1876, but in all these years of pilgrimage and prayer, there have been only sixty-seven official miracle cures. Why so few? Because the faithful understand that praying for health is an entreaty, not a prescription. The core of any miracle is faith—the opposite of proof—a sanctified explanation for remarkably good news that's otherwise inexplicable. In 2008, the doctors of the Lourdes Medical Committee announced they would no longer designate cures as miracles, but simply note cases of "remarkable healing" and let the Church take it from there.

Indeed, when contemplating the promise of healing expectations, it's easy to get carried away and imagine that illness is just a state of mind or something easily banished with enough positive thinking. Ironically, such notions can make illness even harder to bear.

About a decade ago, for example, psychologists counseling cancer patients began to complain about "the tyranny of positive thinking" promoted by self-help gurus and prominent cancer charities. The pressure to stay positive and never consider defeat can stymie honest and necessary conversations between patients and their loved ones about fear and grief and the many uncomfortable what-ifs of life-threatening illness. Then there's the guilt. If a patient's optimism kills cancer, then who is to blame if cancer progresses? Mark Francis, a psychologist at Abramson Cancer Center of the University of Pennsylvania, says his patients are often troubled by the fact that they can't be more positive. "They literally think they are killing themselves," he says.

Researchers are just starting to unpack the expectations of health and healing, and the going is slow. The promise of simplicity and easy answers may be the most enduring placebo deception. The origins and interactions of expectations on the body are multiple. They require as much study as any new therapeutic, if not more. While expectations can affect our health in many profound and surprising ways, the word "can" is a very important one. It's a mindful word, conveying possibility but distinct from the mindless "will." Optimism can be just as mindless as pessimism.

In the three decades since Langer's monastery study, she has published a slew of experiments on the potential of mindful expectations. Collectively, the promise of these studies is that we don't need to fully unravel and categorize all the expectations that influence health and healing to take advantage of their potential. We don't need to know how, or if, a change in our expectations will affect our health in order to try it. The change may be small, nearly imperceptible, just enough to crack open the doors of our assumptions.

In a 2010 study led by Langer, subjects' vision improved after they read a bogus yet authoritative-sounding medical memo about improving vision through eye exercises and then did those exercises. Other people's vision improved simply by flipping the eye chart used to test them, so that the lines grew easier to read toward the bottom of the chart and more difficult toward the top. Years of eye exams using the standard chart have led us to expect that we should be able to read the first few lines with ease. Conversely, we are habituated to not being able to see the eye chart's bottom lines. Flipping the chart shook up these expectations. Jolted out of their usual, mindless eye-exam assumptions, subjects could read significantly more letters in the smallest fonts when they appeared at the top of the chart.

A few years ago, Langer and one of her students, Alia Crum, now a clinical psychology researcher at Yale, spoke about exercise to scores of women who clean hotel rooms for a living. They told the women that the surgeon general recommends thirty minutes of daily exercise. Then they asked the women how frequently they exercised and gave them a physical. The chambermaids worked at seven different hotels, and Langer and Crum told the women at four of these hotels that the work they did every day—cleaning an average of fifteen hotel rooms and hauling their supply carts up and down the hallways—was in fact exercise. They also gave them some calorie-burning particulars, such as 40 calories for changing linens, 50 calories for 15 minutes of vacuuming, and 60 calories for cleaning a bathroom.

Four weeks later, the women who were told that their work was "exercise" showed significant improvements in every single measure of fitness. They lost weight and body fat. They also had lower blood pressure, smaller waist-to-hip ratios, and healthier body mass indices. The women hadn't changed their routines. They reported no extra exercise outside of work. The control group women showed no improvements.

Langer acknowledges that there's no biological or physiological model to explain effects like these. Indeed, it should be noted that attempts in 2011 by other researchers to replicate the exercise results in adolescents and university service workers failed. Langer emphasizes that she's not trying to develop a specific new therapy with a defined likelihood of success. She seems to be an advocate for belief, but is in fact calling for more skepticism about everything we take for granted.

"It's about trying. That's different from me saying that if you do three hours of mindfulness every two days, you'll be healed," she says. "Mindfulness is an antidote to learned helplessness."

Among Langer's favorite expectations to challenge is the inevitable decline of old age. In one study, Langer and several colleagues followed up on an earlier experiment that focused on the cognitive and behavioral influences from implicit bits of suggestion—known as priming. In the earlier study, subjects unscrambled anagrams into words. The solutions to the experimental group's anagrams were disproportionately related to stereotypes about old age, words such as forgetful, helpless, gray, rigid, lonely, and wrinkled, while the control group's words were not age-related. After solving the anagrams, the subjects were told they could leave.

A confederate of the researchers sat in the hall outside the lab. Ostensibly, she was a student waiting to speak with the professor, but she was actually timing how long the subjects took to make their way down the hall to the elevator. In two experiments, the subjects primed with old folks stereotypes walked more slowly.

Langer's group asked their young research participants (average age twenty-four) to sort photographs of faces multiple times. The faces were of people more than sixty-five years old and younger than thirty, so age was an unspoken prime.

People in the control group sorted photos four times according to the obvious split between old and young. A "low mindfulness" group sorted by gender. The "moderate mindfulness" group sorted according to four assigned categories—age, gender, attractive versus unattractive, and white versus nonwhite. The final, "high mindfulness," group chose their own categories. After the sorting task, the researchers covertly timed their subjects' walking speed, just as in the earlier study. They found that the moderate and high mindfulness photograph sorters walked much faster than the controls or the low mindfulness subjects.

"We expected [the more mindful sorters] to come to see the person in the photo as many things and not just old," Langer writes in *Counterclockwise: Mindful Health and the Power of Possibility* (2009). "We were looking to see whether the mindful action of recategorizing would lead people to be immune to the 'old age' prime." At least judged by subjects' walking speed, it worked.

Elsewhere in her book, Langer advises us to be skeptical of absolute certainty when it comes to our health, and to pay attention to the expectations built into the words we use to describe ourselves. "We need to learn how to integrate what the medical world knows to be generally true," she writes, "with what we know, or can find out, about ourselves."

TURNING EXPECTATIONS INTO MEDICINE

If doctors are to make greater use of the placebo effect, then a modicum of clinical consistency is a must. As individuals, we are free to pretend we're twenty years younger, or flip the eye chart, or whatever we damn well please. Clinicians, however, have a duty to offer the best available care to their patients.

The herculean task of untangling the various sources of placebo expectations is the central research focus of Harvard placebo guru Ted Kaptchuk. Among medical school professors, Kaptchuk has a unique background. After graduating from Columbia, he traveled to Macau and earned a doctorate in oriental medicine. He returned to the States and opened an alternative medicine clinic in a Boston hospital. Soon, however, he began to wonder how much the placebo effect factored into his treatments. He taught himself to do clinical trials and eventually won support from the National Institutes of Health as well as a spot on Harvard's faculty. In 2011, he became the founding director of the Program in Placebo Studies and the Therapeutic Encounter at Boston's Beth Israel Hospital.

In his research, Kaptchuk tries to tease apart the slivers of "psychosocial context" that may spur self-healing. Sometimes that means pitting one type of placebo against another—a saline injection may elicit stronger effects than sugar pills, for example. More recently, he's focused on the doctor-patient relationship.

There's a scattered history to this research, which has taken on new relevance recently, because the declining number of general practitioners and the efficiency priorities of managed health care have curtailed the time that doctors can spend with individual patients. In the late 1980s, a British general practitioner randomly sorted two hundred of his patients who complained of various symptoms but had no apparent illness. He gave some a definite diagnosis and told them confidently that they would feel better in a few days. He gave the others neither a diagnosis nor a prognosis. These two groups were further subdivided into patients given a placebo prescription and those sent home empty-handed. Two weeks later, the doctor's office checked up on how all the patients were faring.

Getting a diagnosis and a few comforting words from the doctor led to more healing than having a medicine to take. Nearly two thirds of the patients to whom the doctor gave a positive consultation said they felt better, compared to 39 percent of the rest. By comparison, the difference in symptom relief between those who took a placebo and those who didn't was much more modest, 53 to 50 percent.

While most people don't go to a doctor for a common cold, several hundred folks did so for a 2009 study. In fact, they went three times—at the onset of symptoms, two days later, and when they were symptom free. They scored their doctors using a Consultation and Relational Empathy (CARE) survey, assessing whether the doctor let them "tell their story," helped them take control, and several similar items. Patients of doctors with the highest CARE scores got over their colds faster, and their colds were less severe, although the latter finding was not statistically significant.

By contrast, Margaret Kemeny, a psychologist at the University of California, San Francisco, found no effects from varying doctor-patient interactions in a 2007 placebo study of asthmatics, although she did find that placebo inhalers could open up constricted airways.

"What it tells me is that it's not a simple story," Kemeny says. "You can't just go in there and be really nice to your patient and believe that's going to facilitate a placebo response." In other words, it takes some know-how. And whether it's called "bedside manner" or the more current "people skills," medical schools have lately been paying more attention to it. In recent years, about two dozen medical schools in the United States and Canada have started putting candidates through nine "mini interviews," à la speed dating, specifically to weed out people with lackluster social and communication skills. In addition, Harvard Medical School launched a new clerkship program in 2004, in which medical students become advocates and sympathetic ears for a handful of specific patients with chronic care needs.

Writing about the usefulness of such programs in the *Boston Globe,* one newly minted doctor admitted that bedside manner basics learned in medical school went by the wayside when she and her classmates began to work in hospitals.

"Schedules were tight. Our focus on connecting with patients faded as we scrambled to fit in and observed the way things were *really done,*" she wrote.

In 2008, Kaptchuk took a more fine-grained look at the doctor-patient relationship in a six-week study of people with irritable bowel syndrome. Some patients were kept on a waiting list.

Others were given placebo acupuncture but "limited" patient-practitioner interaction—no chitchatting, just needles. A third group was given placebo acupuncture as well as an "augmented" interaction with a practitioner who asked a lot of questions, listened closely to the answers, was very empathetic, and displayed a lot of confidence in the treatment.

After six weeks, the "augmented" group felt the most relief. Overall, 62 percent of them improved, which is comparable to most drugs used to treat irritable bowel syndrome. By contrast, sham acupuncture didn't do much for the "limited" group. At the final follow-up, they were feeling only marginally better than the patients kept on the wait list. Still, that's a lot of possibilities to consider.

"Was it the twenty seconds of thoughtful silence? Was it the touch? Was it being an empathetic listener and witness?" Kaptchuk says. "Shit, I don't know."

RESTORING TRUST

The placebo may be considered a lie among many medical professionals. Still, it is a lie oft told. Survey after anonymous survey show that doctors are using placebos or "placebo-like treatments," such as prescribing antibiotics for someone with a nonbacterial diagnosis, despite the ethical prohibitions. In 2010, a meta-analysis of these surveys, spanning four decades, reported that about half of doctors and nurses had used a placebo at some point in their career.

The debate over what exactly counts as deception and when it's okay for a doctor or a nurse to tiptoe up to one ethical line or another gets complicated really fast. However, we could cut through the ethical brambles if we could just tell people that they're getting placebos. It's not as crazy as it sounds.

One of the most promising routes is the conditioning work pioneered by Robert Ader, which we touched on in the previous chapter. Again, the expectations of conditioning are automatic, self-generated, and often—though not always—impervious to conscious knowledge. Everybody can know the truth, in other words, and the conditioned response won't change a wit.

With patients' consent, doctors could condition them to expect certain drug effects from a very specific cue, such as a medicinal taste or a pungent odor. Then they could gradually reduce the amount of active drug paired with the cue, letting the conditioned placebo effects pick up the slack. Patients would need fewer drugs and would likely experience fewer side effects, while getting the same therapeutic benefits.

Ader's first chance to test the idea came a little over a decade after his rat experiments, when he learned of a thirteen-year-old girl with severe lupus who suffered from seizures and internal bleeding. In fact, every so often the girl's heart stopped. The girl was quite sensitive to drug side effects, but her pediatrician feared she might not live another year without chemotherapy. The girl's mother was a psychologist who knew Ader's work and contacted him about using a conditioned placebo response to help her daughter endure the treatments. Ader agreed, and the hospital approved the plan on an emergency basis.

Once a month, for three months, the girl sipped cod liver oil and sniffed rose perfume—her choice—while the chemo drug dripped intravenously into her foot. Then came the switcheroo. The cod liver sipping and perfume sniffing continued every month, but the drug was administered only every third month. The girl improved, despite getting only one third the standard dose of chemotherapy. While her health remained delicate, she lived to be twenty-four, outlasting her original prognosis by more than a decade.

Two decades later, Ader finally won approval for a clinical trial of the conditioned placebo response among patients with the skin disease psoriasis. In the 2009 study, Ader and colleagues showed that by pairing active medication with a smelly, yellowish salve, they were able to cut the amount of medication mixed into the salve by half (and later by 75 percent) over several weeks without hurting the patient's recovery.

The success of the psoriasis study allowed Ader to begin work on a larger trial using conditioned placebo effects to cut down the medication required to manage hypertension. Ader died in December 2011, before receiving final approval for that study from the National Institutes of Health.

Still, conditioning is time intensive. It fits most neatly into repeated, chronic care, and it's not always impervious to learning that the active medication has been reduced or is absent. A more direct route toward honest placebo effects would be to have sufficient confidence in our self-healing mechanisms that nobody need pretend that the treatments are "real." Could we have anywhere near the same faith in our ability to self-heal as we have in the medicines that placebos mimic?

When I began writing this book, many of the experts I asked were skeptical. They figured that anybody with actual symptoms who was openly prescribed placebos would toss the dummy pills back in the doctor's face: "You think I'm not really suffering? Choke on 'em!"

In a 2003 study, researchers didn't use the word "placebo" when giving an inert pill to people with irritable bowel syndrome. Still, they didn't say it was medicine, either.

"The agent you have just been given is known to significantly reduce pain in some patients," they told subjects, which was true enough. Indeed, the placebo worked just as well as the real medicine given to other patients.

In another case, in 1965, two psychiatrists actually told a group of psychiatric outpatients they were getting placebos, although they used the term "sugar pill" instead.

"Many people with your kind of condition have been helped by what are sometimes called 'sugar pills,'" they said. "A sugar pill is a pill with no medicine in it at all. I think this pill will help you as it has helped so many others. Are you willing to try this pill?" All but one of the patients did, and again, the pills worked.*

Oddly, nobody followed up on those findings for decades until Kaptchuk and a team of researchers affiliated with his new placebo center finally did. The study, published in 2010, enrolled patients with irritable bowel syndrome. The researchers gave half of these patients no treatment and the other half placebo pills. Before the patients were randomized, they heard a researcher explain that placebo pills had no active medication but did trigger natural healing responses in some people. The placebo group received a three-week supply of blue and maroon gelatin capsules in a bottle labeled "Placebo Pills: Take Twice Daily." And according to a follow-up questionnaire, all but one of the subjects said they believed that the pills they were taking were inert.

In the end, about 60 percent of the patients who knowingly took the placebos reported adequate symptom relief, compared to just over a third of those in the no-treatment group. There were also significant improvements in symptom severity and quality-of-life measures among the placebo group. According to the researchers, the improvements were "comparable with the responder rates in clinical trials of drugs currently used in [treating irritable bowel syndrome]."

The idea of prescribing placebos openly once again highlights the doctor-patient relationship. Keeping placebos covert and hidden may make them more effective overall, but the implication is that they aren't really trusted. Neither is the patient's self-healing mechanisms, which seemingly work only in the shadowy realm of imagination and dissolve in the clear light of truth. While clinicians openly offering placebos do risk insulting the patient, they are also saying, "I trust this treatment, and I trust your ability to help your body heal. You can, too."

Naturally, caveats apply. Authentic expectations tend to transfer

---

* Several of the patients were paranoid and suspected the doctors lied and actually gave them real medication, but the placebos also worked for the others.

best, and placebos are far from a panacea. At the very least, however, open-label placebos offer a new way to study the healing potential of doctors trusting their patients, and patients trusting themselves.

THE POWER OF QUESTIONS

With animal magnetism, Mesmer claimed to have grasped the beating heart of the universe, but the truly marvelous thing about his cures—the power of imagination—undercut his grandiose claims. We've seen the many ways that changing our expectations can bend reality, but the overarching message of their influence is how easily everything we take for granted, everything that seems so solid and permanent, can shift, and potentially even crumble.

The research in this book doesn't promise mind control or unlimited success or freedom from struggle and loss. Its greatest value may be to encourage us to stand back and challenge our assumptions from time to time. We might be bold enough to compare that pricey wine we've grown so attached to with a cheaper bottle in a blind taste test. We might question whether we truly are shy, or not great with numbers, or a poor public speaker. Maybe we'll try to walk a little taller or reinterpret our jitters before a test as extra motivation.

Hopefully, through all this questioning, we will gradually build up more trust in ourselves. It might give us the confidence to take our medicine and know that we can help it do its healing work. It may help us summon the energy for the marathon's final mile or give us one more day of resisting unhealthy temptations.

Even if we don't have all the answers, we can be a little less insistent on separating what we imagine and what's real. Our fast-forward minds are busy making all sorts of self-fulfilling hypotheses about who we are and the world we live in. The least we can do is try the occasional experiment.

ACKNOWLEDGMENTS

This book is the work of many hands and many minds. For starters, I am long overdue in thanking my parents for the support that began many years before this project was a glimmer in my eye. Without their encouragement, I would never have dared.

I benefited greatly from the sage advice of Seth Shulman and Toby Lester as I took my first tentative steps toward writing this book. I'm also grateful to Paul Reyes for the inspiration of his writing and for introducing me to my agent, David Patterson, who has gone above and beyond for me from day one.

Thanks to all the incredible staffers at Current. First and foremost, this book benefited from the insights of three editors. David Moldawer's creative mind got things started, and I am grateful to him for the opportunity. Courtney Young endured the early drafts and helped steer them toward coherence. Niki Papadopoulos took over the editing at a critical stage, reenergized a tired author, and shaped the project into a book. Meanwhile, their excellent assistants, Eric Meyers and Natalie Horbachevsky, guided me through publishing's nitty-gritty. Finally, this book could not have found a better advocate than publicist Tiffany Liao.

Many thanks to my friend Jessica Ullian-Lacount, who took time from her own book writing to read my manuscript and offer astute editorial feedback. My writing was likewise much improved by the superb fact checking of Hilary McLellan.

I am indebted to the many scientists and scholars who let me glom on to their hard work and expertise. Many were as generous with their time as they were with their research, including Joshua Aronson, Orley Ashenfelter, Jeremy Bailenson, Moshe Bar, Roy Baumeister, Chris Beedie, Sian Beilock, Fabrizio Benedetti, Kent Berridge, Geoffroy Berthelot, Sarah Brosnan, Dana Carney, Joshua Clarkson, Jim Coyne, Amy Cuddy, Anna Dreber, Carol Dweck, Jennifer Dysart, Timothy Fong, Mark Francis, Ayelet Gneezy, Rob Gray, Geir Jordet, Ted Kaptchuk, Margaret Kemeny, Irving Kirsch, Ellen Langer, Jakob Linnet, David Mann, Tim Noakes, Michael Norton, Terrance Odean, Lisa Ordóñez, Alvaro Pascual-Leone, William Potter, Antonio Rangel, Alan Reifman, Robert Rosenthal, Nick Rule, Laurie Santos, Daniel Schacter, Geoffrey Schoenbaum, Wolfram Schultz, Tali Sharot, Mel Slater, Jon Stoessl, Jack Tsao, Tor Wager, John Waller, Roman Weil, Rhona Weinstein, Timothy Wilson, Kielan Yarrow, Martin Zack, and Jon-Kar Zubieta.

Robert Ader, the pioneer of psychoneuroimmunology, spoke to me about his research on conditioned placebos by phone and also invited me over to his house for a lengthy follow-up talk, despite his failing health. Sadly, he passed away in December 2011 before I could thank him properly.

Anne Harrington introduced me to Franz Anton Mesmer's life and works in her excellent book, *The Cure Within*. Dan Moerman's *Meaning, Medicine and the "Placebo Effect"* was equally thought-provoking, and wickedly funny. My description of J. S. G. Boggs is based on Lawrence Weschler's delightful book, *Boggs: A Comedy of Values*.

I received just as much help from sources beyond the library and the lab. Jeri B.'s eloquent account of her gambling problems gave me unique insights into the addicted mind. Jeri was also good enough to ask her Gamblers Anonymous meeting if I could join them one evening, and they were kind enough to permit it. Thanks also to Fernando Bermudez and his wife, Crystal, for bringing me into their lives.

While researching this book, I was delighted to meet two guys nicknamed "Pooch." Both are class acts. Lieutenant Commander John Pucillo, who lost a leg in Iraq, trusted me with his remarkable story. Meanwhile, G. M. Pucilowski, the head wine judge at the California State Fair, not only let me pester him on the busiest morning of his year, he also let me eavesdrop on his judges.

I am also grateful to Bob Hodgson and his wife, Judy, for hosting me at the beautiful Fieldbrook Winery. Another highlight of that trip was spending time with Robin Goldstein and Alexis Herschkowitsch, foodie phenoms and coeditors of the *Fearless Critic* restaurant guides.

Robin and Alexis inspired me to host my own blind wine tasting. I promised everyone who participated and followed my silly rules that the evening would be off the record; they know who they are, and I thank them all.

I save my biggest thank-you for my wife, Meaghan. No matter how tough her own workday was, Meaghan always came home ready to hear about my progress (or lack thereof). It was the best part of my day. Her enthusiasm for these conversations never flagged, even though I told her about every little snag and snafu, and not enough about the joy and the gratitude I felt for the privilege of doing this work and the fun of sharing it with my best friend.

NOTES

PRELUDE: A MARVELOUS THING

1 **a healer named Franz Anton Mesmer:** Benjamin Franklin et al., *Report of Dr. Franklin and other commissioners charged by the King of France with the examination of the animal magnetism as practiced at Paris,* trans. H. Perkins (Philadelphia, 1831), 2–44. Alfred Binet and Charles Féré, *Animal Magnetism* (New York: D. Appleton, 1894), 1–32. Anne Harrington, *The Cure Within* (New York: W. W. Norton, 2008), 39–53.

9 **flipping the eye chart:** Ellen Langer et al., "Believing Is Seeing: Using Mindfulness (Mindfully) to Improve Visual Acuity, *Psychological Science* 18:2 (2007): 165–71.

9 **sugar pills heal ulcers in French patients but not in Brazilians:** Daniel Moerman, *Meaning, Medicine and the "Placebo Effect"* (Cambridge, UK: Cambridge University Press, 2002), 80–81.

9 **people feel full after eating imaginary cheese:** Carey Morewedge, Young Eun-Huh, and Joachim Vosgerau, "Thought for Food: Imagined Consumption Reduces Actual Consumption," *Science* 330:6010 (December 2010): 1530–33.

9 **wearing knockoff sunglasses can turn people into cheaters:** Francesca Gino, Michael Norton, and Dan Ariely, "The Counterfeit Self: The Deceptive Costs of Faking It," *Psychological Science* 21:5 (2010): 712–20.

9 **blurry vision can help cricket batters:** David Mann, Bruce Abernathy, and Damian Farrow, "Visual Information Underpinning Skilled Anticipation: The Effect of Blur on a Coupled and Uncoupled In Situ Anticipatory Response," *Attention, Perception & Psychophysics* 72:5 (2010): 1317–26.

9 **reviewing their résumés on heavier clipboards:** Joshua Ackerman, Christopher Nocera, and John Bargh, "Incidental Haptic Sensations Influence Social Judgments and Decisions," *Science* 328:5986 (June 2010): 1712–15.

CHAPTER 1: RUNNING ON EMPTY

13 **On a breezy day in May 1954:** Roger Bannister, *The Four-Minute Mile,* rev. ed. (Guilford, CT: Lyons Press, 2004), 171.

14 **Consider how much better the "best" is now:** High school track and field

records accessed online at *Track & Field News* (May 30, 2012), http://www
.trackandfieldnews.com/records/outdoor/men/hs_outdoor_records.html.

14 **"My body had long since exhausted all its energy":** Bannister, *Four-Minute Mile*, 172.

15 **extrapolating the trends in world record times:** Andrew J. Tatem et al., "Momentous Sprint at the 2156 Olympics?," *Nature* 431 (September 30, 2004): 525.

15 **"If you just extrapolate the data":** Author interview, April 20, 2011.

15 **Actually, Berthelot seems to know fairly precisely:** Geoffroy Berthelot et al., "The Citius End: World Records Progression Announces the Completion of a Brief Ultra-Physiological Quest," *PLoS ONE* 3:2 (February 2008): e1552.

15 **top ten performances each year:** Geoffroy Berthelot et al., "Athlete Atypicity on the Edge of Human Achievement: Performances Stagnate After the Last Peak, in 1988," *PLoS ONE* 5:1 (January 2010): e8800.

15 **some world beaters likely cheated:** Nour El Helou et al., "Tour de France, Giro, Vuelta, and Classic European Races Show a Unique Progression of Road Cycling Speed in the Last 20 Years," *Journal of Sports Sciences* 28:7 (May 14, 2010): 789–96.

16 **a federal grand jury:** Ian Austen, "Inquiry on Lance Armstrong Ends with No Charges," *New York Times*, February 3, 2012.

16 **nearly all of the cyclists who finished second and third:** "Teammate: Lance Armstrong Cheated," *60 Minutes*, CBS (May 19, 2011).

17 **authorized the introduction of angled starting blocks:** Geoffroy Berthelot et al., "Technology & Swimming: 3 Steps Beyond Physiology," *Materials Today* 13:11 (November 2010): 46–51.

18 **"But you're just resampling the curve":** Author interview, April 20, 2011.

18 **"If there are no more world records":** Ibid.

19 **"When the oxygen supply becomes inadequate":** A. V. Hill, C. H. N. Long, and H. Lupton, "Muscular Exercise, Lactic Acid and the Supply and Utilization of Oxygen: Parts VII–VIII," *Proceedings of the Royal Society of London*, Series B, Containing Papers of a Biological Character 97 (1924): 144–76.

20 **the theory of "teleoanticipation":** H. V. Ulmer, "Concept of an Extracellular Regulation of Muscular Metabolic Rate During Heavy Exercise in Humans by Psychophysiological Feedback," *Experientia* 52 (1996): 416–20.

20 **expert cyclists ride a stationary bike:** Ross Tucker et al., "The Rate of Heat Storage Mediates an Anticipatory Reduction in Exercise Intensity During Cycling at a Fixed Rating of Perceived Exertion," *The Journal of Physiology* 574 (August 1, 2006): 905–15.

21 **energy drinks aren't what you think:** E. S. Chambers, M. W. Bridge, and D. A. Jones, "Carbohydrate Sensing in the Human Mouth: Effects on Exercise Performance and Brain Activity," *The Journal of Physiology* 587 (April 15, 2009): 1779–94.

22 **intravenously given either a carbohydrate solution or a placebo:** James M. Carter, Asker E. Jeukendrup, and David A. Jones, "The Effect of Carbohydrate Mouth Rinse on 1-h Cycle Time Trial Performance," *Medicine & Science in Sports & Exercise* 36:12 (December 2004): 2107–11.

22 **admitted to doctoring stopwatches:** "Coach Gallagher," *The Sports Factor,* ABC Radio National (January 18, 2002).

23 **This ruse may backfire:** Martin E. P. Seligman et al., "Explanatory Style as a Mechanism of Disappointing Athletic Performance," *Psychological Science* 1:2 (March 1990): 143–46.

23 **In the first of these studies:** Gideon Ariel and William Saville, "Anabolic Steroids: The Physiological Effects of Placebos," *Medicine & Science in Sports & Exercise* 4:2 (Summer 1972): 124–26.

23 **follow-ups on the weight-lifting research:** R. Gary Ness and Robert W. Patton, "The Effects of Beliefs on Maximum Weight-Lifting Performance," *Cognitive Therapy and Research* 3:2 (1979): 205–11. See also: P. A. Fitzsimmons et al., "Does Self-Efficacy Predict Performance in Experienced Weightlifters?," *Research Quarterly for Exercise and Sport* 62:4 (1991): 424–31, and C. N. Maganaris, D. Collins, and M. Sharp, "Expectancy Effects and Strength Training: Do Steroids Make a Difference?," *Sport Psychologist* 14:3 (2000): 272–78.

24 **evidence that you can think yourself stronger:** Vinoth K. Ranganathan, "From Mental Power to Muscle Power—Gaining Strength by Using the Mind," *Neuropsychologia* 42 (2004): 944–56. See also: Vlodek Siemionow et al., "Relationship Between Motor Activity-Related Cortical Potential and Voluntary Muscle Activation," *Experimental Brain Research* 133 (2000) 303–11, and Florent Lebon, Christian Collet, and Aymerie Guillot, "Benefits of Motor Imagery Training on Muscle Strength," *Journal of Strength & Conditioning Research* 24:6 (June 2010): 1680–87.

24 **"You must be strong willed to do it":** Author interview, October 12, 2010.

24 **researchers tested the Power Balance bracelet:** John Porcari et al., "Can the Power Balance Bracelet Improve Balance, Flexibility, Strength, and Power?," *Journal of Sports Science and Medicine* 10 (2011): 230–31. Mary Wiley, "The Placebo Effect of the Power Balance Band on Muscle Strength, Agility, Power, and RPE," Research Poster, Exercise Science Laboratories, University of Texas, Arlington (February 21, 2012).

24 **according to the bracelet's makers:** Quoted in Porcari et al.

25 **a federal court hit the bracelet's makers with a $57 million judgment:** Jessica Misener, "Power Balance Bracelet Company Hit with $57 Million Settlement, Expected to Go Bankrupt," *Huffington Post* (November 21, 2011), http://www.huffingtonpost.com/2011/11/21/power-bracelets-lawsuit_n_1105559.html.

25 **two different placebo doses of caffeine:** Chris Beedie et al., "Placebo Effect of Caffeine in Cycling Performance," *Medicine & Science in Sports & Exercise* 38:12 (2006): 2159–64.

25 **Researchers gave weight lifters a placebo dose:** Antonella Pollo, Elisa Carlino, and Fabrizio Benedetti, "The Top-Down Influence of Ergogenic Placebos on Muscle Work and Fatigue," *European Journal of Neuroscience* 28 (2008): 379–88.

26 **"you remove anxiety and people just perform better":** Author interview, April 15, 2011.

26 **raise and lower the performance of cyclists:** Chris Beedie et al., "Positive and Negative Placebo Effects Resulting from the Deceptive Administration

of an Ergogenic Aid," *International Journal of Sport* 17:3 (June 2007): 259–69.

26 **omens and good luck charms:** Lysann Damisch et al., "Keep Your Fingers Crossed! How Superstition Improves Performance," *Psychological Science* 21:7 (2010): 1014–20.

26 **AND THIS HOW YOU DO ME!!!!!:** Tim Graham, "Whirl Interrupted: Steve Johnson Drops the Ball," ESPN.com (November 28, 2010), http://espn.go .com/blog/afceast/post/_/id/22378/whirl-interrupted-steve-johnson-drops-ball.

27 **a friendly pain-tolerance competition:** Fabrizio Benedetti, Antonella Pollo, and Luana Colloca, "Opioid-Mediated Placebo Responses Boost Pain Endurance and Physical Performance: Is It Doping in Sport Competitions?," *The Journal of Neuroscience* 27:44 (October 31, 2007): 11934–39.

CHAPTER 2: IN THE ZONE

29 **85 percent of on-target penalty shots score:** Michael Bar-Eli and Ofer Azar, "Penalty Kicks in Soccer: An Empirical Analysis of Shooting Strategies and Goalkeepers' Preferences," *Soccer Society* 10:2 (2009): 183–91.

32 **"The irony is that I'm not that interested in penalties":** Author interview, October 30, 2010.

33 **"Someone will get the bullet":** Quoted in Timothy Farrell, "Attacker Defender Goalkeeper: A New Alternative to the Penalty Kick Shootout" (2008), http://www.theadgalternative.com/PDFS/ADG_EN.pdf.

33 **telltale behaviors of players who miss critical penalties:** Geir Jordet and Esther Hartman, "Avoidance Motivation and Choking Under Pressure in Soccer Penalty Shootouts," *Journal of Sport and Exercise Psychology* 30 (2008): 452–59.

33 **kryptonite for soccer superstars:** Geir Jordet, "When Superstars Flop: Public Status and Choking Under Pressure in International Soccer Penalty Shootouts," *Journal of Applied Sport Psychology* 21:2 (April 2009): 125–30.

34 **"Terry's their superstar":** Author interview, October 30, 2010.

35 **The higher a team's overall status:** Geir Jordet, "Why Do English Players Fail in Soccer Penalty Shootouts? A Study of Team Status, Self-Regulation, and Choking Under Pressure," *Journal of Sports Sciences* 27:3 (January 2009): 97–106.

36 **"inexorable sense of expectation":** James Corbett, *England Expects: A History of the England Football Team* (London: Aurum Press, 2006), x.

36 **"It lurks in your mind somewhere":** Ashley Cole, *My Defence: Winning, Losing, Scandals and the Drama of Germany 2006* (London: Headline Book Publishing, 2006): 248.

36 **based on their team shootout history:** Geir Jordet, Esther Hartman, and Pieter Jelle, "Team History and Choking Under Pressure in Major Soccer Penalty Shootouts," *British Journal of Psychology* 103:2 (May 2011): 268–83.

37 **a potential home field *disadvantage*:** Roy Baumeister and Andrew Steinhilber, "Paradoxical Effects of Supportive Audiences on Performance Under

Pressure: The Home Field Disadvantage in Sports Championships," *Journal of Personality and Social Psychology* 47 (1984): 85–93.

38 **the evidence of a home choke had disappeared:** Barry Schlenker et al., "Where Is the Home Choke?," *Journal of Personality and Social Psychology* 68 (1995): 649–52.

38 **a 2010 meta-analysis spanning ten sports:** Jeremy Jamieson, "The Home Field Advantage in Athletics: A Meta-Analysis," *Journal of Applied Social Psychology* 40:7 (2010): 1819–48.

38 **Baumeister questioned the methodology of home choke critics:** Roy Baumeister, "Disputing the Effects of Championship Pressures and Home Audiences," *Journal of Personality and Social Psychology* 68:4 (1995): 644–48.

38 **the *potential* to endanger performance:** Jennifer Butler and Roy Baumeister, "The Trouble with Friendly Faces: Skilled Performance with a Supportive Audience," *Journal of Personality and Social Psychology* 75:5 (1998): 1213–30.

39 **According to Baumeister, choking is worse than expected performance:** Roy Baumeister, "Choking Under Pressure: Self-Consciousness and Paradoxical Effects of Incentives on Skillful Performance," *Journal of Personality and Social Psychology* 46:3 (1984): 610–20.

39 **this definition is too mild:** Denise Hill et al., "A Re-examination of Choking in Sport," *European Journal of Sport Science* 9:4 (2009): 203–12. Denise Hill et al., "Choking in Sport: A Review," *International Review of Sport and Exercise Psychology* 3:1 (2010): 24–39.

40 **reaction time by pro or Joe alike:** David Epstein, "It's All About Anticipation," *Sports Illustrated,* August 8, 2011: 54.

40 **highly skilled athletes outpredict novices:** Salvatore Aglioti et al.,"Action Anticipation and Motor Resonance in Elite Basketball Players," *Nature Neuroscience* 11:9 (September 2008): 1109–16.

41 **"common coding" theory:** Wolfgang Prinz, "Perception and Action Planning," *European Journal of Cognitive Science* 9:2 (1997): 129–54.

41 **the monkey reached for a peanut:** Vittorio Gallese et al., "Action Recognition in the Premotor Cortex," *Brain* 119:2 (1996): 593–609.

41 **they collectively represent "action ideas":** Günther Knoblich and Rüdiger Flach, "Predicting the Effects of Actions: Interactions of Perception and Action," *Psychological Science* 12:6 (2001): 467–72. Daniel Wolpert and J. Randall Flanagan, "Motor Prediction," *Current Biology* 11:18 (2001): R729–R732. Daniel Wolpert, Kenji Doya, and Mitsuo Kawato, "A Unifying Computational Framework for Motor Control and Social Interaction," *Philosophical Transactions of the Royal Society* 358:1431 (March 2003): 593–602. Cosimo Ugesi et al., "Simulating the Future of Actions in the Human Corticospinal System," *Cerebral Cortex* 20:11 (2010): 2511–21.

41 **expert and novice badminton players:** Michael Wright et al., "Functional MRI Reveals Expert-Novice Differences During Sport-Related Anticipation," *NeuroReport* 21 (2010): 94–98.

41 **direct evidence for human mirror neurons:** Roy Mukamel et al., "Single-Neuron Responses in Humans During Execution and Observation of Actions," *Current Biology* 20:8 (April 2010): 750–56.

42 **Gray set up a home plate in his lab:** Rob Gray, Sian Beilock, and Thomas Carr, "'As Soon as the Bat Met the Ball, I Knew It Was Gone': Outcome Prediction, Hindsight Bias, and the Representation and Control of Action in Expert and Novice Baseball Players," *Psychonomic Society* 14:4 (2007): 669–75.

43 **"when the expert players went through a period of misses":** Author interview, April 7, 2011.

43 **sports medicine and coaching conference:** David Mann, Bruce Abernathy, and Damian Farrow, "A Novel Training Tool for Batters to 'Watch the Ball,'" Conference of Science, Medicine & Coaching in Cricket (Canberra, Australia, June 1–3, 2010).

44 **blurry vision:** David Mann, Bruce Abernathy, and Damian Farrow, "The Resilience of Natural Interceptive Actions to Refractive Blur," *Human Movement Science* 29:3 (2010): 386–400.

44 **wrapped up in a player's practiced reactions:** David Mann, Bruce Abernathy, and Damian Farrow, "Action Specificity Increases Anticipatory Performance and the Expert Advantage in Natural Interceptive Tasks," *Acta Psychologica* 135 (2010): 17–23. David Mann, Bruce Abernathy, and Damian Farrow, "Visual Information Underpinning Skilled Anticipation: The Effect of Blur on a Coupled and Uncoupled In Situ Anticipatory Response," *Attention, Perception & Psychophysics* 72:5 (2010): 1317–26.

44 **study of blur on tennis players:** Robin Jackson, Bruce Abernathy, and Simon Wernhart, "Sensitivity to Fine-Grained and Coarse Visual Information: The Effect of Blurring on Anticipation Skill," *International Journal of Sport Psychology* 40 (2009): 461–75.

45 **"point-light videos":** Michael Wright et al., "Cortical fMRI Activation to Opponents' Body Kinematics in Sport-Related Anticipation: Expert-Novice Differences with Normal and Point-Light Video," *Neuroscience Letters* 21:2 (2011): 94–98.

45 **"They use it as a training tool":** Author interview, April 5, 2011.

46 **slowing things down can make things worse:** Sian Beilock et al., "When Does Haste Make Waste? Speed-Accuracy Tradeoff, Skill Level, and the Tools of the Trade," *Journal of Experimental Psychology* 14:4 (2008): 340–52.

46 **warded off choking with a little distraction:** Robin Thomas et al., "Choking Under Pressure: Multiple Routes to Skill Failure," *Journal of Experimental Psychology* 140:3 (2011): 390–406. Christopher Mesagno, Daryl Marchant, and Tony Morris, "Alleviating Choking: The Sounds of Distraction," *Journal of Applied Sport Psychology* 21:2 (April 2009): 131–47.

47 **One study of free throws:** Chris Lonsdale and Jimmy Tam, "On the Temporal and Behavioural Consistency of Pre-Performance Routines: An Intra-Individual Analysis of Elite Basketball Players' Free Throw Shooting Accuracy," *Journal of Sports Sciences* 26:3 (October 17, 2007): 259–66.

47 **This "implicit learning" approach:** Gabriele Wulf, "Directing Attention to Movement Effects Enhances Learning: A Review," *Psychonomic Bulletin & Review* 8:4 (2001): 648–60.

47 **change our expectations about our ability to perform under pressure:** Brad McKay, Rebecca Lewthwaite, and Gabriele Wulf, "Enhanced Expectancies Improve Performance Under Pressure," *Frontiers in Psychology* 3:8 (2012).

48 **reinterpret symptoms of anxiety:** Yet to be published research by sports psychologist Andrew Lane, University of Wolverhampton (UK), described during author interview on March 16, 2012.

48 **ratchet up anxiety during practice:** Raôul Oudejans and J. Rob Pijpers, "Training with Anxiety Has a Positive Effect on Expert Perceptual-Motor Performance Under Pressure," *The Quarterly Journal of Experimental Psychology* 62:8 (2008): 1631–47. Raôul Oudejans and J. Rob Pijpers, "Training with Mild Anxiety May Prevent Choking Under Higher Levels of Anxiety," *Psychology of Sport and Exercise* 11 (2010): 44–50.

49 **"but the coaches are the biggest escape artists of all":** Author interview, October 30, 2010.

49 **basketball shooters can get "hot":** Thomas Gilovich, Robert Vallone, and Amos Tversky, "The Hot Hand in Basketball: On the Misperception of Random Sequences," *Cognitive Psychology* 17 (1985): 295-314.

51 **statistical support for the hot hand is "considerably limited":** Michael Bar-Eli, Simcha Avugos, and Markus Raab, "Twenty Years of 'Hot Hand' Research: Review and Critique," *Psychology of Sport and Exercise* 7 (2006): 525–53.

51 **another found one in volleyball:** Markus Raab, Bartosz Gula, and Gerd Gigerenzer, "The Hot Hand Exists and Is Used for Allocation Decisions," *Journal of Experimental Psychology* 18:1 (March 2012): 81–94.

52 **the skeptics don't simply argue:** Steven Hales, "An Epistemologist Looks at the Hot Hand in Sports," *Journal of the Philosophy of Sport* 26 (1999): 79–87.

53 **"positive or negative vicarious experiences":** Jordet, Hartman, and Jelle, "Team History and Choking Under Pressure in Major Soccer Penalty Shootouts," *British Journal of Psychology* 103:2 (May 2012): 268–283.

53 **"your body simply doesn't belong to you":** Michael Owen, *Off the Record* (London: HarperCollins, 2005), 98.

CHAPTER 3: THE BIG WANT

57 **"I was there the day Foxwoods opened":** Author interview, November 3, 2010.

58 **The world is fat:** "Obesity and the Economics of Prevention: Fit Not Fat," Organisation for Economic Co-operation and Development, September 23, 2010, http://www.oecd.org/document/31/0,3746,en_2649_33929_45999775_1_1_1_1,00.html#Executive_Summary.

59 **a novel way to slim us down:** Daniel Bernstein et al., "False Beliefs About Fattening Foods Can Have Healthy Consequences," *PNAS* 102:39 (September 2005): 13724–31.

60 **Even monkeys crave discovery:** Ethan Bromberg-Martin and Okihide Hikosaka, "Midbrain Dopamine Neurons Signal Preference for Advance Information about Upcoming Rewards," *Neuron* 63 (July 2009): 119–26.

60 **the brains of self-reported dieters:** Todd Hare et al., "Dissociating the Role of the Orbitofrontal Cortex and the Striatum in the Computation of Goal Values and Prediction Errors," *The Journal of Neuroscience* 28:22 (May 2008): 5623–30.

62 consuming a mix of real calories and placebo calories: Jeffrey Brunstrom et al., "'Expected Satiety' Changes Hunger and Fullness in the Inter-Meal Interval," *Appetite* 56 (2011): 310–15.

62 placebo calories can have real effects: Alia Crum et al., "Mind over Milkshakes: Mindsets, Not Just Nutrients, Determine Ghrelin Response," *Health Psychology* 30:4 (July 2011): 424–29.

63 dieters often overeat a food they believe is lower in fat: Brian Wansink and Pierre Chandon, "Can 'Low-Fat' Nutrition Labels Lead to Obesity?," *Journal of Marketing Research* 43 (November 2006): 605–17.

63 imagine doing two simple tasks repeatedly: Carey Morewedge, Young Eun-Huh, and Joachim Vosgerau, "Thought for Food: Imagined Consumption Reduces Actual Consumption," *Science* 330:6010 (December 2010): 1530–33.

64 watch a sitcom with or without commercials: Leif Nelson, Tom Meyvis, and Jeff Galak, "Enhancing the Television-Viewing Experience Through Commercial Interruptions," *Journal of Consumer Research* 36 (August 2009): 160–72.

64 Underestimating adaptation: Daniel Gilbert and Timothy Wilson, "Miswanting: Some Problems in the Forecasting of Future Affective States," in *Feeling and Thinking: The Role of Affect in Social Cognition*, ed. J. Forgas (Cambridge: Cambridge University Press, 2000), 178–97.

65 wealth brings happiness only up to a point: Daniel Kahneman et al., "Would You Be Happier If You Were Richer? A Focusing Illusion," *Science* 312 (2006): 1908–10.

65 a Gallup survey of one thousand Americans: Daniel Kahneman and Angus Deaton, "High Income Improves Evaluation of Life but Not Emotional Well-Being," *PNAS* 107:38 (2010): 16489–93.

65 Richard Easterlin replicated results he first published in the 1970s: Richard Easterlin et al., "The Happiness-Income Paradox Revisited," *PNAS* 107:52 (2010): 22463–68. Richard Easterlin, "Does Money Buy Happiness," *The Public Interest* (Winter 1973): 3–10.

65 Otto Tinklepaugh found: Otto Tinklepaugh, "An Experimental Study of Representative Factors in Monkeys," *Journal of Comparative Psychology* 8:3 (June 1928): 197–36.

66 playing a Pac-Man-esque video game: Dean Mobbs et al., "Choking on the Money: Reward-Based Performance Decrements Are Associated with Midbrain Activity," *Psychological Science* 20:8 (August 2009): 955–62.

67 an ambitious goal for the number of words: Maurice Schweitzer, Lisa Ordóñez, and Bambi Douma, "Goal Setting as a Motivator of Unethical Behavior," *Academy of Management Journal* 47:3 (2004): 422–32.

67 intrinsic motivators can backfire on us: Iris Mauss et al., "Can Seeking Happiness Make People Unhappy? Paradoxical Effects of Valuing Happiness," *Emotion* 11:4 (August 2011): 807–15.

69 It is the brain's anticipation juice: Kent Berridge, "The Debate Over Dopamine's Role in Reward: The Case for Incentive Salience," *Psychopharmacology* 191 (2007): 391–431. Kent Berridge, Terry Robinson, and J. Wayne Aldridge, "Dissecting Components of Reward: 'Liking,' 'Wanting,' and

Learning," *Current Opinion in Pharmacology* 9:1 (February 2009): 65–73. Kent Berridge and J. Wayne Aldridge, "Decision Utility, the Brain, and Pursuit of Hedonic Goals," *Social Cognition* 26:5 (2008) 621–46. Morten L. Kringelbach, "The Human Orbitofrontal Cortex: Linking Reward to Hedonic Experience," *Nature Reviews* 6 (September 2005): 691–702. Morten Kringelbach and Kent Berridge, "Towards a Functional Neuroanatomy of Pleasure and Happiness," *Trends in Cognitive Sciences* 13:11 (2009): 479–87.

69 **About 17 percent of them develop an impulse control disorder:** Christina Rabinak and Melissa Nirenberg, "Dopamine Agonist Withdrawal Syndrome in Parkinson Disease," *Archives of Neurology* 67:1 (January 2010): 58–63.

70 **hypersensitive to a jackpot's allure:** Ruth J. van Holst et al., "Distorted Expectancy Coding in Problem Gambling: Is the Addictive in the Anticipation?," *Biological Psychiatry* 71:8 (April 2012): 741–48.

70 **"In my mind, the disease somehow became its own cure":** Author interview, November 3, 2010.

71 **a randomly generated series of squares and circles:** Scott Huettel, Peter Mack, and Gregory McCarthy, "Perceiving Patterns in Random Series: Dynamic Processing of Sequence in Prefrontal Cortex," *Nature Neuroscience* 5:5 (2002): 485–90.

71 **near-miss expectations in frequent gamblers:** Luke Clark, "Decision-Making During Gambling: An Integration of Cognitive and Psychobiological Approaches," *Philosophical Transactions of the Royal Society* 365 (2010): 319–30.

72 **"It's the anticipation that you've got a method this time":** Author interview, November 3, 2010.

72 **uncertainty intensifies emotional reactions:** Yoav Bar-Anan, Timothy Wilson, and Daniel Gilbert, "The Feeling of Uncertainty Intensifies Affective Reactions," *Emotion* 9:1 (February 2009): 123–27.

72 **"Dopamine engaging motivation is not a simple mechanistic process":** Author interview, November 11, 2010.

73 **less than 10 percent of gamblers who join the program:** Ruth Stewart and R. Lain Brown, "An Outcome Study of Gamblers Anonymous," *British Journal of Psychiatry* 152 (February 1988): 284–88.

74 **"the dreamworld of the compulsive gambler":** Gamblers Anonymous, *Yellow Book*, revised (2009): 11.

74 **a failed stockbroker named Bill Wilson:** Brendan Koerner, "Secret of AA: After 75 Years, We Don't Know How It Works," *Wired* 18:7 (July 2010).

75 **"The meetings are amazing, and I don't know how they work":** Author interview, November 3, 2010.

CHAPTER 4: ACCOUNTING FOR TASTE

78 **"Trade morality has come to such a pass":** H. Warner Allen, *The Romance of Wine* (New York: Dover, 1971), 243.

78 **eighteenth-century Château Lafite:** Patrick Radden Keefe, "The Jefferson Bottles," *The New Yorker*, September 3, 2007, 106–17.

78 Tesco sold bottles of counterfeit Louis Jadot Pouilly-Fuissé: Jane Hamilton, "You Plonkers," *The Sun* (London), June 21, 2010.

78 hundreds of bottles of fake Jacob's Creek wine: Victoria Moore, "Fake Wines: Don't Keep Concerns Bottled Up," *Telegraph* (London), April 7, 2011.

79 fooled French sommeliers: Frédéric Brochet, "Chemical Object Representation in the Field of Consciousness," Working Paper, General Oenology Laboratory, Bordeaux School of Oenology, France, 2001.

79 According to one flavor textbook: Henk Maarse, ed., *Volatile Compounds in Foods and Beverages* (New York: Marcel Dekker, 1991), 30. See also: Raffi Khatchdourian, "The Taste Makers," *The New Yorker*, November 23, 2009, 86–99.

80 "cheddar cheese" or "body odor": Ivan de Araujo et al., "Cognitive Modulation of Olfactory Processing," *Neuron* 46:4 (May 2005): 671–79.

80 our brains anticipate smells: Christina Zelano, Aprajita Mohanty, and Jay Gottfried, "Olfactory Predictive Codes and Stimulus Templates in Piriform Cortex," *Neuron* 72:1 (October 2011): 178–87.

80 do we dislike what we expect to dislike?: Leonard Lee, Shane Frederick, and Dan Ariely, "Try It, You'll Like It: The Influence of Expectation, Consumption, and Revelation on Preferences for Beer," *Psychological Science* 17:12 (December 2006): 1054–58.

81 In one early study of brand power: Ralph Allison and Kenneth Uhl, "Influence of Beer Brand Identification on Taste Perception," *Journal of Marketing Research* 1:3 (1964): 36–39.

82 her "monkeynomics" research: M. Keith Chen, Venkat Lakshminarayanan, and Laurie Santos, "How Basic Are Behavioral Biases? Evidence from Capuchin Monkey Trading Behavior," *Journal of Political Economy* 114:3 (2006): 517–37.

82 "They understand what price means": Author interview, January 17, 2012.

83 taste five Cabernets while in a brain scanner: Hilke Plassmann et al., "Marketing Actions Can Modulate Neural Representations of Experienced Pleasantness," *PNAS* 105:3 (January 2008): 1050–54.

84 a selection of *New Yorker* cartoons: Timothy Wilson et al., "Preferences as Expectation-Driven Inferences: Effects of Affective Expectations on Affective Experience," *Journal of Personality and Social Psychology* 56:4 (1989): 519–30.

86 "Blind Tasting Manifesto": Robin Goldstein, "The Blind Tasting Manifesto," in Robin Goldstein, Alexis Herschkowitsch, and Tyce Walters, eds., *The Wine Trials 2011* (New York: Fearless Critic Media, 2011), 5–70.

86 more than six thousand blind tastings: Robin Goldstein et al., "Do More Expensive Wines Taste Better? Evidence from a Large Sample of U.S. Blind Tastings," *Journal of Wine Economics* 3:1 (2008): 1–10.

87 "I can make or break a wine": "An Hour About Wine with Critic Robert Parker," *Charlie Rose*, PBS (April 24, 2001). Viewed online (May 30, 2012), http://www.charlierose.com/view/interview/3151.

87 "smells barnyardy and tastes decayed": Robin Goldstein, "What Does It

Take to Get a Wine Spectator Award of Excellence?" *Blind Taste* (August 15, 2008), http://blindtaste.com/2008/08/15/what-does-it-take-to-get-a-wine-spectator-award-of-excellence/.

88   **descriptions of both wines written by the same critic:** Roman Weil, "Debunking Critics' Wine Words: Can Amateurs Distinguish the Smell of Asphalt from the Taste of Cherries?," *Journal of Wine Economics* 2:2 (2007): 136–44.

88   **culled wine descriptors from top critics:** Richard Quandt, "On Wine Bullshit: Some New Software," *Journal of Wine Economics* 2:2 (2007): 129–35.

89   **In 2011, Goldstein collaborated with economists:** Orley Ashenfelter, Robin Goldstein, and Craig Riddel, "Do Expert Ratings Measure Quality?: The Case of Restaurant Wine Lists," American Association of Wine Economists, 4th annual conference (Davis, CA), June 2010.

89   **superimposed their results onto a 100-point rating system:** Goldstein et al., "Do More Expensive Wines Taste Better?,"4.

89   **The Center for Sensory Perception and Behavior:** Robin Goldstein, "The Culinary Institute of America Center for Sensory Perception and Behavioral Economics," Draft Proposal, February 2011, 4.

90   **"Ours is a more modest project":** Author interview, June 1, 2011.

90   **"a dangerous path toward a bland convergence":** Goldstein, "The Blind Tasting Manifesto," 45.

91   **"There's a huge amount of bullshit in the wine world":** Author interview, June 1, 2011.

93   **This did nothing to improve consistency:** Robert Hodgson, "An Examination of Judge Reliability at a Major U.S. Wine Competition," *Journal of Wine Economics* 3:2 (2008): 105–13.

93   **"Are Wine Competitions a Hoax?":** Interview with California State Fair chief wine judge G. M. "Pooch" Pucilowski, February 2009, produced by California Exposition & State Fair News Bureau, http://www.youtube.com/watch?v=qQoy4bX_foM (accessed May 2, 2012).

94   **"Award winners truly are the best of the best!":** This quote is no longer on the California State Fair Web site, but it's archived online in several places, such as: http://classicwinesofcalifornia.com/images/CA_St_Fair_MP_Mrlt_06_91_Pts.pdf

94   **"their integrity is above reproach":** Author interview, May 31, 2011.

94   **"It's about how an ordinary person, or a wine buyer, would approach wine":** Ibid.

95   **"I tell people, just drink what you like":** Author interview, June 1, 2011.

96   **"It is vital for professional wine judges":** Maynard Amerine and Edward Roessler, *Wines: Their Sensory Evaluation* (New York: W. H. Freeman, 1976), 14.

96   **In a nutshell, the new system failed:** Robert Hodgson, "How to Improve Wine Judge Consistency Using the ABS Matrix," American Association of Wine Economists, 5th annual conference (Bolzano, Italy), June 23, 2011.

96   **"This is a work in progress":** Author interview, June 17, 2011.

97   **"Any number of conscious or unconscious influences":** Jeffrey Postman,

"Blind Tasting," Letter to the Editor, *Journal of Wine Economics* 5:1 (2010): 184–87.

97 **"It is the sensory quality of the wine in the glass"**: Amerine and Roessler, *Wines*, 7.

97 **"Trying to eliminate all external factors"**: Eric Asimov, "Judging the Judging," "Diner's Journal: Notes on Eating, Drinking, and Cooking," NYTimes .com, September 17, 2007.

98 **wines compiled on www.cellartracker.com**: Omer Gokcekus and Dennis Nottebaum, "The Buyer's Dilemma: Whose Rating Should a Wine Drinker Pay Attention To?," American Association of Wine Economists, Working Paper No. 91, September 2011.

98 **"contrast effect" in wine tasters' reactions to prices**: Ayelet Gneezy and Uri Gneezy, "Price-Based Expectations," Behavioral Decision Research and Management conference (Pittsburgh, PA), June 11, 2010.

99 **"You have to make sure that you at least live up to the threshold of expectations"**: Author interview, April 25, 2011.

101 **"Even if you don't want to take the time"**: Author interview, June 1, 2011.

CHAPTER 5: *E PLURIBUS UNUM*

102 **constables barged into a London art gallery**: Lawrence Weschler, *Boggs: A Comedy of Values* (Chicago: University of Chicago Press, 1999), 5.

103 **Bitcoin that has no physical form**: Benjamin Wallace, "Bitcoin's Rise and Fall," *Wired* 19:12 (November 23, 2011): 99–113.

104 **If you have a morbid sense of humor**: David Lereah, *Why the Real Estate Boom Will Not Bust—And How You Can Profit from It* (New York: Crown Business, 2005), http://www.amazon.com/Real-Estate-Boom-Will-Bust/dp/0385514352/ref=sr_1_3?ie=UTF8&qid=1335989960&sr=8-3 (accessed May 1, 2012).

106 **the brain's optimism switch**: Tali Sharot et al., "Neural Mechanisms Mediating Optimism Bias," *Nature* 450 (November 2007): 102–5.

106 **mildly depressed people are more accurate**: Tali Sharot, *The Optimism Bias: A Tour of the Irrationally Positive Brain* (New York: Pantheon, 2011), 89.

106 **Our brains process good and bad news differently**: Tali Sharot et al., "How Unrealistic Optimism Is Maintained in the Face of Reality," *Nature Neuroscience* 14 (2011): 1475–79.

107 **we know nothing lasts**: Ajit Varki, "Human Uniqueness and the Denial of Death," *Nature* 460 (August 2009): 684.

107 **"No one sees the barn"**: Don Delillo, *White Noise*, rev. ed. (New York: Penguin, 1999), 12.

108 **compared the relative length of different line segments**: Solomon Asch, "Studies of Independence and Conformity: A Minority of One Against a Unanimous Majority," *Psychological Monographs: General and Applied* 70 (1956): 1–70.

108 **rate photographs of women**: Jamil Zaki, Jessica Schirmer, and Jason Mitchell, "Social Influence Modulates the Neural Computation of Value," *Psychological Science* 22:7 (July 2011): 894–900.

109 **"We have reached the third degree":** John Maynard Keynes, *The General Theory of Employment, Interest, and Money*, rev. ed. (New Delhi: Atlantic Publishers and Distributors, 2006), 140.

109 **two economists combed through thousands of news stories:** Tomasz Wisniewski and Brendan Lambe, "The Role of Media in the Credit Crunch: The Case of the Banking Sector," *Journal of Economic Behavior & Organization*, Article in Press (2011).

110 **an algorithm that distills Twitter feeds:** Johan Bollen, Huina Mao, and Xiao-Jun Zeng, "Twitter Mood Predicts the Stock Market," *Journal of Computational Science* 2:1 (March 2011): 1–8. Jack Jordan, "Hedge Fund Will Track Twitter to Predict Stock Moves," Bloomberg.com, December 22, 2010, http://www.bloomberg.com/news/2010-12-22/hedge-fund-will-track-twitter-to-predict-stockmarket-movements.html (accessed May 2, 2012).

110 **"Investors wait for a stock to catch their attention":** Author interview, April 7, 2011.

110 **analyzed thousands of accounts at a large discount broker:** Brad Barber and Terrance Odean, "Trading Is Hazardous to Your Wealth: The Common Stock Investment Performance of Individual Investors," *The Journal of Finance* 55:2 (April 2000): 773–806.

111 **Up to 70 percent of U.S. stock trades are now triggered by computers:** Timothy Lavin, "Monsters in the Market," *Atlantic Monthly* (July/August 2010), 21.

111 **the stock market forecasts of chief financial officers:** Itzhak Ben-David, John Graham, and Campbell Harvey, "Managerial Miscalibration," Charles A. Dice Center, Working Paper No. 2010-2012, November 8, 2010.

111 **In a study of about 1,600 investors:** Brad Barber and Terrance Odean, "Online Investors: Do the Slow Die First?," *The Review of Financial Studies* 15:2 (2002): 455–88.

111 **"Overconfidence gives you the courage to act on your misguided convictions":** Author interview, April 7, 2011.

111 **awaiting their host:** Roger Farmer, *How the Economy Works: Confidence, Crashes, and Self-Fulfilling Prophecies* (New York: Oxford University Press, 2010), 1–3.

112 **"I don't want to be the mug left without my savings":** Joe Bolger and Marcus Leroux, "Northern Rock Savers Rush to Empty Accounts," *The Times* (London), September 14, 2007, retrieved from Times Online.

112 **Credit, they point out, derives from the Latin *credo*:** George Akerlof and Robert Shiller, *Animal Spirits* (Princeton: Princeton University Press, 2010), 12.

113 **people playing a "prisoner's dilemma" game:** James Rilling et al., "A Neural Basis for Cooperation," *Neuron* 35 (July 2002): 395–405.

113 **brains assess the value of fairness in the same way:** Alan Sanfey et al., "The Neural Basis of Economic Decision-Making in the Ultimatum Game," *Science* 300 (June 2003): 1755–58.

114 **a series of "public goods" games:** James Fowler and Nicholas Christakis, "Cooperative Behavior Cascades in Human Social Networks," *PNAS* 107:12 (March 2010): 5334–38.

114   **Trust can evaporate just as easily:** Laetitia Mulder et al., "Undermining Trust and Cooperation: The Paradox of Sanctioning Systems in Social Dilemmas," *Journal of Experimental Social Psychology* 42 (2006): 147–62.

115   **college students taking a math exam:** Francesca Gino, Shahar Ayal, and Dan Ariely, "Contagion and Differentiation in Unethical Behavior," *Psychological Science* 20:3 (March 2009): 393–98.

115   **compared chimpanzees, orangutans, and toddlers:** Esther Herrmann, "Humans Have Evolved Specialized Skills of Social Cognition: The Cultural Intelligence Hypothesis," *Science* 317 (September 2007): 1360–66.

116   **characters in vignettes who inflicted grievous harm:** Liane Young et al., "Disruption of the Right Temporoparietal Junction with Transcranial Magnetic Stimulation Reduces the Role of Beliefs in Moral Judgments," *PNAS* 107:15 (April 2010): 6753–58.

117   **more likely to reuse their towels:** Noah Goldstein, Robert Cialdini, and Vladas Griskevicius, "A Room with a Viewpoint: Using Social Norms to Motivate Environmental Conservation in Hotels," *Journal of Consumer Research* 35 (October 2008): 472–82.

117   **Radiohead let fans download their latest release:** Ju-Young Kim, Martin Natter, and Martin Spann, "Pay What You Want: A New Participative Pricing Mechanism," *Journal of Marketing* 73 (January 2009): 44–58. Jagmohan Raju and Z. John Zang, *Smart Pricing: How Google, Priceline and Leading Businesses Use Pricing Innovation for Profitability* (Philadelphia: Wharton School Publishing, 2010), 19–40.

118   **market-based and social norms:** James Heyman and Dan Ariely, "Effort for Payment: A Tale of Two Markets," *Psychological Science* 15:11 (2004): 787–93.

118   **an amusement park concession stand:** Ayelet Gneezy et al., "Shared Social Responsibility: A Field Experiment in Pay-What-You-Want Pricing and Charitable Giving," *Science* 329 (July 2010): 325–27.

119   **"Nobody could see what the customer paid":** Author interview, April 25, 2011.

120   **"conceptual consumption":** Dan Ariely and Michael Norton, "Conceptual Consumption," *Annual Review of Psychology* 60 (2009): 475–99.

120   **"They're making a mistake in some sense":** Author interview, April 8, 2011.

120   **choose more expensive, feature-filled electronics:** Debora Thompson and Michael Norton, "The Social Utility of Feature Creep," *Journal of Market Research* 48 (June 2011): 555–65.

121   **"It's not just in their heads":** Author interview, April 8, 2011.

121   **Secret Service agents and local police:** Weschler, *Boggs*, 141.

CHAPTER 6: THE FINE LINE BETWEEN YOU AND ME

125   **"Though seeing and hearing":** Richard Gregory, "Brainy Mind," *British Medical Journal* 317 (1998): 1693–95.

126   **"you either get the bomb, or the bomb gets you":** Author interview, March 31, 2011.

127   **a life-sized rubber hand:** Matthew Botvinick and Jonathan Cohen, "Rubber Hands 'Feel' Touch That Eyes See," *Nature* 391 (February 1998): 756.

127   **trick an amputee's brain:** Vilayanur Ramachandran, Diane Rogers-Ramachandran, and Steve Cobb, "Touching the Phantom Limb," *Nature* 377 (1995): 489–90. Vilayanur Ramachandran and Diane Rogers-Ramachandran, "Synesthesia in Phantom Limbs, Induced with Mirrors," *Proceedings of the Royal Society* 263 (1996): 377–86.

128   **a study of eighteen veterans:** Brenda Chan et al., "Mirror Therapy for Phantom Limb Pain," *The New England Journal of Medicine* 357:21 (November 2007): 2206–7.

129   **expanding mirror therapy into the virtual world:** Craig Murray et al., "The Treatment of Phantom Limb Pain Using Immersive Virtual Reality: Three Case Studies," *Disability & Rehabilitation* 29:18 (2007): 1645–49.

129   **regained their lost limb in virtual reality:** Catherine Mercer and Angela Sirigu, "Training with Virtual Visual Feedback to Alleviate Phantom Limb Pain," *Neurorehabilitation and Neural Repair* 20:10 (2009): 587–94.

129   **a prosthetic limb that could talk to the brain:** Michael Zeher et al., "Using a Virtual Integration Environment in Treating Phantom Limb Pain," *Studies in Health Technology and Informatics* 163 (2011): 730–36.

130   **"What is most surprising about this illusion":** K. Carrie Armel and Vilayanur Ramachandran, "Projecting Sensations to External Objects: Evidence from Skin Conductance Response," *Proceedings of the Royal Society* 270 (2003): 1499–1506.

130   **the brushstrokes on the rubber hand and the real hand:** H. Henrik Ehrsson et al., "Threatening a Rubber Hand That You Feel Is Yours Elicits a Cortical Anxiety Response," *PNAS* 104:23 (June 2007): 9828–33.

131   **lunge at the mannequin with a knife:** Valerie Petkova and H. Henrik Ehrsson, "If I Were You: Perceptual Illusion of Body Swapping," *PLoS ONE* 3:12 (2008): e3832.

133   **the much penalized Oakland Raiders:** Mark Frank and Thomas Gilovich, "The Dark Side of Self and Social Perception: Black Uniforms and Aggression in Professional Sports," *Journal of Personality and Social Psychology* 54:1 (1998): 74–85.

134   **a large group of women tried on sunglasses:** Francesca Gino, Michael Norton, and Dan Ariely, "The Counterfeit Self: The Deceptive Costs of Faking It," *Psychological Science* 21:5 (2010): 712–20.

135   **work off the computer-generated flab:** Jim Blascovich and Jeremy Bailenson, *Infinite Reality* (New York: HarperCollins, 2011), 110–11.

135   **77, 000 *World of Warcraft* players:** Nick Yee, Jeremy Bailenson, and Nicolas Ducheneaut, "The Proteus Effect: Implications of Transformed Digital Self-Representation on Online and Offline Behavior," *Communication Research* 36:2 (2009): 285–312.

135   **wearing better-looking avatars:** Nick Yee and Jeremy Bailenson, "The Difference Between Being and Seeing: The Relative Contribution of Self-Perception and Priming to Behavioral Changes Via Digital Self-Representation," *Media Psychology* 12:2 (2009): 195–209.

136 **in a virtual ultimatum game:** Yee, Bailenson, and Ducheneaut, "The Proteus Effect."

136 **"We thought baseline measures of self-esteem would be a very big mediator":** Author interview, January 26, 2011.

136 **Women whose avatars visibly pudged:** Jesse Fox, Jeremy Bailenson, and Joseph Binney, "Virtual Experiences, Physical Behaviors: The Effect of Presence on Imitation of an Eating Avatar," *Presence* 18:4 (2009): 294–303.

136 **the recent rise of cybertherapy:** Alessandra Gorini et al., "A Second Life for eHealth: Prospects for the Use of 3-D Virtual Worlds in Clinical Psychology," *Journal of Medical Internet Research* 10:3 (2008): e21. Benedict Carey, "In Cybertherapy, Avatars Assist with Healing," *New York Times*, November 22, 2010.

136 **short of what they'll need for a secure retirement:** "Restoring Americans' Retirement Security: A Shared Responsibility," McKinsey & Company, 2009, http://www.retirementmadesimpler.org/Library/Retirement_Security .pdf.

137 **showed this future-self estrangement:** Emily Pronin, Christopher Olivola, and Kathleen Kennedy, "Doing unto Future Selves as You Would Do unto Others: Psychological Distance and Decision Making," *Personality and Social Psychology Bulletin* 34:2 (2008): 224–36.

137 **how close people felt to their future selves:** Hal Ersner-Hershfield, G. Elliott Wimmer, and Brian Knutson, "Saving for the Future Self: Neural Measures of Future Self-Continuity Predict Temporal Discounting," *Social Cognitive and Affective Neuroscience* 4:1 (2009): 85–92.

137 **delay discounting evaporated:** Jans Peters and Christian Büchel, "Episodic Future Thinking Reduces Reward Delay Discounting Through an Enhancement of Prefrontal-Mediotemporal Interactions," *Neuron* 66:1 (April 2010): 138–48.

138 **seventy-year-old versions of their college student subjects:** Hal Ersner-Hershfield et al., "Increasing Saving Behavior Through Age-Progressed Renderings of the Future Self," *Journal of Marketing Research* 48 (2011): S23–S37.

138 **the "chameleon effect":** Tanya Chartrand and John Bargh, "The Chameleon Effect: The Perception-Behavior Link and Social Interaction," *Journal of Personality and Social Psychology* 76:6 (1999): 893–910.

138 **inadvertently it can be triggered:** David DeSteno and Piercarlo Valdesolo, "Synchrony and the Social Tuning of Compassion," *Emotion* 11:2 (April 2011): 262–66.

139 **agents mirrored participants' head movements:** Jeremy Bailenson and Nick Yee, "Digital Chameleons: Automatic Assimilation of Nonverbal Gestures in Immersive Virtual Environments," *Psychological Science* 16 (2005): 814–19.

139 **blend a candidate's face with the participant's face:** Jeremy Bailenson, Shanto Iyengar, and Nick Yee, "Facial Similarity Between Voters and Candidates Causes Influence," *Public Opinion Quarterly* 72:5 (2008): 935–61.

140 **"I crumbled":** Author interview, March 31, 2011.

CHAPTER 7: YOU THINK, THEREFORE I AM

143 **nearly three hundred violent crime convictions overturned:** Reported on the Web site of The Innocence Project (accessed May 2, 2012): http://www.innocenceproject.org/know/.

143 **a horse named Hans:** Robert Rosenthal, ed., *Clever Hans (The Horse of Mr. Von Osten)* by Oskar Pfungst, rev ed. (New York: Holt, Rinehart & Winston, 1965).

144 **"The Horse Actually Reasons":** "'Clever Hans' Again. Expert Commission Decides That the Horse Actually Reasons" (from *The London Standard*, September 13, 1904), *New York Times*, October 2, 1904.

144 **Pfungst tested these unintentional cues:** Rosenthal, ed., *Clever Hans*, 102–40.

145 **"Many experimenters over the years":** Ibid., xxii–xxiii.

146 **"There were already treatment effects from treatments they had yet to receive":** Author interview, September 23, 2011.

146 **Rosenthal set up more photo-judging experiments:** Rosenthal, ed., *Clever Hans*, xxiv–xxv.

149 **"who sat together and discussed his photograph":** John Cataldo, J.S.C., *People v. Bermudez*, Supreme Court of New York State, ruling, November 9, 2009.

149 **multisite field study of eyewitness identification:** Gary Wells, Nancy Steblay, and Jennifer Dysart, "A Test of the Simultaneous vs. Sequential Lineup Methods: An Initial Report of the AJS National Eyewitness Identification Field Studies," American Judicature Society, 2011.

150 **witnesses to mock crimes:** Sarah Greathouse and Margaret Bull Kovera, "Instruction Bias and Lineup Presentation Moderate the Effects of Administrator Knowledge on Eyewitness Identification," *Law and Human Behavior* 33 (2009): 70–82.

151 **studies comparing simultaneous and sequential lineups:** Nancy Steblay, Jennifer Dysart, and Gary Wells, "Seventy-two Tests of the Sequential Lineup Superiority Effect: A Meta-Analysis and Policy Discussion," *Psychology, Public Policy, and Law* 17:1 (February 2011): 99–139.

151 **"There's a clear difference between eyewitness choices and eyewitness identifications":** Author interview, November 3, 2011.

152 **the National Institute of Justice recommended:** U.S. Department of Justice, National Institute of Justice, "Eyewitness Evidence: A Guide for Law Enforcement," Technical Working Group for Eyewitness Evidence, 1999, http://www.ojp.usdoj.gov/nij/puns-sum/178240.htm.

153 **Hollerith Tabulating Machine:** Joseph Jastrow, *Faith and Fable in Psychology* (Boston: Houghton Mifflin, 1900), 301–3.

153 **a book-length treatment of his two-year study:** Robert Rosenthal and Lenore Jacobson, *Pygmalion in the Classroom: Teacher Expectation and Pupils' Intellectual Development*, rev. ed. (New York: Irvington, 1992).

153 **That's an oversimplification:** Lee Jussim and Kent Harber, "Teacher Expectations and Self-Fulfilling Prophecies: Knowns and Unknowns, Resolved and

Unresolved Controversies," *Personality and Social Psychology Review* 9:2 (2005): 131–35.

154 **they can be major influences:** Ibid.

154 **"There's an expectation in scientific research that if a phenomenon exists":** Author interview, November 15, 2011.

154 **self-fulfilling prophecies of adult performance:** Dov Eden, *Pygmalion in Management: Productivity as a Self-Fulfilling Prophecy* (Lexington, MA: Lexington, 1990), 19–68.

154 **spent many years observing classrooms:** Rhona Weinstein, *Reaching Higher: The Power of Expectations in Schooling* (Cambridge: Harvard University Press, 2002), 89–174.

156 **"The question is, do we focus on identifying the star talents":** Author interview, November 15, 2011.

156 **in the top 15 percent:** Vicky Walters (director, Media Relations, California Charter Schools Association), e-mail to author, December 27, 2011.

156 **coined the term "stereotype threat":** Claude Steele and Joshua Aronson, "Stereotype Threat and the Intellectual Test Performance of African Americans," *Journal of Personality and Social Psychology* 69:5 (1995): 797–811.

157 **white male Stanford students with high math SATs:** Joshua Aronson et al., "When White Men Can't Do Math: Necessary and Sufficient Factors in Stereotype Threat," *Journal of Experimental Social Psychology* 35 (1999): 29–46.

158 **Asian American female college students:** Todd Pittinsky, Margaret Shih, and Nalini Ambady, "Identity Adaptiveness: Affect Across Multiple Identities," *Journal of Social Issues* 55:3 (1999): 503–18.

158 **using a similar experiment with Asian American women:** Sapna Cheryan and Galen Bodenhausen, "When Positive Stereotypes Threaten Intellectual Performance: The Psychological Hazards of 'Model Minority' Status," *Psychological Science* 11:5 (2000): 399–402.

159 **expert male golfers:** Sian Beilock et al., "On the Causal Mechanisms of Stereotype Threat: Can Skills That Don't Rely Heavily on Working Memory Still Be Threatened?," *Personality and Social Psychology Bulletin* 32:8 (2006): 1059–71.

159 **math word problems to male and female students:** Michal Johns, Toni Schmader, Andy Martens, "Knowing Is Half the Battle: Teaching Stereotype Threat as a Means of Improving Women's Math Performance," *Psychological Science* 16:3 (2005): 175–78.

160 **a real-world intervention with high school kids:** Gerardo Ramirez and Sian Beilock, "Writing About Testing Worries Boosts Exam Performance in the Classroom," *Science* 331:6014 (January 2011): 211–13.

160 **given the right spin:** Jeremy Jaimeson, "Turning the Knots in Your Stomach into Bows: Reappraising Arousal Improves Performance on the GRE," *Journal of Experimental Social Psychology* 46 (2010): 208–12.

161 **positive motivational energy:** Adam Alter et al., "Rising to the Threat: Reducing Stereotype Threat by Reframing the Threat," *Journal of Experimental Social Psychology* 46 (2010): 166–71.

161 **"It's not just removing the anxiety, it's turning that arousal into a motivator":** Author interview, October 25, 2011.

161 **growing up in the 1950s:** Lenore Skenazy, *Free-Range Kids: How to Raise Safe, Self-Reliant Children* (San Francisco: Jossey-Bass, 2010), 120.

162 **In one of Dweck's landmark studies:** Claudia Mueller and Carol Dweck, "Praise for Intelligence Can Undermine Children's Motivation and Performance," *Journal of Personality and Social Psychology* 75:1 (1998): 33–52.

163 **"I am an important person":** Jeanne Twenge and W. Keith Campbell, *The Narcissism Epidemic: Living in the Age of Entitlement,* paperback ed. (New York: Free Press, 2010), 35.

163 **a nation's math performance was inversely related:** Tom Loveless, "2006 Brown Center Report on American Education: How Well Are American Students Learning?," *Brown Center Report on American Education* 2:1 (October 2006).

163 **the same trends were found with science:** Tom Loveless, "2008 Brown Center Report on American Education: How Well Are American Students Learning?," *Brown Center Report on American Education* 2:4 (February 2009).

163 **"stunning finding":** U.S. Department of Education, "Secretary Arne Duncan's Remarks at OECD's Release of the Program for International Student Assessment (PISA) 2009 Results," December 7, 2010, http://www.ed.gov /news/speeches/secretary-arne-duncans-remarks-oecds-release-program-international-student-assessment-.

163 **The problem is especially acute at private colleges:** Stuart Rojstaczer and Christopher Healy, "Grading in American Colleges and Universities," *Teachers College Record* (March 4, 2010), http://www.tcrecord.org.

164 **dozens of valedictorians:** Winnie Hu, "How Many Graduates Can Be No. 1? Ask the 30 Valedictorians," *New York Times,* June 27, 2010.

164 **a self-esteem intervention:** Donelson Forsyth et al., "Attempting to Improve the Academic Performance of Struggling College Students by Bolstering Their Self-Esteem: An Intervention That Backfired," *Journal of Social and Clinical Psychology* 26 (2007): 447–59.

164 **overestimate the role our talents and intelligence:** Zoë Chance et al., "Temporal View of the Costs and Benefits of Self-Deception," *PNAS* 108 (March 2011): 15655–59.

165 **pry apart expectations and fantasies:** Gabriele Oettingen and Doris Mayer, "The Motivating Function of Thinking About the Future: Expectations Versus Fantasies," *Journal of Personality and Social Psychology* 83:5 (2002): 1198–1212.

166 **failure was a favorite theme:** Peter J. Gomes, *The Good Life: Truths That Last in Times of Need* (New York: HarperCollins, 2002), 73–97.

166 **"Self-esteem without true competence is worthless":** Author interview, November 15, 2011.

166 **tried teaching a growth mindset:** Lisa Blackwell, Kali Trzesniewski, and Carol Dweck, "Implicit Theories of Intelligence Predict Achievement Across Adolescent Transition: A Longitudinal Study and an Intervention," *Child Development* 78:1 (2007): 246–63.

CHAPTER 8: WHAT IT TAKES

168 **spent more than $100,000:** Peter Elkind, *Rough Justice: The Rise and Fall of Eliot Spitzer* (New York: Penguin, 2010).

169 **"I'm a fucking steamroller":** Steve Fishman, "The Steamroller in the Swamp: Is Eliot Spitzer Changing Albany or Is Albany Changing Him?," *New York* 40:26 (July 14, 2007): 22.

169 **the news of Spitzer's D.C. dalliance:** Danny Hakim and William K. Rashbaum, "Spitzer Is Linked to Prostitution Ring," *New York Times*, March 10, 2008.

169 **"I brought myself down":** *Client 9: The Rise and Fall of Eliot Spitzer,* directed by Alex Gibney (2010; New York, Magnolia Pictures).

170 **the "Johnson Treatment":** All of these photos can be seen online at several Web sites dedicated to nonverbal communication, including http://www .uiowa.edu/commstud/resources/nonverbal/lbj.htm and http://www .carlosbaena.com/resource/resource_tips_status.html.

171 **people who are given a warm drink:** Joshua Ackerman, Christopher Nocera, and John Bargh, "Incidental Haptic Sensations Influence Social Judgments and Decisions," *Science* 328:5986 (June 2010): 1712–15.

171 **"When we evolved the capacity to be disgusted":** Robert Sapolsky, "This Is Your Brain on Metaphors," *New York Times*, November 4, 2010.

172 **"We feel sorry because we cry":** William James, *Principles of Psychology,* Volume II (London: Macmillan, 1891), 450.

172 **smiling increases happiness:** Robert Soussignan, "Duchenne Smile, Emotional Experience, and Autonomic Reactivity: A Test of the Facial Feedback Hypothesis," *Emotion* 2 (2002): 52–74.

172 **hold expansive or hunched poses:** Dana Carney, Amy Cuddy, and Andy Yapp, "Power Posing: Brief Nonverbal Displays Affect Neuroendocrine Levels and Risk Tolerance," *Psychological Science* 21:10 (2010):1363–68.

173 **market testing ergonomic chairs:** Li Huang et al., "Powerful Postures Versus Powerful Roles: Which Is the Proximate Correlate of Thought and Behavior?," *Psychological Science* 22:1 (2011): 95–102.

174 **give an impromptu speech:** Amy Cuddy, Caroline Wilmuth, Dana Carney, "Fake It 'Til You Make It: Power Posing Before a Mock Job Interview Boosts Performance," article in preparation.

174 **"It was all about how engaging and captivating people were when delivering them":** Author interview, November 11, 2011.

175 **easier for people to lie about stealing money:** Dana Carney et al., "How Power Corrupts: Power Buffers the Emotional, Cognitive, and Physiological Stress of Lying," article in preparation.

176 **researchers approached people:** Andy Yap et al., "The Perils of an Expansive Posture: The Effect of Everyday, Incidental Posture on Stealing, Cheating and Parking Violations (Results from the Lab and Field)," article in preparation.

177 **"Power is an intoxicant":** Author interview, November 20, 2011.

178 **In studies of winners:** See, for example: Malcolm Gladwell, "The Talent Myth," *The New Yorker,* July 22, 2002. Geoff Colvin, *Talent Is Overrated* (New

York: Penguin, 2008). Jonah Lehrer, "The Truth About Grit: Modern Science Builds the Case for an Old-Fashioned Virtue—And Uncovers New Secrets to Success," *Boston Globe*, August 2, 2009. Angela Duckworth, "The Significance of Self-Control," *PNAS* 108:7 (February 2011): 2639–40.

178 **tests of willpower and self-control":** Angela Duckworth et al., "Grit: Perseverance and Passion for Long-Term Goals," *Journal of Personality and Social Psychology* 92:6 (2007): 1087–01. Angela Duckworth and Martin Seligman, "Self-Discipline Outdoes IQ in Predicting Academic Performance of Adolescents," *Psychological Science* 16:12 (2005): 939–44. Angela Duckworth et al., "Deliberate Practice Spells Success: Why Grittier Competitors Triumph at the National Spelling Bee," *Social Psychology and Personality Science* 2:2 (March 2011): 174–81. Terrie Moffitt et al., "A Gradient of Childhood Self-Control Predicts Health, Wealth, and Public Safety," *PNAS* 108:7 (February 2011): 2693–98.

179 **resisting chocolate chip cookies:** Roy Baumeister et al., "Ego Depletion: Is the Active Self a Limited Resource?," *Journal of Personality and Social Psychology* 74:5 (May 1998): 1252–65.

179 **20 percent of the body's daily glucose consumption:** Daniel Goleman, *Consciousness, the Brain, States of Awareness, and Alternate Realities* (New York: Harper & Row, 1979), 6.

179 **drank sugar-sweetened lemonade:** Matthew Gailliot and Roy Baumeister, "The Physiology of Willpower: Linking Blood Glucose to Self-Control," *Journal of Personality and Social Psychology Review* 11 (2007): 303–27. Matthew Gailliott et al., "Self-Control Relies on Glucose as a Limited Energy Source: Willpower Is More than a Metaphor," *Journal of Personality and Social Psychology* 92 (2007): 325–36.

179 **while the willpower muscle tires after strenuous use, it can also be strengthened:** Roy Baumeister and John Tierney, *Willpower: Rediscovering the Greatest Human Strength* (New York: Penguin, 2011), 124–41.

180 **believing willpower was actually an unlimited resource:** Veronika Job, Carol Dweck, and Gregory Walton, "Ego-Depletion—Is It All in Your Head? Implicit Theories About Willpower Affect Self-Regulation," *Psychological Science* 21:11 (September 2010): 1686–93.

182 **placebos could replenish willpower:** Patrick Egan, Joshua Clarkson, and Edward Hirt, "From Mental Depletion to Spontaneous Replenishment: A Regulatory Stimulant Hypothesis," *Journal of Personality and Social Psychology*, article in press, 2012.

184 **swishing and spitting a glucose solution:** Daniel Molden et al., "The Motivational Versus Metabolic Effects of Carbohydrates on Self-Control," *Psychological Science*, article in press, 2012.

184 **"We just think we're redefining strength":** Author interview, October 10, 2011.

CHAPTER 9: FAITH IN A BOTTLE

189 **analyzed more than a dozen drug studies:** Henry Beecher, "The Powerful Placebo," *Journal of the American Medical Association* 159:17 (1955): 1602–6.

190 **"He had an ethical motive, but he wasn't objective":** Author interview, October 13, 2010.

191 **"I shall please":** Daniel Moerman, *Meaning, Medicine and the "Placebo Effect"* (Cambridge, UK: Cambridge University Press, 2002), 10–11.

192 **overzealous swig of scalding clam chowder:** Stewart Wolf, "Effects of Suggestion and Conditioning on the Action of Chemical Agents in Human Subjects—The Pharmacology of Placebos," *Journal of Clinical Investigations* 29:1 (January 1950): 100–109. Stewart Wolf, *The Stomach* (New York: Oxford University Press, 1965).

192 **secretly injecting some patients with naloxone:** Jon Levine, Newton Gordon, and Howard Fields, "The Mechanism of Placebo Analgesia," *The Lancet* 312:8091 (September 1978): 654–57.

193 **confirmed the existence of a conditioned placebo response:** Robert Ader and Nicholas Cohen, "Behaviorally Conditioned Immunosuppression," *Psychosomatic Medicine* 37:4 (1975): 333–40.

194 **more than one way to think away pain:** Martina Amanzio and Fabrizio Benedetti, "Neuropharmacological Dissection of Placebo Analgesia: Expectation-Activated Opioid Systems Versus Conditioning-Activated Specific Subsystems," *The Journal of Neuroscience* 19:1 (1999): 484–91.

195 **patients recovering from surgery:** Antonella Pollo et al., "Response Expectancies in Placebo Analgesia and Their Clinical Relevance," *Pain* 93:1 (July 2001): 77–84.

195 **placebo dopamine drugs:** Fabrizio Benedetti, *Placebo Effects: Understanding the Mechanisms in Health and Disease* (New York: Oxford University Press, 2008), 99–121.

195 **wiped out if the patient is told the truth:** Donald Price et al., "An Analysis of Factors That Contribute to the Magnitude of Placebo Analgesia in an Experimental Paradigm," *Pain* 83:2 (November 1999): 147–56.

195 **placebo treatment of hormonal deficiencies:** Benedetti, *Placebo Effects*, 163–70.

195 **"You don't need to trust your doctor":** Author interview, September 25, 2010.

196 **a strong nocebo component:** Benedetti, *Placebo Effects*, 154–62.

196 **secretly cut the morphine drips:** Luana Colloca and Fabrizio Benedetti, "Nocebo Hyperalgesia: How Anxiety Is Turned into Pain," *Current Opinion in Anesthesiology* 20:5 (October 2007): 435–39.

197 **a chemical called proglumide:** Fabrizio Benedetti, "The Opposite Effects of the Opiate Antagonist Naloxone and the Cholecystokinin Antagonist Proglumide on Placebo Analgesia," *Pain* 64:3 (March 1996): 535–43.

197 **men with enlarged prostates:** Nicola Mondaini et al., "Finasteride 5 mg and Sexual Side Effects: How Many of These Are Related to a Nocebo Phenomenon?," *The Journal of Sexual Medicine* 4:6 (November 2007): 1708–12.

197 **different types of migraine drugs:** Martina Amanzio et al., "A Systematic Review of Adverse Events in Placebo Groups of Anti-Migraine Clinical Trials," *Pain* 146:3 (December 2009): 261–69.

198 **fear swept the shores of Lake Victoria:** A. M. Rankin and P. J. Philip, "An

Epidemic of Laughing in the Bukoba District of Tanganyika," *Central African Journal of Medicine* 9:5 (1963): 167–70.

199   **the dancing plagues:** John Waller, *A Time to Dance, a Time to Die: The Extraordinary Story of the Dancing Plague of 1518* (London: Icon, 2008).

201   **That suspicion didn't sit well:** Susan Dominus, "What Happened to the Girls in Le Roy," *New York Times Magazine*, March 7, 2012.

201   **a rare lab study of nocebo contagion:** William Lorber, Giulliana Mazzoni, and Irving Kirsch, "Illness by Suggestion: Expectancy, Modeling, and Gender in the Production of Psychosomatic Symptoms," *Annals of Behavioral Medicine* 33:1 (2007): 112–16.

202   **Placebos can also be contagious:** Luana Colloca and Fabrizio Benedetti, "Placebo Analgesia Induced by Social Observational Learning," *Pain* 144: 1–2 (July 2009): 28–34.

203   **that anticipated reward is symptom relief:** Sarah Lidstone, Raul de la Fuente-Fernandez, and A. Jon Stoessl, "The Placebo Response as a Reward Mechanism," *Seminars in Pain Medicine* 3 (2005) 37–42. Predrag Petrovic et al., "Placebo in Emotional Processing—Induced Expectations of Anxiety Relief Activate a Generalized Modulatory Network," *Neuron* 46 (June 2005): 957–69. Jon-Kar Zubieta and Christian Stohler, "Neurobiological Mechanisms of Placebo Responses," *Annals of the New York Academy of Sciences* 1156 (March 2009): 198–210. Petra Schweinhardt et al., "The Anatomy of the Mesolimbic Reward System: A Link Between Personality and the Placebo Analgesic Response," *The Journal of Neuroscience* 29:15 (April 2009): 4882–87.

203   **people whose reward circuits were more active:** David Scott et al., "Individual Differences in Reward Responding Explain Placebo-Induced Expectations and Effects," *Neuron* 55 (July 2007): 325–36.

204   **men and women who were recently dumped:** Ethan Kross et al., "Social Rejection Shares Somatosensory Representations with Physical Pain," *PNAS* 108:15 (April 2011): 6270–75.

204   **photos of a new love:** Jarred Younger et al., "Viewing Pictures of a Romantic Partner Reduces Experimental Pain: Involvement of Neural Reward Systems," *PLoS ONE* 5:10 (2010): e13309.

204   **people who were about to get a painful shock:** Tor Wager et al., "Predicting Individual Differences in Placebo Analgesia: Contributions of Brain Activity During Anticipation and Pain Experience," *The Journal of Neuroscience* 31:2 (2011): 439–52.

205   **"I think the fundamental placebo process is really a decision your brain makes":** Author interview, September 30, 2010.

CHAPTER 10: HEALING REDEFINED

207   **He was going to fake it:** Margaret Talbot, "The Placebo Prescription," *New York Times Magazine,* January 9, 2000.

208   **operation to treat angina:** Irving Kirsch, *The Emperor's New Drugs: Exploding the Antidepressant Myth* (New York: Random House, 2010), 111–12.

209   **vasovagal syncope:** Antonio Raviele et al., "A Randomized, Double-Blind, Placebo Controlled Study of Permanent Cardiac Pacing for the Treatment of

Recurrent Tilt-Induced Vasovagal Syncope," *European Heart Journal* 25:19 (2004): 1741–48.

209 **hypertrophic cardiomyopathy:** Daniel Moerman, *Meaning, Medicine and the "Placebo Effect"* (Cambridge, UK: Cambridge University Press, 2002), 61.

209 **transmyocardial laser revascularization:** Ibid., 63. Martin B. Leon et al., "A Blinded, Randomized, Placebo-Controlled Trial of Percutaneous Laser Myocardial Revascularization to Improve Anging Symptoms in Patients with Severe Coronary Disease," *Journal of the American College of Cardiology* 44:10 (2005): 1812–19.

210 **either saline or proglumide:** Luana Colloca and Fabrizio Benedetti, "Placebos and Painkillers: Is Mind as Real as Matter?," *Nature Reviews* 6 (July 2005): 545–52. Fabrizio Benedetti, Elisa Carlino, and Antonella Pollo, "Hidden Administration of Drugs," *Clinical Pharmacology & Therapeutics* 90 (November 2011): 651–61.

211 **decided to study acupuncture:** Klaus Linde, Karin Niemann, and Karin Meissner, "Are Sham Acupuncture Interventions More Effective than (Other) Placebos? A Re-Analysis of Data from the Cochrane Review on Placebo Effects," *Forschende Komplementärmedizin* 17 (2010). Michael Haake et al., "German Acupuncture Trials (GERAC) for Chronic Low Back Pain," *Archives of Internal Medicine* 167:17 (2007): 1892–98.

211 **confronting a placebo crisis:** Steve Silberman, "Placebos Are Getting More Effective. Drugmakers Are Desperate to Know Why," *Wired*, August 24, 2009. William Potter, Testimony before the Committee on Oversight and Government Reform, Domestic Policy Subcommittee, United States House of Representatives, September 29, 2010.

212 **Speaking before a congressional oversight committee:** Potter, Testimony.

212 **"there was no viable business model for developing novel psychiatric drugs":** Author interview, October 27, 2010.

213 **"You could get rich on those, and everybody did":** Ibid.

213 **the true placebo component of drugs:** Irving Kirsch and Guy Sapirstein, "Listening to Prozac but Hearing Placebo: A Meta-Analysis of Antidepressant Medication," *Prevention & Treatment* 1, posted June 26, 1998, http://psychrights.org/research/Digest/CriticalThinkRxCites/KirschandSapirstein1998.pdf. Irving Kirsch et al., "Initial Severity and Antidepressant Benefits: A Meta-Analysis of Data Submitted to the Food and Drug Administration," *PLoS Medicine* 5:2 (2008): e45. Kirsch, *The Emperor's New Drugs*, 23–34.

213 **selective publication of positive results:** Erick Turner et al., "Selective Publication of Antidepressant Trials and Its Influence on Apparent Efficacy," *The New England Journal of Medicine* 358:3 (January 2008): 252–60.

214 **men hospitalized for depression:** Helen Mayberg, "The Functional Neuroanatomy of the Placebo Effect," *American Journal of Psychiatry* 159 (2002): 728–37.

214 **increased suicidal thoughts and behaviors:** Shankar Vendantam, "FDA Urged Withholding Data on Antidepressants: Makers Were Dissuaded from Labeling Drugs as Ineffective in Children," *Washington Post*, September 10, 2004.

214 **New York sued GlaxoSmithKline:** Brooke Masters, "N.Y. Sues Paxil Maker

Over Studies on Children: Negative Data Withheld, Attorney General Says," *Washington Post,* June 3, 2004.

215 **"the best intervention is probably time, structure, and support":** Author interview, October 27, 2010.

215 **French and Brazilian patients with ulcers:** Moerman, *Meaning, Medicine and the "Placebo Effect,"* 80–81.

216 **rooted in our most basic beliefs:** Ibid., 47–53.

216 **inexplicable loss of efficacy:** Ibid., 45–46.

216 **aspirin soothed headaches better:** Alan Branthwaite and Peter Cooper, "Analgesic Effects of Branding in Treatment of Headaches," *British Medical Journal* 282 (May 1981): 1576–78.

216 **Even price matters:** Baba Shiv, Ziv Carmon, and Dan Ariely, "Placebo Effects of Marketing Actions: Consumers May Get What They Pay For," *Journal of Marketing Research* 42 (November 2005): 383–93.

217 **shuffled aboard a bus:** Ellen Langer, *Counterclockwise: Mindful Health and the Power of Possibility* (New York: Ballantine Books, 2009), 35–37; 164–79.

220 **no longer designate cures as miracles:** Jamey Keaten, "Lourdes Doctors Leave Ruling on 'Miracles' up to Church," Associated Press, December 4, 2008.

220 **"the tyranny of positive thinking":** Jimmie Holland and Sheldon Lewis, *The Human Side of Cancer: Living with Hope, Coping with Uncertainty* (New York: Harper, 2000), 13.

220 **"They literally think they are killing themselves":** Author interview, December 10, 2010.

221 **subjects' vision improved:** Ellen Langer et al., "Believing Is Seeing: Using Mindfulness (Mindfully) to Improve Visual Acuity," *Psychological Science* 21:5 (2010): 661–66.

221 **women who clean hotel rooms:** Alia Crum and Ellen Langer, "Mind-set Matters: Exercise and the Placebo Effect," *Psychological Science* 18:2 (2007): 165–71.

222 **adolescents and university service workers:** Mark Beauchamp et al., "Testing the Effects of an Expectancy-Based Intervention Among Adolescents: Can Placebos Be Used to Enhance Physical Health?," *Psychology, Health, and Medicine* 16:4 (2011): 405–17. Dixie Stanforth et al., "An Investigation of Exercise and the Placebo Effect," *American Journal of Health Behavior* 35:3 (2011): 257–68.

222 **"It's about trying":** Author interview, October 26, 2011.

222 **sort photographs of faces:** Maja Dijikic, Ellen Langer, and Sarah Fulton Stapleton, "Reducing Stereotyping Through Mindfulness: Effects on Automatic Stereotype-Activated Behaviors," *Journal of Adult Development* 15:2 (2008): 106–11.

223 **"see the person in the photo as many things and not just old":** Ellen Langer, *Counterclockwise,* 86.

223 **"learn how to integrate what the medical world knows to be generally true":** Ibid, 86.

224 **pitting one type of placebo against another:** Ted Kaptchuk et al., "Do Medical Devices Have Enhanced Placebo Effects?," *Journal of Clinical Epidemiology* 53 (2000) 786–92. Ted Kaptchuk et al., "Sham Device v. Inert Pill: Randomised Controlled Trial of Two Placebo Treatments," *British Medical Journal* 332 (February 2006): 391–97.

224 **randomly sorted two hundred of his patients:** K. B. Thomas, "General Practice Consultations: Is There Any Point in Being Positive?," *British Medical Journal* 294 (May 1987): 1200–1202.

224 **go to a doctor for a common cold:** David Rakel et al., "Practitioner Empathy and the Duration of the Common Cold," *Family Medicine* 41:7 (2009): 494–501.

225 **placebo study of asthmatics:** Margaret Kemeny et al., "Placebo Response in Asthma: A Robust and Objective Phenomenon," *Journal of Allergy and Clinical Immunology* 119:6 (2007): 1375–81.

225 **"What it tells me is that it's not a simple story":** Author interview, November 11, 2010.

225 **nine "mini interviews":** Gardiner Harris, "New for Aspiring Doctors, the People Skills Test," *New York Times,* July 10, 2011.

225 **a new clerkship program:** Ishani Ganguli, "Building Better Doctors: Can a Unique Training Program Help Medical Students Keep in Step with Their Patients," *Boston Globe Magazine,* October 30, 2011.

225 **a more fine-grained look:** Ted Kaptchuk et al., "Components of Placebo Effect: Randomised Controlled Trial in Patients with Irritable Bowel Syndrome," *British Medical Journal* 336 (2008): 999–1003.

226 **"Was it the twenty seconds of thoughtful silence?":** Author interview, October 13, 2010.

226 **Survey after anonymous survey:** Rachel Sherman and John Hickner, "Academic Physicians Use Placebos in Clinical Practice and Believe in the Mind-Body Connection," *Journal of General Internal Medicine* 23:1 (2007) 7–10. Jon Tilburt et al., "Prescribing 'Placebo Treatments': Results of National Survey of US Internists and Rheumatologists," *British Medical Journal* 337 (2008): a1938.

226 **a meta-analysis of these surveys:** Magrit Fässler et al., "Frequency and Circumstances of Placebo Use in Clinical Practice—A Systematic Review of Empirical Studies," *BMC Medicine* 8:15 (2010).

227 **thirteen-year-old girl with severe lupus:** Karen Olness and Robert Ader, "Conditioning as an Adjunct in the Pharmacotherapy of Lupus Erythematosus," Case Report, *Developmental and Behavioral Pediatrics* 13:2 (April 1992): 124–25.

227 **clinical trial of the conditioned placebo response:** Robert Ader et al., "Conditioned Pharmacotherapeutic Effects: A Preliminary Study," *Psychosomatic Medicine* 72:2 (February/March 2010): 192–97.

228 **researchers didn't use the word "placebo":** Lene Vase et al., "The Contributions of Suggestion, Desire, and Expectation to Placebo Effects in Irritable Bowel Syndrome Patients. An Empirical Investigation," *Pain* 105:1–2 (September 2003): 17–25.

228 **a group of psychiatric outpatients:** Lee Park and Lino Covi, "Nonblind Placebo Trial: An Exploration of Neurotic Patients' Responses to Placebo When Its Inert Content Is Disclosed," *Archives of General Psychiatry* 12:4 (1965): 336–45.

229 **"Placebo Pills: Take Twice Daily":** Ted Kaptchuk et al., "Placebos Without Deception: A Randomized Controlled Trial in Irritable Bowel Syndrome," *PLoS ONE* 5:12 (2010): e15591.

INDEX

action ideas, 41–42
acupuncture, 211, 226
addictions, 57–58, 68–75
  cybertherapy for, 136
  prescription drug, 195
  see also gambling addicts
Ader, Robert, 193–94, 195, 201, 226–28
Afghanistan, 127
aging, 222–23
  "1959" monastery study of, 217–19
  in virtual reality, 136–37, 138
Akerlof, George, 112
Alcoholics Anonymous (AA), 74
allergens, fake, 196
allergies, 196
Almenberg, Johan, 86–87
Amazon.com, 104–5
Amerine, Maynard, 95–96, 97
Andreu, Frankie, 16
animal acts, "thinking," 143–44
"animal magnetism," 1–8, 230
Animal Spirits (Akerlof and
  Shiller), 112
antidepressants, 211–15
Ariely, Dan, 80–81, 118, 120
Armstrong, Lance, 16
Aronson, Joshua, 156–57
arthroscopic knee surgery, 207–8, 217
Asch, Solomon, 108
Ashenfelter, Orley, 89
Asimov, Eric, 97
asthma inhalers, 225
athletes, 13–28
  anticipation by, 31, 39–43

doping of, 15–16, 23–24, 25
energy drinks for, 21–22, 180
fatigue of, 19–22
female, 15, 49
focus of, 33, 46
motion predictions of, 45
Olympic, 13, 14, 15, 17, 18, 22, 39–40
pain tolerance of, 27
physical limits of, 13–14, 15–18,
  19, 23
prayers of, 26
reflexes of, 40
routines of, 32, 47
world records set by, 13–14,
  15–18, 28
see also sports
athletes, precompetition anxiety of,
  25–26, 29–53, 159
anticipation skills affected by,
  39–43
blurry vision and, 43–45
counterstrategies for, 45–49
focus altered by, 42–45, 46
in home games, 37–39
"hot hand" and "cold hand" theory
  of, 49–53
and laws of probability, 50–53
practice and, 33, 48–49
pre-shot routines and, 32
supportive audiences and, 38–39
time pressure in, 46–47
see also soccer penalty kickers
Australia, 13*n*, 22, 79
Australian Wine Institute, 90–91

261